Middle School 3-2

기말고사 완벽대비

적중100

영어 기출 문제집

중3

동아 | 이병민

Best Collection

구성과 특징

교과서의 주요 학습 내용을 중심으로 학습 영역별 특성에 맞춰 단계별로 다양한 학습 기회를 제공하여
단원별 학습능력 평가는 물론 중간 및 기말고사 시험 등에 완벽하게 대비할 수 있도록 내용을 구성

Words & Expressions

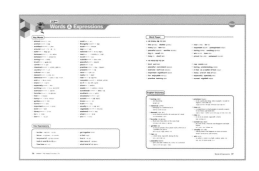

Step1   Key Words 단원별 핵심 단어 설명 및 풀이
         Key Expression 단원별 핵심 숙어 및 관용어 설명
         Word Power 반대 또는 비슷한 뜻 단어 배우기
         English Dictionary 영어로 배우는 영어 단어

Step2   실력평가 단원별 수시평가 대비 주관식, 객관식 문제풀이

Step3   서술형 대비 학업성취도 및 수행능력평가 대비 서술형 문제풀이

Conversation

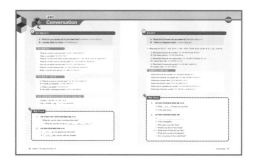

Step1   핵심 의사소통 소통에 필요한 주요 표현 방법 요약
         핵심 Check 기본적인 표현 방법 및 활용능력 확인

Step2   대화문 익히기 교과서 대화문 심층 분석 및 확인

Step3   교과서 확인학습 빈칸 채우기를 통한 문장 완성 능력 확인

Step4   기본평가 시험대비 기초 학습 능력 평가

Step5   실력평가 단원별 수시평가 대비 주관식, 객관식 문제풀이

Step6   서술형 대비 학업성취도 및 수행능력평가 대비 서술형 문제풀이

Grammar

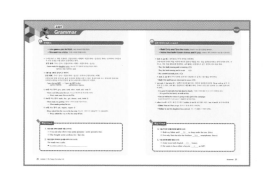

Step1   주요 문법 단원별 주요 문법 사항과 예문을 알기 쉽게 설명
         핵심 Check 기본 문법사항에 대한 이해 여부 확인

Step2   기본평가 시험대비 기초 학습 능력 평가

Step3   실력평가 단원별 수시평가 대비 주관식, 객관식 문제풀이

Step4   서술형 대비 학업성취도 및 수행능력평가 대비 서술형 문제풀이

Reading

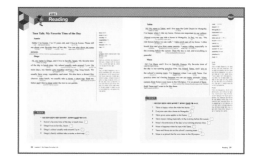

Step1   구문 분석 단원별로 제시된 문장에 대한 구문별 분석과 내용 설명
         확인문제 문장에 대한 기본적인 이해와 인지능력 확인

Step2   확인학습A 빈칸 채우기를 통한 문장 완성 능력 확인

Step3   확인학습B 제시된 우리말을 영어로 완성하여 작문 능력 키우기

Step4   실력평가 단원별 수시평가 대비 주관식, 객관식 문제풀이

Step5   서술형 대비 학업성취도 및 수행능력평가 대비 서술형 문제풀이
         교과서 구석구석 교과서에 나오는 기타 문장까지 완벽 학습

Composition

|영역별 핵심문제|

단어 및 어휘, 대화문, 문법, 독해 등 각 영역별 기출문제의 출제 유형을 분석하여 실전에 대비하고 연습할 수 있도록 문제를 배열

|단원별 예상문제|

기출문제를 분석한 후 새로운 시험 출제 경향을 더하여 새롭게 출제될 수 있는 문제를 포함하여 시험에 완벽하게 대비할 수 있도록 준비

|서술형 실전 및 창의사고력 문제|

학교 시험에서 점차 늘어나는 서술형 시험에 집중 대비하고 고득점을 취득하는데 만전을 기하기 위한 학습 코너

|단원별 모의고사|

영역별, 단계별 학습을 모두 마친 후 실전 연습을 위한 모의고사

교과서 파헤치기

- **단어Test1~3** 영어 단어 우리말 쓰기, 우리말을 영어 단어로 쓰기, 영영풀이에 해당하는 단어와 우리말 쓰기
- **대화문Test1~2** 대화문 빈칸 완성 및 전체 대화문 쓰기
- **본문Test1~5** 빈칸 완성, 우리말 쓰기, 문장 배열연습, 영어 작문하기 복습 등 단계별 반복 학습을 통해 교과서 지문에 대한 완벽한 습득
- **구석구석지문Test1~2** 지문 빈칸 완성 및 전문 영어로 쓰기

Lesson 7

Feel the Wonder

🎙 의사소통 기능

- 궁금함 표현하기

  A: I wonder where the bus stop is.

  B: It's in front of the police station.

- 보고하기

  A: Is there anything interesting?

  B: This article says scientists have discovered a new planet.

🎙 언어 형식

- 소유격 관계대명사 whose

  This small fish **whose** favorite food is clams uses a tool to open them.

- 시간을 나타내는 접속사

  Humpback whales stand on their tails **while** they sleep.

Words & Expressions

Key Words

- ☐ **abroad** [əbrɔ́ːd] 부 해외에, 해외로
- ☐ **against** [əgénst] 전 ~에 대고, ~에 반대하여
- ☐ **Arctic** [ɑ́ːrktik] 명 북극 (지방)
- ☐ **article** [ɑ́ːrtikl] 명 기사
- ☐ **average** [ǽvəridʒ] 형 평균의, 보통의
- ☐ **blood** [blʌd] 명 피
- ☐ **blow** [blou] 동 (입으로) 불다
- ☐ **breathe** [briːð] 동 숨을 쉬다
- ☐ **calculate** [kǽlkjulèit] 동 계산하다
- ☐ **camel** [kǽməl] 명 낙타
- ☐ **careful** [kέərfəl] 형 조심스러운
- ☐ **clam** [klæm] 명 조개
- ☐ **communicate** [kəmjúːnəkèit] 동 소통하다
- ☐ **complete** [kəmplíːt] 동 완성하다
- ☐ **completely** [kəmplíːtli] 부 완전히
- ☐ **cute** [kjuːt] 형 귀여운
- ☐ **desert** [dézərt] 명 사막
- ☐ **discover** [diskʌ́vər] 동 발견하다
- ☐ **distance** [dístəns] 명 거리
- ☐ **dive** [daiv] 동 뛰어들다, 다이빙하다
- ☐ **enemy** [énəmi] 명 적
- ☐ **fat** [fæt] 명 지방
- ☐ **finally** [fáinəli] 부 마침내
- ☐ **fool** [fuːl] 동 속이다, 기만하다 명 바보
- ☐ **forecast** [fɔ́ːrkæst] 명 예측, 예보
- ☐ **friendly** [fréndli] 형 친절한
- ☐ **guess** [ges] 동 추측하다
- ☐ **hide** [haid] 동 숨다

- ☐ **join** [dʒɔin] 동 합류하다
- ☐ **million** [míljən] 명 100만 형 100만의, 수많은
- ☐ **monster** [mɑ́nstər] 명 괴물
- ☐ **mop** [mɑp] 동 대걸레로 닦다
- ☐ **nearby** [nìərbái] 형 인근의, 가까운 곳의 부 인근에, 가까운 곳에
- ☐ **ocean** [óuʃən] 명 대양, 바다
- ☐ **octopus** [ɑ́ktəpəs] 명 문어
- ☐ **planet** [plǽnit] 명 행성
- ☐ **probably** [prɑ́bəbli] 부 아마
- ☐ **rainy** [réini] 형 비가 내리는
- ☐ **scenery** [síːnəri] 명 경치, 풍경
- ☐ **serve** [səːrv] 동 (음식을) 제공하다, 차려 주다
- ☐ **smash** [smæʃ] 동 때려 부수다, 깨뜨리다
- ☐ **snowy** [snóui] 형 눈이 내리는
- ☐ **species** [spíːʃiːz] 명 (분류상의) 종
- ☐ **spot** [spɑt] 동 발견하다, 찾아내다
- ☐ **solar** [sóulər] 형 태양의
- ☐ **sunny** [sʌ́ni] 형 화창한
- ☐ **surface** [sə́ːrfis] 명 수면, 표면
- ☐ **surround** [səráund] 동 둘러싸다
- ☐ **temperature** [témpərətʃər] 명 온도, 기온
- ☐ **the South Pole** 남극
- ☐ **tightly** [táitli] 부 단단히, 꽉
- ☐ **tool** [tuːl] 명 도구
- ☐ **vacuum** [vǽkjuəm] 동 진공청소기로 청소하다
- ☐ **weather forecast** 일기 예보
- ☐ **whale** [hweil] 명 고래
- ☐ **wonder** [wʌ́ndər] 명 경이, 경탄, 놀라움 동 궁금하다

Key Expressions

- ☐ **be covered with** ~로 덮여 있다
- ☐ **be different from** ~와 다르다
- ☐ **be full of** ~로 가득 차다
- ☐ **check out** (흥미로운 것을) 살펴보다, 확인하다
- ☐ **fall asleep** 잠들다
- ☐ **give up** 포기하다
- ☐ **go on a picnic** 소풍가다
- ☐ **go without** ~ 없이 지내다
- ☐ **grow up** 자라다, 성장하다

- ☐ **How about -ing?** ~하는 것이 어떠니?
- ☐ **in a line** 한 줄로
- ☐ **in the end** 마침내, 결국
- ☐ **in front of** ~ 앞에
- ☐ **keep -ing** 계속 ~하다
- ☐ **millions of** 수백만의
- ☐ **melt away** 차츰 사라지다
- ☐ **smash A against B** A를 B에 내리치다
- ☐ **this time of year** 이맘때는, 이맘때쯤이면

Word Power

※ 서로 비슷한 뜻을 가진 어휘

- □ **abroad** 해외에 – **overseas** 해외에
- □ **calculate** 계산하다 – **count** 세다
- □ **complete** 완성하다 – **finish** 끝내다
- □ **forecast** 예측 – **prediction** 예측
- □ **scenery** 경치, 풍경 – **landscape** 풍경
- □ **tightly** 단단히 – **firmly** 단단히

- □ **article** 기사 – **column** 기사
- □ **careful** 조심스러운 – **thoughtful** 사려 깊은
- □ **finally** 마침내 – **lastly** 마지막으로
- □ **probably** 아마 – **perhaps** 아마
- □ **smash** 때려 부수다 – **shatter** 산산이 조각내다

※ 서로 반대의 뜻을 가진 어휘

- □ **against** ~에 반대하여 ↔ **for** ~에 찬성하여
- □ **careful** 조심스러운 ↔ **careless** 부주의한
- □ **enemy** 적 ↔ **friend** 친구
- □ **nearby** 인근의 ↔ **faraway** 멀리 떨어진

- □ **Arctic** 북극 (지방) ↔ **Antarctic** 남극 지방
- □ **discover** 발견하다 ↔ **hide** 숨기다
- □ **friendly** 친절한 ↔ **unfriendly** 불친절한
- □ **probably** 아마 ↔ **improbably** 있음직 하지 않게

※ 동사 – 명사

- □ **bleed** 피를 흘리다 – **blood** 피
- □ **calculate** 계산하다 – **calculation** 계산
- □ **complete** 완성하다 – **completion** 완성

- □ **breathe** 숨을 쉬다 – **breath** 호흡
- □ **communicate** 소통하다 – **communication** 소통
- □ **discover** 발견하다 – **discovery** 발견

※ 명사 – 형용사

- □ **care** 조심 – **careful** 조심스러운, **careless** 부주의한
- □ **friend** 친구 – **friendly** 친절한
- □ **rain** 비 – **rainy** 비가 내리는
- □ **sun** 태양 – **sunny** 맑은

- □ **cloud** 구름 – **cloudy** 구름 낀
- □ **monster** 괴물 – **monstrous** 괴물 같은
- □ **snow** 눈 – **snowy** 눈이 내리는
- □ **wonder** 경이, 경탄, 놀라움 – **wonderful** 놀라운

English Dictionary

- □ **Arctic** 북극 (지방)
  → the area around the North Pole
  북극의 주변 지역

- □ **blow** (입으로) 불다
  → to send out air from the mouth
  입에서 공기를 내보내다

- □ **breathe** 숨을 쉬다
  → to move air into and out of your lungs
  공기를 폐 안팎으로 움직이다

- □ **distance** 거리
  → the amount of space between two places or things
  두 개의 장소나 물건 사이에 있는 공간의 양

- □ **dive** 뛰어들다, 다이빙하다
  → to jump into water, especially with your arms and head going in first
  특히 머리와 팔이 먼저 가도록하여 물속으로 뛰어들다

- □ **forecast** 예측, 예보
  → a statement about what you think is going to happen in the future
  당신이 생각하기에 미래에 무엇이 일어날지에 대한 언급

- □ **million** 100만
  → the number 1,000,000
  1,000,000이라는 수

- □ **smash** 때려 부수다, 깨뜨리다
  → to break something into many pieces
  무언가를 많은 조각으로 깨뜨리다

- □ **species** (분류상의) 종
  → a set of animals or plants that have similar characteristics to each other
  서로 유사한 특성을 가진 동물이나 식물의 집합

- □ **surface** 수면, 표면
  → the upper layer of an area of land or water
  땅이나 물의 위층

- □ **tool** 도구
  → a piece of equipment you use with your hands for a particular task
  특정한 일을 위하여 손으로 사용하는 기구

- □ **whale** 고래
  → a very large mammal that lives in the sea
  바다에 사는 거대한 포유동물

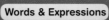

01 다음 밑줄 친 부분의 의미가 다른 하나를 고르시오.

① The plane landed at the airport.

② The bird landed on the water.

③ The pilot managed to land the aircraft safely.

④ The land in this town is good for farming.

⑤ There's a plane coming in to land now.

02 다음 밑줄 친 부분의 의미로 알맞지 않은 것은?

① People are looking at the camel in the zoo. (낙타)

② Students must complete the course. (경쟁하다)

③ Katya will make her first trip abroad next month. (해외로)

④ My parents sometimes seem to treat me as if I were their enemy. (적)

⑤ I cut this article out of the newspaper. (기사)

03 다음 제시된 단어를 사용하여 자연스러운 문장을 만들 수 없는 것은?

> away   from   up   with

① London was different _____ most European capitals.

② We spent half an hour looking for the keys, but eventually gave _____ and went home.

③ The ice hotel will melt _____ completely and flow into the river.

④ His desk was covered _____ books and papers.

⑤ They were stuck _____ a line of traffic.

04 다음 밑줄 친 부분과 의미가 가장 가까운 것을 고르시오.

> From the hill, he looked down on the peaceful landscape.

① horizon   ② local   ③ climate
④ scenery   ⑤ environment

05 다음 영영풀이가 어색한 것은?

① Arctic: the area around the South Pole

② surface: the upper layer of an area of land or water

③ whale: a very large mammal that lives in the sea

④ dive: to jump into water, especially with your arms and head going in first

⑤ breathe: to move air into and out of your lungs

01 빈칸을 주어진 영영풀이에 해당하는 말을 이용하여 채우시오.

> to break something into many pieces

➡ They repeatedly _____ the shellfish against the rock until it breaks open.

 02 다음 우리말에 맞도록 빈칸에 알맞은 말을 쓰시오. (철자가 주어진 경우 주어진 철자로 시작할 것)

(1) 너 근처에 사니?
  ➡ Do you live n_____?
(2) 지금부터 10년 후의 회사 판매에 대한 정확한 예측을 하는 것은 불가능하다.
  ➡ It is impossible to give an accurate f_____ of company sales 10 years from now.
(3) 마침내 우리가 빚을 다 청산했다.
  ➡ We are _____ clear of debt.
(4) Marie는 아이를 그녀의 팔로 단단히 잡았다.
  ➡ Marie held the baby _____ in her arms.

[03~04] 다음 빈칸에 공통으로 들어갈 말을 쓰시오. (철자가 주어진 경우 주어진 철자로 시작할 것)

03
• She is _____ing her new song in the studio.
• She set an Olympic _____.

04
• Anyone who thinks TV news gives you enough information is a f_____.
• You can't f_____ me. I know he's already given you the money.

05 다음 빈칸에 들어갈 말을 〈보기〉에서 찾아 쓰시오. (필요하면 어형을 바꿀 것)

> ─┤ 보기 ├─
> blow   dive   serve   spot

(1) I _____ a police car behind us a moment ago.
(2) I saw her _____ onto her coffee to cool it down.
(3) _____ off the cliffs is dangerous.
(4) Teacakes should be _____ hot with butter.

06 우리말 해석에 맞게 주어진 단어를 알맞게 배열하시오.

(1) 매년 이맘때는 날씨가 변덕이 아주 심하다.
  (at, very, of, year, this, the weather, time, changeable, is)
  ➡ _____
    _____
(2) 학부모들이 학교를 둘러볼 기회가 있을 것이다.
  (there, to, around, parents, school, chance, the, be, look, a, will, for)
  ➡ _____
    _____

Conversation

① 궁금함 표현하기

> **A** I wonder where the bus stop is. 나는 버스 정류소가 어디인지 궁금해.
> **B** It's in front of the police station. 그것은 경찰서 앞에 있어.

- 어떤 것에 대한 궁금증을 표현할 때는 wonder(궁금하다), curious(궁금한, 호기심이 많은), want to know(알고 싶다) 등의 표현을 이용하여 'I wonder ~.(나는 ~이 궁금하다.)' 또는 'I'm curious about ~.(나는 ~이 궁금해.)'라고 말한다. 또한 궁금한 내용을 알고 싶다는 의미를 'I would like to know ~.', 'I want to know ~.', 'I don't know why ~.' 등으로 표현할 수도 있다.

- 'I wonder ~'를 사용할 때의 어순은 'I wonder+의문사+주어+동사 ~.', 'I wonder+if/whether+주어+동사 ~.'이고, 명사(구)와 함께 나타낼 때는 'I wonder+명사(구)'이다. 궁금함을 나타내는 'I'm curious'와 명사구를 같이 쓸 때는 'I'm curious about+명사구'이고, 명사절과 함께 쓸 때는 'I'm curious if/whether ~.' 또는 'I'm curious 의문사(+주어)+동사.'이다.

- 궁금한 점에 대하여 알고 싶을 때는 'Can you tell me about ~?(~에 대하여 이야기해 줄 수 있니?)', 'I'm interested to know ~.(나는 ~를 아는 것에 관심 있어.)'와 같이 표현할 수 있고, 'Can I ~?', 'Can/Could you ~?' 등과 같이 요구/요청을 나타내는 조동사 표현을 사용하여 'Can I ask you ~?' 또는 'Can you tell me ~?'와 같이 궁금한 점에 대하여 물어볼 수 있다. 그 외에 궁금증을 나타낼 때는 'Do you know ~?' 등을 사용할 수도 있다.

궁금함 표현하기

- I wonder+의문사/if/whether 주어+동사 ~. ~인지 궁금하다.
- I would like/want to know ~. 나는 ~이 알고 싶다.
- I am curious about ~. 나는 ~이 궁금하다.
- I'm curious if/whether 주어+동사 ~. 나는 ~가 궁금하다.
- Can you tell me about ~? ~에 대해 말해 줄 수 있니?
- I want to know 명사구/명사절. 나는 ~을 알고 싶다.

핵심 Check

1. 괄호 안에 주어진 말을 바르게 배열하여 대화를 완성하시오.

(1) B: (where, wonder, is, the museum, I).
   G: It is next to the bank.
   ➡ _____

(2) B: (wonder, long, the Amazon River, I, how, is).
   G: It's about 7,000km long.
   ➡ _____

② 보고하기

> **A** Is there anything interesting? 재미있는 뭔가가 있니?
> **B** This article says scientists have discovered a new planet.
> 이 기사에 따르면 과학자들이 새로운 행성을 발견했어.

■ 'This article says ~.(이 기사에 따르면 ~이다.)'처럼 '~ says (that) …(~에 따르면 …이다)'는 어딘가에서 보거나 들은 내용을 상대방에게 보고하거나 전달할 때 사용하는 표현이다. 동사 'say'는 '~라고 말하다'라는 뜻으로 흔히 사용되지만, 여기에서는 '~라고 되어[쓰여] 있다, ~라고 나와 있다, (글, 표지판 등이) ~을 나타내다, ~에 따르면 …이다' 등의 의미로 사용되었다.

■ 무엇을 통해서 보고 들은 내용을 상대방에게 보고하는가에 따라서 'This article says ~.' 형태의 표현에서 This article 대신 The Internet, The book, People, Someone 등을 쓸 수 있다. 어떤 사람이 전해준 말일 때는 'He[She] said ~'의 형태로 상대방에게 보고하거나 전달한다. 전달자에 따라 he를 people, someone, my friend 등으로 바꿔 말할 수 있으며, He told me ~., I've heard ~ from him. 등으로 말할 수도 있다.

■ '~에 따르면'이라는 뜻으로 'according to'를 사용할 수 있다. 'according to'는 전치사구 취급하여 명사(구), 동명사를 목적어로 가져서 'according to 명사/동명사'의 형태가 된다.

보고하기

- This article says ~. 이 기사에 따르면 ~.
- The book says ~. 그 책에 따르면 ~.
- Someone says/said ~. 누군가 ~라고 한다.
- The Internet says ~. 인터넷에 따르면 ~.
- People say/said~. 사람들이 ~라고 한다.
- According to ~, … ~에 따르면 …이다.

핵심 Check

2. 다음 우리말과 일치하도록 빈칸에 알맞은 말을 쓰시오.

   (1) 인터넷에 따르면 목성은 지구보다 11배 이상 더 크다고 한다.

   ➡ _____ Jupiter is over 11 times bigger than Earth.

   (2) 그 책에 따르면 남극의 평균 기온은 약 영하 49℃라고 한다.

   ➡ _____ the average temperature of the South Pole is about -49℃.

3. 다음 대화의 밑줄 친 부분의 의도로 알맞은 것을 고르시오.

   A: Can you check the weather?

   B: Oh, no! The weather forecast says it'll be rainy in the afternoon.

   ① 당부하기　　　② 동의하기　　　③ 보고하기

   ④ 거절하기　　　⑤ 감사하기

Listen and Speak 1 A

B: ❶We're almost at the top of the mountain.

G: ❷I wonder how high this mountain is.

B: It's ❸about 2,000m high.

G: Wow! This is a really high mountain.

B: Yes, it is. Let's ❹keep going.

B: 우리는 산 정상에 거의 다 왔어.
G: 나는 이 산이 얼마나 높은지 궁금해.
B: 이 산은 높이가 약 2,000미터야.
G: 우와! 정말 높은 산이구나.
B: 응, 맞아. 계속 올라가자.

❶ almost: 거의, 장소 앞에 전치사 at을 사용할 수 있다. at the top of: ~의 맨 위에
❷ 'I wonder ~.'는 '나는 ~이 궁금하다.'라는 뜻으로 어떤 것에 대해 궁금할 때 사용하는 표현이다. wonder 다음에는 의문사절이나 if/whether절이 온다. wonder: 궁금해하다
❸ about: 대략, 약
❹ keep 동사ing: 계속해서 ~하다

Check(√) True or False

(1) They already reached the top of the mountain.   T ☐ F ☐

(2) The girl wants to know how high the mountain is.   T ☐ F ☐

Listen and Speak 2 A

B: The weather is so nice outside.

G: Yeah. ❶How about going on a picnic this afternoon?

B: Good idea. Can you ❷check the weather?

G: Oh, no! ❸The weather forecast says ❹it'll be rainy in the afternoon.

B: Let's go another time, ❺then.

B: 바깥 날씨가 아주 좋아.
G: 응. 오늘 오후에 소풍 갈래?
B: 좋은 생각이야. 날씨를 확인해 주겠니?
G: 오, 안 돼! 일기 예보에 따르면 오후에 비가 올 거래.
B: 그러면 다음에 가자.

❶ How about 다음에 동사구를 ~ing 형태로 사용하여 상대방에게 제안·권유할 수 있다. go on a picnic: 소풍 가다
❷ check: 확인하다
❸ '~가 …라고 말하다'라는 의미의 '주어+say(s)+that+주어+동사 ~.' 구문을 이용해 주어가 한 말인 that절의 내용을 상대방에게 보고하거나 전해줄 수 있다. 이때 접속사 that은 생략 가능하다. 정보 제공자에 따라 'The weather forecast' 대신에 'The Internet', 'The book', 'People', 'Someone' 등을 쓸 수 있다.
❹ 시간, 거리, 계절, 요일, 명암, 날씨, 날짜 등을 이야기할 때 비인칭 주어 it을 사용한다. 여기서는 '날씨'로 비인칭 주어 it을 사용했다.
❺ then: (논리적인 결과를 나타내어) 그러면[그렇다면]

Check(√) True or False

(3) It is fine now, but is going to be rainy in the afternoon.   T ☐ F ☐

(4) They are going to go on a picnic this afternoon.   T ☐ F ☐

Listen and Speak 1 C

A: We're finally here.

B: Yes, I'm so excited. Let's ❶look around.

A: ❷I wonder where the bus stop is.

B: It's ❸in front of the police station.

A: You're right. Let's go.

A: 마침내 다 왔어.
B: 맞아. 매우 신나. 주위를 둘러 보자.
A: 나는 버스 정류장이 어디에 있는지 궁금해.
B: 경찰서 앞에 있어.
A: 맞아. 가자.

❶ look around: 둘러보다

❷ 'I wonder ~.'는 '나는 ~이 궁금하다.'라는 뜻으로 어떤 것에 대해 궁금할 때 사용하는 표현이다. wonder 다음에는 의문사절이나 if/whether절이 온다. 여기서는 '의문사(where)+주어(the bus stop)+동사(is)'인 의문사절을 wonder의 목적어로 사용했다. 궁금증을 나타내는 다른 표현으로 '어떤 일에 대해 호기심이 생기다, 궁금해지다'라는 의미는 'be[become] curious about+명사'로 나타낼 수 있으며, 'be interested in ~, want to know ~' 등으로도 표현할 수도 있다. 위의 문장인 'I wonder where the bus stop is.'를 'I'm curious where the bus stop is.', 'I'm interested in where the bus stop is.', 'I want to know where the bus stop is.'로 바꿔 쓸 수 있다.

❸ in front of ~: ~ 앞에

Check(√) True or False

(5) They are looking for the police station.   T ☐ F ☐

(6) A wants to know where the bus stop is.   T ☐ F ☐

Real Life Talk Step 2

A: Where is ❶the coldest place on Earth?

B: I thinks it's ❷the South Pole.

A: ❸I wonder ❹how cold it is.

B: ❺The book says ❻the average temperature of the South Pole is about -49°C.

A: ❼That's amazing!

A: 지구에서 가장 추운 곳이 어디니?
B: 남극이라고 생각해.
A: 얼마나 추울지 궁금해.
B: 책에 따르면 남극의 평균 온도가 영하 49도래.
A: 굉장하다!

❶ the coldest는 형용사 cold의 최상급으로 '가장 추운'의 의미이다.

❷ the South Pole: 남극 (the North Pole, the Arctic: 북극)

❸ I wonder+의문사절 또는 if/whether 주어 동사: 나는 ~이 궁금하다.

❹ how 뒤에 형용사나 부사가 오면 how는 '얼마나'의 의미로 사용된다.

❺ 'The book says ~.'는 '책에 따르면 ~.'이라는 뜻으로 어딘가에서 보거나 들은 내용을 상대방에게 보고하거나 전달할 때 사용하는 표현이다. average: 평균; 평균의

❻ says와 the average temperature 사이에 접속사 that이 생략되어 있다. the average temperature가 단수 주어이므로 단수동사인 is가 사용되었다.

❼ 놀람을 표현할 때는 'That's amazing.' 'That's surprising.' 'I can't believe it.' 등으로 말할 수 있다.

Check(√) True or False

(7) B searches the temperature of the South Pole in the book.   T ☐ F ☐

(8) There is a place colder than the South Pole.   T ☐ F ☐

Listen and Speak 1 B

B: Look at the baby penguins on TV. They're so cute.

G: Yes, but they ❶look very cold out there.

B: Yeah, the South Pole is the coldest place ❷on Earth.

G: ❸I wonder how cold it is there.

B: The average temperature is ❹about -58℃ in July and -26℃ in December.

G: Oh, then, July is ❺colder than December there. Interesting!

B: Yes. ❻Although it's very cold there, it doesn't snow much.

G: That's interesting, too!

❶ look+형용사: ~하게 보이다
❷ on Earth: 지구상에서
❸ 궁금증을 표현할 때 '~를 궁금해하다'라는 의미를 가진 동사 wonder를 이용하여 'I wonder ~.'라고 말한다. I wonder 뒤에는 간접의문문의 어순인 '의문사(how cold)+주어(it)+동사(is)'의 순서로 문장을 쓴다.
❹ about: 대략, 약. 연도나 달 앞에는 전치사 in을 사용한다.
❺ colder than ~: ~보다 더 추운(cold의 비교급)
❻ although는 접속사로 '비록 ~일지라도', '~이긴 하지만'의 의미로 뒤에 주어와 동사가 나온다.

Listen and Speak 2 B

B: Sumin, ❶what are you going to do on Sunday?

G: I'm going to go hiking. Do you want to join me?

B: I'd love to. Where do you want to go?

G: ❷I'm thinking of going to Namsan.

B: Oh, the ❸scenery there is so beautiful ❹this time of year.

G: Right. ❺I heard that it's covered with red autumn leaves now.

B: Great. How long does the shortest hiking course ❻take?

G: ❼The Internet says it takes about two hours.

B: Okay, see you on Sunday!

❶ 상대방에게 무엇을 할 계획인지(또는 어떤 계획이 있는지) 물어볼 때 'What are you planning[going] to+동사원형 ~?'을 사용할 수 있다.
❷ 'I'm thinking of ~.'는 '나는 ~할까 생각 중이다.'라는 뜻으로 of 뒤에 동명사를 취해 의도나 계획을 나타낼 때 쓰는 표현이다. 'I'm considering ~ing.' 또는 'I intend to ~.'와 바꿔 쓸 수 있다.
❸ scenery: 경치, 풍경

❹ this time of year: 이맘때는, 이맘때쯤이면
❺ 어떤 내용을 들어서 알고 있음을 표현할 때 'I heard that+주어+동사 ~.'의 형태로 말할 수 있다. heard 대신에 현재완료형의 형태인 have heard를 사용할 수도 있다. be covered with: ~로 덮여 있다 autumn leaves: 단풍
❻ take: (얼마의 시간이) 걸리다
❼ 'The Internet says ~.'는 '인터넷에 따르면 ~.'이라는 뜻으로 어딘가에서 보거나 들은 내용을 상대방에게 보고하거나 전달할 때 사용하는 표현이다.

Listen and Speak 2 C

A: What are you doing?

B: I'm reading the newspaper.

A: Is there ❶anything interesting?

B: ❷This article says scientists have discovered a new planet.

❶ -thing, -body, -one으로 끝나는 부정대명사는 형용사가 뒤에 나온다.
❷ 'This article says ~.'는 '이 기사에 따르면 ~.'이라는 뜻으로 어딘가에서 보거나 들은 내용을 상대방에게 보고하거나 전달할 때 사용하는 표현이다. 정보 제공자에 따라 This article 대신 The Internet, The book, People, Someone 등을 쓸 수 있다.

Real Life Talk Watch a Video

Suji: ❶Check out this picture!

Tony: Wow! ❷The camels are walking in a line in the desert.

Suji: Yeah. The desert ❸looks very hot and dry.

Tony: ❹I wonder how long camels can go without water in the desert.

Suji: Let's ❺find out ❻on the Internet.

Tony: Okay. ❼The Internet says they can go about two weeks without water.

Suji: Wow, that's amazing! Camels are really ❽interesting animals.

Tony: ❾I want to travel with them in the desert someday.

❶ check out: (흥미로운 것을) 살펴보다, 확인하다
❷ camel: 낙타 in a line: 한 줄로 desert: 사막
❸ look+형용사: ~하게 보이다
❹ 궁금증을 표현할 때 '~를 궁금해하다'라는 의미를 가진 동사 wonder를 이용하여 'I wonder ~.'라고 말한다. wonder 다음에는 의문사절이나 if/whether절이 온다. without: ~ 없이
❺ find out: 찾아내다, (조사하여) 발견하다
❻ on the Internet: 인터넷에서
❼ '~가 …라고 말하다'라는 의미의 '주어+say(s)+that+주어+동사 ~.' 구문을 이용해 주어가 한 말인 that절의 내용을 상대방에게 보고하거나 전해줄 수 있다. 이때 접속사 that은 생략 가능하다.
❽ interesting은 '흥미로운'의 뜻으로 animals가 감정을 유발함을 나타내기 때문에 현재분사형으로 사용했다.
❾ want는 to부정사를 목적어로 취하는 동사이다. travel: 여행하다 someday: 언젠가, 훗날

● 다음 우리말과 일치하도록 빈칸에 알맞은 말을 쓰시오.

Listen and Speak 1 A

B: We're _____ _____ the top of the mountain.

G: I _____ _____ _____ this mountain is.

B: _____ _____ 2,000m high.

G: Wow! This is a really high mountain.

B: Yes, it is. Let's _____ _____ .

Listen and Speak 1 B

B: Look _____ the baby penguins _____ TV. They're so cute.

G: Yes, but they _____ very cold out there.

B: Yeah, the South Pole _____ _____ _____ _____ Earth.

G: I wonder _____ _____ _____ _____ there.

B: The _____ temperature _____ about -58℃ _____ July and -26℃ _____ December.

G: Oh, _____, July is _____ _____ December there. Interesting!

B: Yes. _____ very cold there, it _____ snow much.

G: That's _____, too!

Listen and Speak 1 C

1. A: We're _____ here.

   B: Yes, I'm so _____ . Let's _____ _____ .

   A: I _____ _____ the bus stop is.

   B: It's _____ _____ _____ the police station.

   A: You're right. Let's go.

2. A: We're _____ _____ .

   B: Yes, I'm so excited. Let's look around.

   A: I _____ _____ _____ _____ _____ is.

   B: It's _____ the library.

   A: You're right. Let's go.

3. A: We're finally here.

   B: Yes, I'm so excited. Let's look around.

   A: _____ _____ _____ Green Park _____ .

   B: It's _____ _____ the school.

   A: You're right. Let's go.

Listen and Speak 2 A

B: The weather is _____ nice outside.

G: Yeah. How _____ _____ _____ _____ _____ this afternoon?

B: Good idea. Can you _____ the weather?

G: Oh, no! The weather _____ _____ _____ _____ in the afternoon.

B: Let's go _____ _____, then.

B: 바깥 날씨가 아주 좋아.
G: 응. 오늘 오후에 소풍 갈래?
B: 좋은 생각이야. 날씨를 확인해 주겠니?
G: 오, 안 돼! 일기 예보에 따르면 오후에 비가 올 거래.
B: 그러면 다음에 가자.

Listen and Speak 2 B

B: Sumin, what are you going _____ _____ on Sunday?

G: I'm going to go hiking. Do you want to _____ _____?

B: I'd love to. _____ _____ _____ _____ _____ go?

G: I'm _____ _____ _____ to Namsan.

B: Oh, the _____ there is so beautiful _____ _____ _____ year.

G: Right. _____ _____ _____ _____ _____ _____ _____ red autumn leaves now.

B: Great. _____ _____ does the shortest hiking course _____?

G: _____ _____ _____ _____ _____ about two hours.

B: Okay, see you _____ Sunday!

B: 수민아, 일요일에 무엇을 할 거니?
G: 나는 등산을 갈 거야. 나와 함께 가겠니?
B: 그러고 싶어. 어디로 가고 싶어?
G: 나는 남산에 가려고 생각 중이야.
B: 오, 매년 이맘때 그곳 경치는 아주 아름다워.
G: 맞아. 지금 빨간 단풍잎으로 덮여 있다고 들었어.
B: 좋아. 가장 짧은 등산 코스는 얼마나 걸리니?
G: 인터넷 정보에 따르면 약 두 시간 정도 걸린대.
B: 알겠어, 일요일에 봐!

Listen and Speak 2 C

1. A: _____ are you _____?

   B: I'm reading the newspaper.

   A: Is there _____ _____?

   B: _____ _____ _____ _____ _____ _____ _____ a new planet.

2. A: What are you doing?

   B: I'm reading _____ _____.

   A: Is there _____ _____?

   B: _____ _____ _____ a whale family _____ _____ _____ _____ _____ _____.

1. A: 뭐 하고 있니?
   B: 신문을 읽는 중이야.
   A: 흥미로운 것이 있니?
   B: 이 기사에 따르면 과학자들이 새로운 행성을 발견했대.

2. A: 뭐 하고 있니?
   B: 신문을 읽는 중이야.
   A: 흥미로운 것이 있니?
   B: 이 기사에 따르면 고래 가족이 동해에서 발견됐대.

Real Life Talk Watch a Video

Suji: _____ _____ this picture!

Tony: Wow! The _____ are walking _____ _____ _____ _____ the desert.

Suji: Yeah. The desert looks very hot and dry.

Tony: I _____ _____ _____ _____ _____ _____ without water in the desert.

Suji: Let's find _____ on the Internet.

Tony: Okay. _____ _____ _____ they can go about two weeks without water.

Suji: Wow, that's amazing! _____ _____ really _____ animals.

Tony: I want to _____ _____ _____ in the desert someday.

Real Life Talk Step 2

1. **A:** _____ is the coldest place on Earth?
   B: I thinks it's the South Pole.
   A: _____ _____ _____ _____ it is.
   B: The book _____ the _____ _____ of the South Pole is _____ -49°C.
   A: That's _____!

2. **A:** Which planet is the biggest in the _____ _____?
   B: I thinks it's Jupiter.
   A: _____ _____ _____ _____ it is.
   B: _____ _____ _____ Jupiter is over 11 _____ _____ _____ Earth.
   A: That's amazing!

3. **A:** Where is the hottest desert _____ Earth?
   B: I thinks it's the Sahara Desert.
   A: I wonder _____ _____ _____ _____.
   B: The newspaper _____ the temperature of the Sahara Desert can _____ _____ _____ 50°C.
   A: That's amazing!

해석

수지: 이 사진을 봐!
Tony: 우와! 낙타들이 사막에서 한 줄로 걸어가고 있네.
수지: 응. 사막은 매우 덥고 건조해 보여.
Tony: 낙타들이 사막에서 물 없이 얼마나 오래 갈 수 있는지 궁금해.
수지: 인터넷에서 찾아보자.
Tony: 그래. 인터넷 정보에 따르면 낙타는 물 없이 2주 정도 갈 수 있대.
수지: 우와, 굉장하다! 낙타는 정말 흥미로운 동물이구나.
Tony: 나는 언젠가 사막에서 그들과 함께 여행하고 싶어.

1. A: 지구에서 가장 추운 곳이 어디니?
   B: 남극이라고 생각해.
   A: 나는 그곳이 얼마나 추운지 궁금해.
   B: 책에 따르면 남극의 평균 온도가 섭씨 영하 49도래.
   A: 굉장하다!

2. A: 태양계에서 가장 큰 행성이 어느 것이니?
   B: 목성이라고 생각해.
   A: 나는 그것이 얼마나 큰지 궁금해.
   B: 인터넷에 따르면 목성은 지구보다 11배 이상 크다고 해.
   A: 굉장하다!

3. A: 지구에서 가장 더운 사막이 어디게?
   B: 사하라 사막이라고 생각해.
   A: 나는 그곳이 얼마나 더운지 궁금해.
   B: 신문에 따르면 사하라 사막 온도가 섭씨 50도까지 이룰 수 있다고 해.
   A: 굉장하다!

01 다음 대화의 밑줄 친 부분과 바꿔 쓸 수 있는 것을 고르시오.

> B: We're almost at the top of the mountain.
> G: <u>I wonder how high this mountain is.</u>
> B: It's about 2,000m high.
> G: Wow! This is a really high mountain.
> B: Yes, it is. Let's keep going.

① I know exactly how high this mountain is.
② I'm curious how high this mountain is.
③ Do you know if this mountain is high?
④ I'd like to know whether this mountain is high.
⑤ Can you check whether this mountain is high?

02 다음 대화의 빈칸에 알맞은 것을 고르시오.

> B: The weather is so nice outside.
> G: Yeah. How about going on a picnic this afternoon?
> B: Good idea. Can you check the weather?
> G: Oh, no! The weather forecast _____ it'll be rainy in the afternoon.
> B: Let's go another time, then.

① hears   ② heard   ③ have heard
④ says   ⑤ is said

03 다음 대화의 밑줄 친 부분과 바꿔 쓸 수 <u>없는</u> 것은?

> A: Which planet is the biggest in the solar system?
> B: I thinks it's Jupiter.
> A: <u>I wonder how big it is.</u>
> B: The Internet says Jupiter is over 11 times bigger than Earth.
> A: That's amazing!

① I'm sure how big it is.
② Can you tell me how big it is?
③ I want to know how big it is.
④ I'd be very interested to know how big it is.
⑤ I'm curious about how big it is.

[01~03] 다음 대화를 읽고 물음에 답하시오.

> B: We're almost at the top of the mountain.
> G: I ___(A)___ how high this mountain is.
> B: It's about 2,000m high.
> G: Wow! This is a really high mountain.
> B: Yes, it is. Let's keep ___(B)___ (go).

01 빈칸 (A)에 알맞은 말을 고르시오.

① wonder   ② know   ③ curious
④ strange   ⑤ create

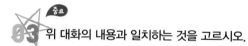

02 괄호 안의 단어를 문맥에 맞게 고쳐 빈칸 (B)를 채우시오.

➡ _____

03 위 대화의 내용과 일치하는 것을 고르시오.

① To get to the top of the mountain, they have to climb for about 2 hours.
② The boy doesn't know how high the mountain is.
③ They think that the mountain which they are climbing up is not high.
④ They have just reached the top of the mountain.
⑤ The girl wants to know how high the mountain is.

04 다음 빈칸에 알맞은 말을 고르시오.

> A: I wonder what the highest mountain in the world is.
> B: It's Mt. Everest. _____

① The weather forecast says it'll be rainy in the afternoon.
② The Internet says that it's about 8,850m high.
③ The Internet says they can go about two weeks without water.
④ This article says scientists have discovered a new planet.
⑤ This article says a whale family was seen in the East Sea.

05 다음 중 짝지어진 대화가 <u>어색한</u> 것은?

① A: How did Ann become a member of the orchestra?
　B: She said she played the violin 8 hours a day.
② A: My grandma said that a brand-new computer was so expensive.
　B: Really? How much is it?
③ A: I wonder who sang this song.
　B: The Internet says Jack wrote it.
④ A: I wonder where noodles come from.
　B: The book says they are from China.
⑤ A: Websites are very useful for doing homework, aren't they?
　B: Yes, they are. I wonder how people did their homework before the Internet.

06 다음 빈칸 (A)와 (B)에 알맞은 말을 쓰시오.

> A: Mina, is there anything interesting in the newspaper?
> B: The newspaper ___(A)___ the Arctic ice is melting ___(B)___.

(A) _____ (B) _____

[07~10] 다음 대화를 읽고 물음에 답하시오.

B: Look at the baby penguins on TV. They're so cute. (①)
G: Yes, but they look very cold out there. (②)
B: Yeah, the South Pole is the coldest place __(a)__ Earth.
G: _____(A)_____
B: The average temperature is about -58℃ in July and -26℃ in December. (③)
G: Oh, then, July is colder __(b)__ December there. Interesting! (④)
B: Yes. (⑤)
G: That's interesting, too!

07 위 대화의 ①~⑤ 중 주어진 문장이 들어갈 알맞은 곳은?

> Although it's very cold there, it doesn't snow much.

①   ②   ③   ④   ⑤

08 위 대화의 빈칸 (A)에 알맞지 <u>않은</u> 말을 고르시오.

① I'm curious about how cold it is there.
② Can you tell me how cold it is there?
③ I wonder how cold it is there.
④ I heard how cold it is there.
⑤ I would like to know how cold it is there.

서답형
09 위 대화의 빈칸 (a)와 (b)에 알맞은 말을 쓰시오.

(a) _____ (b) _____

중요
10 위 대화를 읽고 답할 수 <u>없는</u> 질문을 고르시오.

① How cold is it in the South Pole?
② What are they watching on TV?
③ What is the average temperature for the year in the South Pole?
④ Where is the coldest place on Earth?
⑤ Does it snow much in the South Pole?

11 다음 대화의 빈칸에 들어갈 말을 〈보기〉에서 골라 순서대로 옳게 배열한 것은?

B: Sumin, what are you going to do on Sunday?
G: _____
B: _____
G: _____
B: _____
G: Right. I heard that it's covered with red autumn leaves now.
B: Great. How long does the shortest hiking course take?
G: The Internet says it takes about two hours.
B: Okay, see you on Sunday!

> (A) Oh, the scenery there is so beautiful this time of year.
> (B) I'm thinking of going to Namsan.
> (C) I'm going to go hiking. Do you want to join me?
> (D) I'd love to. Where do you want to go?

① (B) – (A) – (C) – (D)
② (B) – (C) – (A) – (D)
③ (C) – (A) – (B) – (D)
④ (C) – (B) – (A) – (D)
⑤ (C) – (D) – (B) – (A)

[01~03] 다음 대화를 읽고 물음에 답하시오.

Suji: Check __(A)__ this picture!

Tony: Wow! The camels are walking in a line in the desert.

Suji: Yeah. The desert looks very hot and dry.

Tony: I wonder _____ⓐ_____ camels can go without water in the desert.

Suji: Let's find __(B)__ on the Internet.

Tony: Okay. The Internet says they can go about two weeks without water.

Suji: Wow, that's amazing! Camels are really interesting animals.

Tony: I want to travel with ⓑthem in the desert someday.

01 빈칸 (A)와 (B)에 공통으로 들어갈 말을 쓰시오.

➡ _____

02 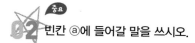 빈칸 ⓐ에 들어갈 말을 쓰시오.

➡ _____

03 밑줄 친 ⓑthem이 가리키는 것을 대화에서 찾아 쓰시오.

➡ _____

[04~05] 다음 대화를 읽고 물음에 답하시오.

B: Sumin, what are you going to do on Sunday?

G: I'm going to go hiking. Do you want to join me?

B: I'd love to. Where do you want to go?

G: I'm thinking of going to Namsan.

B: Oh, the scenery there is so beautiful this time of year.

G: Right. 지금 빨간 단풍잎으로 덮여 있다고 들었어. (heard, leaves, covered, I, red, that, autumn, is, now, with, it)

B: Great. How long does the shortest hiking course take?

G: The Internet __(A)__ it __(B)__ about two hours.

B: Okay, see you on Sunday!

04 빈칸 (A)와 (B)에 들어갈 말을 <보기>에서 찾아 어법에 맞게 쓰시오.

┌─── 보기 ───┐

get   know   make   say

speak   take

(A) _____   (B) _____

05 밑줄 친 우리말과 일치하도록 괄호 안에 주어진 단어를 알맞게 배열하시오.

➡ _____

_____

06 다음 밑줄 친 우리말과 일치하도록 주어진 단어를 이용하여 영작하시오.

A: We're finally here.

B: Yes, I'm so excited. Let's look around.

A: 나는 Green Park가 어디에 있는지 궁금해.

B: It's next to the school.

A: You're right. Let's go.

➡ _____ (be, wonder)

Grammar

① 소유격 관계대명사 whose

- This small fish **whose** favorite food is clams uses a tool to open them.
  가장 좋아하는 먹이가 조개인 이 작은 물고기는 조개를 열기 위해 도구를 사용한다.

■ 관계대명사의 소유격은 선행사가 그 뒤에 나오는 문장에서 소유격 형태로 나올 때 두 문장을 하나로 이어주어 '접속사'와 '대명사의 소유격'의 역할을 한다. 소유격 관계대명사는 생략할 수 없으며, 관계대명사절은 형용사 역할을 하여 바로 앞의 선행사를 꾸며준다.

- He's a man. I respect his opinion.
  = He's a man, and I respect his opinion.
  = He's a man **whose** opinion I respect. 그는 내가 그의 의견을 존중하는 남자이다.
- It's the house. Its door is painted red.
  = It's the house, and its door is painted red.
  = It's the house **whose** door is painted red. 그것은 문이 빨간색 페인트로 칠해진 집이다.

■ 관계대명사의 소유격은 선행사가 사람 또는 사물인 경우에 whose를 쓸 수 있으며, 선행사가 사물일 경우에는 of which로 바꿔 쓸 수 있으며 사람일 경우에는 of which를 쓸 수 없다. of which를 쓸 경우 of which가 받는 명사 앞에는 정관사 the를 써야 한다.

- The desk did not burn. Its top was made of metal.
  = The desk did not burn and its top was made of metal.
  = The desk, **whose** top was made of metal, did not burn.
  = The desk, **of which** the top was made of metal, did not burn.
  = The desk, the top **of which** was made of metal, did not burn. 그 책상은 표면이 금속제여서 타지 않았다.

■ 소유격을 대신하기 때문에 whose 뒤에 명사가 오고, 관계사절은 완전한 절이 나온다.

- I saw a sick animal. Its life was in danger.
  = I saw a sick animal **whose** life was in danger. 나는 생명이 위태로운 아픈 동물을 보았다.

■ 의문사 whose(누구의)와 혼동하지 않도록 유의한다.

- He **whose** walk is upright fears the Lord. 걸음이 올바른 사람은 하나님을 두려워한다. (소유격 관계대명사)
- **Whose** house is that? 저것이 누구의 집이죠? (의문사)

핵심 Check

1. 다음 괄호 안에서 알맞은 단어를 고르시오.
   (1) I have several friends (whose / who) jobs are doctors.
   (2) I'd rather work for a company (which / of which) the products I trust.

② 시간을 나타내는 접속사

• Humpback whales stand on their tails **while** they sleep.
혹동고래는 잠을 자는 동안 꼬리로 서 있다.

■ 시간을 나타내는 접속사의 종류와 쓰임: 시간의 접속사는 종속절을 이끌며 주절과 종속절을 이어주는 역할을 한다.

when	~할 때	while	~하는 동안에
before	~하기 전에	until	~할 때까지
after	~한 후에	as soon as	~하자마자

• It hurts **when** I bend my knee. 저는 무릎을 구부리면 아파요.

• It began to rain **before** I got home. 내가 집에 도착하기 전에 비가 내리기 시작했다.

• I've got into the habit of turning on the TV **as soon as** I get home.
나는 집에 오자마자 TV를 켜는 것이 버릇이 되었다.

■ 시간의 접속사가 이끄는 종속절은 주절의 앞이나 뒤에 모두 올 수 있다. 주절의 앞에 올 경우 보통 종속절 끝에 콤마(,)를 찍어 준다.

• We waited inside **until** things calmed down.

= **Until** things calmed down, we waited inside. 우리는 사태가 진정될 때까지 안에서 기다렸다.

■ 시간의 접속사가 이끄는 부사절에서는 미래의 의미일지라도 현재 시제를 쓴다.

• I will look after your affairs **while** you are away. (○)

I will look after your affairs **while** you will be away. (×) 내가 당신이 없는 동안 뒷일을 돌보겠다.

핵심 Check

2. 다음 우리말에 맞게 괄호 안의 어구를 바르게 배열하시오.

(1) 우리는 성질이 가라앉을 때까지 기다려야 할 것 같아. (I, we, think, wait, have, should, cooled, tempers, until)

➡ _____

(2) 도로를 건널 때는 내 손을 잡아라. (we, me, the road, your hand, give, cross, while)

➡ _____

01 다음 빈칸에 들어갈 말로 알맞은 것은?

> This small fish _____ favorite food is clams uses a tool to open them.

① which   ② of which   ③ who

④ whose   ⑤ whom

02 다음 두 문장을 한 문장으로 바꾸어 쓸 때 알맞게 표현한 것을 고르시오.

> • What happened? • I was out.

① What happened while I was out?

② What happened because I was out?

③ What happened although I was out?

④ What happened since I was out?

⑤ What happened if I was out?

03 다음 두 문장을 관계대명사를 이용하여 하나의 문장으로 바르게 쓴 것을 고르시오.

> • I know the woman. • Her last name is Johnson.

① I know the woman who last name is Johnson.

② I know the woman whose last name is Johnson.

③ I know the woman whom last name is Johnson.

④ I know the woman which last name is Johnson.

⑤ I know the woman of which last name is Johnson.

04 다음 괄호 안에서 알맞은 말을 고르시오.

(1) I got a surprise (until / when) I saw the bill.

    ➡ _____

(2) I felt so lonesome (after / although) she left.

    ➡ _____

(3) He repeated it several times over (as soon as / until) he could remember it.

    ➡ _____

01 다음 문장의 밑줄 친 부분 중 어법상 어색한 것은?

> The documentary ①caused ②a lot of bad feeling among the workers ③of which lives ④it ⑤described.

①   ②   ③   ④   ⑤

02 다음 중 어법상 어색한 문장은?

① I learned French after I moved to Paris.
② There was a long pause before she answered.
③ I recognized him as soon as he came in the room.
④ Mr. Cho met many foreigners while he was abroad.
⑤ The female sits on the eggs after they hatch.

서답형
[03~04] 다음 우리말과 일치하도록 괄호 안에 주어진 어구를 바르게 배열하시오.

03
> 나는 나와 이름이 같은 소녀를 만났다.
> (I, a girl, name, the same, mine, whose, met, is, as)

➡ _____

04
> 내가 말하는 동안 조용히 해라.
> (I'm, be, while, quiet, speaking)

➡ _____

[05~06] 다음 우리말과 일치하도록 바르게 영작한 것을 고르시오.

05
> 미술관에 그의 그림이 있는 남자는 나의 삼촌이다.

① The man whose painting is in the museum is my uncle.
② The man who painting is in the museum is my uncle.
③ The man whom painting is in the museum is my uncle.
④ The man which painting is in the museum is my uncle.
⑤ The man of which painting is in the museum is my uncle.

06
> 그는 점심 식사 후에, 친구들과 야구를 했다.

① He played baseball with his friends before he had lunch.
② He played baseball with his friends when he had lunch.
③ He played baseball with his friends after he had lunch.
④ He played baseball with his friends while he had lunch.
⑤ He played baseball with his friends until he had lunch.

서답형
07 다음 문장에서 어법상 어색한 것을 바르게 고치시오.

> This is the picture of which price is unbelievably high.

_____ ➡ _____

08 다음 중 빈칸 ⓐ∼ⓕ에 같은 단어가 들어가는 것끼리 바르게 짝지어진 것은?

> • I know a boy ⓐ_____ dad is a history teacher.
> • The book the cover ⓑ_____ is blue is mine.
> • There is a student ⓒ_____ favorite subject is music.
> • There was a big house the garden ⓓ _____ was very beautiful.
> • She's an artist ⓔ_____ work I really admire.

① ⓐ, ⓒ, ⓓ
② ⓐ, ⓒ, ⓔ
③ ⓑ, ⓒ, ⓔ
④ ⓑ, ⓓ, ⓔ
⑤ ⓒ, ⓓ

09 다음 중 밑줄 친 접속사의 쓰임이 어색한 것은?

① When he was a child, he lived in Busan.
② I was listening to the radio while my husband was taking a shower.
③ He came up as she was speaking.
④ Eddie bought a bottle of water until he was thirsty.
⑤ We'll leave in the morning as soon as it's light.

10 다음 중 밑줄 친 부분의 쓰임이 나머지와 다른 것은?

① The boy whose T-shirt is red is Homin.
② I have several friends whose jobs are doctors.
③ There is a frog whose length is longer than a pencil.
④ A man whose name I didn't know lived there.
⑤ Will you tell me whose side are you on?

11 다음 중 밑줄 친 부분의 쓰임이 어색한 것은?

① We have ten minutes before the train leaves.
② Just ring for the nurse if you need her.
③ I usually go to the gym while my lunch hour.
④ She felt disappointed since she hadn't been invited.
⑤ Strange though it may sound, I was pleased it was over.

12 다음 중 어법상 옳은 문장은?

① Look at the house of which roof is red.
② My favorite sea animal is the beluga whale whose body is white all over.
③ Veronica, of which the hobby is playing the piano, finally received the first prize last week.
④ Teachers tend to be more generous to those students whose the work is neat and tidy.
⑤ We came to a small circular apartment roof of which was a perfect arched dome.

[13~14] 주어진 두 문장을 관계대명사를 사용해서 하나의 문장으로 바르게 고친 것을 고르시오.

13

> • She met the man.
> • His name is Mark.

① She met the man the name of which is Mark.

② She met the man who the name is Mark.

③ She met the man whose the name is Mark.

④ She met the man whom the name is Mark.

⑤ She met the man whose name is Mark.

14

> • War must be a word.
> • Its meaning has to disappear from our understanding.

① War must be a word the meaning of which has to disappear from our understanding.

② War must be a word whose the meaning has to disappear from our understanding.

③ War must be a word of which meaning has to disappear from our understanding.

④ War must be a word the meaning of what has to disappear from our understanding.

⑤ War must be a word who the meaning has to disappear from our understanding.

서답형

15 다음 괄호 안에서 알맞은 말을 고르시오.

(1) I have a watch (whose / of which) price is 9,000 won.

(2) I have a brother (that / whose) name is Tony.

(3) Look at the dog (of which / whose) the tail is very long.

(4) Please make yourself comfortable (while / during) I get some coffee.

(5) I hope you will have a housewarming party when you (are / will be) settled.

(6) I'll wait outside (until / that) the meeting's over.

16 다음 우리말을 영작할 때, 어법상 <u>어색한</u> 문장을 고르시오. (2개)

> 유명한 작가의 소설은 잘 팔린다.
>
> *readily: 즉시, 쉽사리, 순조롭게

① Novels of which the authors are famous sell readily.

② Novels the authors of which are famous sell readily.

③ Novels whose authors are famous sell readily.

④ Novels whose the authors are famous sell readily.

⑤ Novels of which authors are famous sell readily.

⭐01 다음 우리말과 일치하도록 괄호 안에 주어진 어구를 알맞게 배열하시오.

(1) Tony는 머리가 빨간색인 그 소녀를 본 적이 있다. (Tony, the girl, red, hair, has, is, seen, whose)

➡ _____

(2) 그것들은 개인 사업이기 때문에 주요 목적이 돈을 버는 것이다. (businesses, focus, they, money, is, are, private, whose, main, making)

➡ _____
_____

(3) 혹등고래는 잠을 자는 동안 꼬리로 서 있다. (humpback whales, tails, they, their, sleep, stand, while, on)

➡ _____
_____

(4) 우리는 그 섬에 도착하자마자 간절히 탐사가 하고 싶었다. (As, as, we, we, the island, explore, were, arrived, eager, soon, to, on)

➡ _____
_____

02 다음 괄호 안에 주어진 접속사를 사용하여 두 문장을 한 문장으로 바꿔 쓰시오. (주절을 앞에 쓸 것.)

(1) • I met my friend.
• I was on my way to school. (while)

➡ _____

(2) • You will be instructed where to go.
• The plane is ready. (as soon as)

➡ _____
_____

(3) • He grew and grew.
• He was taller than his father. (until)

➡ _____

(4) • You must be careful.
• You are handling chemicals. (when)

➡ _____
_____

03 다음 두 문장을 which를 이용하여 한 문장으로 쓰시오.

(1) • I have a cup.
• The color of the cup is blue.

➡ _____
_____

(2) • I could not solve the science problem.
• Its solution was very difficult.

➡ _____
_____

(3) • I want to enter an international school.
• The students of the school come from many countries.

➡ _____
_____
_____

(4) • Years ago I happened to get a very old-looking jar.
• The owner of the jar is not known up to now.

➡ _____
_____
_____

04 다음 각 문장에서 어법상 <u>어색한</u> 단어를 한 개씩만 찾아 고치시오.

> (1) I know a boy whose the hobby is collecting stamps.
> (2) I used to take care of a cat of which owner went away frequently on business.
> (3) Andy lives in a house which the windows were covered with roses.
> (4) Look at the boy who dog is bigger than him.
> (5) He wanted to honor people whose made the world better.
> (6) Shrek is a friendly monster who body is green.

(1) _____ ➡ _____
(2) _____ ➡ _____
(3) _____ ➡ _____
(4) _____ ➡ _____
(5) _____ ➡ _____
(6) _____ ➡ _____

[05~06] 다음 우리말과 일치하도록 괄호 안에 주어진 단어와 조건을 활용하여 문장을 완성하시오.

05

> 꼭대기가 눈으로 덮인 저 산을 보아라.
> ➡ Look at the mountain _____ snow.
> (the top, cover, with, 어형 변화 가능)

➡ _____

06

> Jinsu가 Mark와 이야기를 하고 있는 동안 Ann은 그녀의 개를 산책시키고 있었다.
> ➡ _____, Ann was walking her dog.
> (talk with, 6 단어, 어형 변화 가능)

➡ _____

07 다음 우리말을 괄호 안에 주어진 어휘를 사용하여 영작하시오. (필요시 단어를 추가할 수 있으나, 변형은 하지 말 것.)

> (1) 'tuskfish'는 조개가 나타날 때까지 모래에 입김을 분다. (a clam, the tuskfish, the sand, blows, appears, on)
> ➡ _____
> _____

> (2) 당신은 표지를 변경하고 싶은 앨범을 선택할 수 있습니다. (you, you'd, the album, cover of, select, like, can, change, to)
> ➡ _____

> (3) 인류는 세상을 다른 시각으로 보는 사람들에게 아주 냉담할 수 있다. (Humanity, eyes, those, be, can, see the world differently, quite cold to)
> ➡ _____

Reading

Under the Sea

Two-thirds of our planet is covered by oceans. They are full of
3분의 2 (분자는 기수, 분모는 서수)   = oceans   ~로 가득 차다
wonder and are home to millions of species. Every day, we are learning
수많은   매일, 날마다(부사) everyday: 일상의, 매일의
new things about them. Let's find out about some interesting sea
animals.

Sweet Dreams

Can you guess what these whales are doing in the picture? It looks
'의문사+주어+동사'의 어순으로 쓰인 간접의문문   ~처럼 보이다
like they are standing up in a group. But they are actually sleeping!
한 무리를 이루어
Humpback whales stand on their tails while they sleep. They sleep near
혹등고래   '~하는 동안에', 동작이나 상태가 계속됨을 나타냄.(접속사)
the surface. Since they are not fish, they need to come up to breathe.
'~이기 때문에', 이유의 부사절을 이끄는 접속사   목적을 나타내는 to부정사의 부사적 용법
Also, they don't fall asleep completely. When they wake up, they come
out of the water for a deep breath and dive back into the sea.
'~을 위해, ~하러'. 목적의 의미를 나타내는 전치사   이전 장소나 상태로 다시 돌려놓는다는 의미를 나타냄.(부사)
*humpback whale: 혹등고래라고 불리며, 북극해를 제외한 모든 대양에서 서식한다.

planet 행성
wonder 경이, 경탄, 놀라움
millions of 수많은
species (분류상의) 종
whale 고래
tail 꼬리
surface 수면, 표면
breathe 숨을 쉬다
breath 숨, 호흡

확인문제

● 다음 문장이 본문의 내용과 일치하면 T, 일치하지 <u>않으면</u> F를 쓰시오.

1 Two-thirds of our planet is covered by oceans. ☐

2 Humpback whales stand on their heads while they sleep. ☐

3 Humpback whales sleep near the surface. ☐

4 Humpback whales don't need to come up to breathe. ☐

5 Humpback whales don't fall asleep completely. ☐

6 When humpback whales sleep, they come out of the water and dive back into the

sea. ☐

Enjoy Your Meal

If you think <u>fish</u> are not smart, take a look at the tuskfish. This small
<small>fish는 단수형과 복수형이 동일한 단어로 뒤에 나온 are를 근거로 fish가 복수임을 알 수 있다.</small>
fish <u>whose</u> favorite food is clams uses a tool <u>to open</u> <u>them</u>. Clams
<small>소유격 관계대명사   목적을 나타내는 to부정사의 부사적 용법   = clams</small>
usually hide under the sand, <u>so</u> they <u>cannot be</u> easily <u>discovered</u>. The
<small>'그래서, 그 결과'(접속사)   조동사가 포함된 수동태: '조동사(cannot)+be+과거분사'의 형태</small>
tuskfish blows on the sand until a clam appears. The clam is closed
tightly, so the fish cannot eat it. But the tuskfish doesn't give up. <u>It</u>
<small>   = the tuskfish</small>
<u>smashes the clam against a rock</u>. <u>In the end</u>, the clam opens and dinner
<small>smash A against B: A를 B에 내리치다   마침내, 결국</small>
is served.

*tuskfish: 놀래깃과의 물고기로 서태평양과 인도양에서 주로 서식한다.

One, Two, Three, Jump!

You have probably <u>seen a bird fly</u> down to the sea <u>to catch a fish</u>.
<small>지각동사 see+목적어+동사원형: (목적어)가 ~하는 것을 보다   to부정사의 부사적 용법(목적)</small>
But have you ever seen a fish jump out of the water to catch a bird?
<u>Well</u>, birds have to be careful when a giant trevally is around. This fish
<small>Well은 감탄사로 실제로 말하고자 하는 것을 소개하기 위해 씀.</small>
can grow <u>up to</u> 170cm and 80kg. But don't <u>let its size fool you</u>. This
<small>'~까지', 숫자, 정도, 위치 등과 함께 사용   사역동사(let)+목적어+동사원형: (목적어)가 ~하도록 허락하다</small>
fish is <u>quick</u> and <u>smart</u>. It can <u>spot</u> a <u>flying</u> bird <u>and</u> <u>calculate</u> its speed
<small>quick(빠른)과 smart(똑똑한)는 형용사로 주격보어   spot (V1)   현재분사   등위접속사 and를 써서 대등하게 연결 calculate (V2)</small>
and distance. When the bird flies <u>nearby</u>, the giant trevally jumps <u>out</u>
<small>   근처에, 가까운 곳에(부사)</small>
<u>of</u> the water and catches it.
<small>out of+명사: ~의 밖으로</small>

*giant trevally: 전갱잇과의 물고기로 서태평양과 인도양에서 서식한다.

---

clam 조개

tool 도구

discover 발견하다

blow (입으로) 불다

tightly 단단히, 꽉

smash 때려 부수다, 깨뜨리다

serve (음식을) 제공하다, 차려 주다

fool 속이다, 기만하다

spot 발견하다, 찾아내다

calculate 계산하다

distance 거리

 확인문제

● 다음 문장이 본문의 내용과 일치하면 T, 일치하지 <u>않으면</u> F를 쓰시오.

1 The favorite food of the tuskfish is clams. ☐

2 Clams usually hide under the rock. ☐

3 The tuskfish smashes the clam against a rock. ☐

4 It is impossible for a bird to fly down to the sea to catch a fish. ☐

5 A giant trevally can grow up to 170cm and 80kg. ☐

6 A giant trevally can't calculate the speed and distance of a flying bird. ☐

● 우리말을 참고하여 빈칸에 알맞은 말을 쓰시오.

1 _____ the Sea

2 _____ of our planet is covered by oceans.

3 They are full of wonder and are home to _____ _____ _____.

4 Every day, we are learning _____ _____ about them.

5 _____ _____ _____ about some interesting sea animals.

6 _____ Dreams

7 Can you guess _____ _____ _____ _____ _____ in the picture?

8 It looks like they are standing up _____ _____ _____.

9 But they are _____ sleeping!

10 Humpback whales _____ _____ _____ _____ while they sleep.

11 They sleep _____ _____ _____.

12 Since they are not fish, they _____ _____ _____ to breathe.

13 Also, they don't _____ _____ completely.

14 When they wake up, they come out of the water _____ _____ _____ _____ and dive back into the sea.

15 _____ Your Meal

16 If you think fish are not smart, _____ _____ _____ the tuskfish.

1	바다 아래에
2	우리 행성의 3분의 2는 대양들로 덮여 있다.
3	대양들은 신기한 것으로 가득 차 있고 수많은 종의 서식지이다.
4	매일 우리는 그들에 관한 새로운 것들을 배우고 있다.
5	몇몇 흥미로운 바다 동물들을 알아보자.
6	좋은 꿈 꿔라
7	여러분은 그림 속 이 고래들이 무엇을 하고 있는지 추측할 수 있는가?
8	그들이 무리를 지어 서 있는 것처럼 보인다.
9	그러나 그들은 실제로는 잠을 자고 있다!
10	혹등고래들은 잠을 자는 동안 꼬리로 서 있다.
11	그들은 수면 근처에서 잠을 잔다.
12	그들은 물고기가 아니기 때문에 숨을 쉬기 위해 위로 나올 필요가 있다.
13	또한 그들은 완전히 잠들지 않는다.
14	그들은 잠에서 깨면 심호흡을 하러 물 밖으로 나왔다가 바다로 다시 뛰어든다.
15	맛있게 먹어라
16	만약 물고기가 똑똑하지 않다고 생각한다면 'tuskfish'를 보아라.

17 This small fish _____ _____ _____ is clams uses a tool to open them.

18 Clams usually hide under the sand, so they _____ _____ _____ _____.

19 The tuskfish blows on the sand _____ a clam _____.

20 The clam _____ _____ _____, so the fish cannot eat it.

21 But the tuskfish doesn't _____ _____.

22 It _____ the clam _____ a rock.

23 In the end, the clam opens and dinner _____ _____.

24 One, Two, Three, _____!

25 You have probably seen a bird _____ _____ to the sea to catch a fish.

26 But have you ever seen a fish _____ _____ _____ _____ _____ to catch a bird?

27 Well, birds have to be careful when a giant trevally _____ _____.

28 This fish can grow _____ _____ 170cm and 80kg.

29 But don't _____ its size _____ you.

30 This fish is _____ _____ _____.

31 It can _____ a flying bird and _____ its speed and distance.

32 When the bird flies _____, the giant trevally _____ out of the water and _____ it.

---

17 가장 좋아하는 먹이가 조개인 이 작은 물고기는 조개를 열기 위해 도구를 사용한다.

18 조개는 대개 모래 아래에 숨어 있어서 쉽게 발견할 수 없다.

19 'tuskfish'는 조개가 나타날 때까지 모래에 입김을 분다.

20 조개가 단단히 닫혀 있어서 물고기는 이것을 먹을 수 없다.

21 그러나 'tuskfish'는 포기하지 않는다.

22 'tuskfish'는 돌에 조개를 내리친다.

23 마침내 조개가 열리고 밥상이 차려진다.

24 하나, 둘, 셋, 뛰어라!

25 여러분은 아마 새가 물고기를 잡기 위해 바다로 날아 내려가는 것을 본 적이 있을 것이다.

26 그러나 물고기가 새를 잡기 위해 물 밖으로 뛰어오르는 것을 본 적이 있는가?

27 자, 새들은 'giant trevally'가 주변에 있을 때 조심해야 한다.

28 이 물고기는 170센티미터에 80 킬로그램까지 자랄 수 있다.

29 그러나 그 크기에 속지 마라.

30 이 물고기는 빠르고 똑똑하다.

31 이것은 날고 있는 새를 발견하고 그 새의 속도와 거리를 계산할 수 있다.

32 새가 근처에 날고 있을 때, 'giant trevally'는 물 밖으로 뛰어올라 새를 잡는다.

● 우리말을 참고하여 본문을 영작하시오.

1 ▸ 바다 아래에

➡ _____

2 ▸ 우리 행성의 3분의 2는 대양들로 덮여 있다.

➡ _____

3 ▸ 대양들은 신기한 것으로 가득 차 있고 수많은 종의 서식지이다.

➡ _____

4 ▸ 매일 우리는 그들에 관한 새로운 것들을 배우고 있다.

➡ _____

5 ▸ 몇몇 흥미로운 바다 동물들을 알아보자.

➡ _____

6 ▸ 좋은 꿈 꿔라

➡ _____

7 ▸ 여러분은 그림 속 이 고래들이 무엇을 하고 있는지 추측할 수 있는가?

➡ _____

8 ▸ 그들이 무리를 지어 서 있는 것처럼 보인다.

➡ _____

9 ▸ 그러나 그들은 실제로는 잠을 자고 있다!

➡ _____

10 ▸ 혹등고래들은 잠을 자는 동안 꼬리로 서 있다.

➡ _____

11 ▸ 그들은 수면 근처에서 잠을 잔다.

➡ _____

12 ▸ 그들은 물고기가 아니기 때문에 숨을 쉬기 위해 위로 나올 필요가 있다.

➡ _____

13 ▸ 또한 그들은 완전히 잠들지 않는다.

➡ _____

14 ▸ 그들은 잠에서 깨면 심호흡을 하러 물 밖으로 나왔다가 바다로 다시 뛰어든다.

➡ _____

15 ▸ 맛있게 먹어라

➡ _____

16 만약 물고기가 똑똑하지 않다고 생각한다면 'tuskfish'를 보아라.

➡ _____

17 가장 좋아하는 먹이가 조개인 이 작은 물고기는 조개를 열기 위해 도구를 사용한다.

➡ _____

18 조개는 대개 모래 아래에 숨어 있어서 쉽게 발견할 수 없다.

➡ _____

19 'tuskfish'는 조개가 나타날 때까지 모래에 입김을 분다.

➡ _____

20 조개가 단단히 닫혀 있어서 물고기는 이것을 먹을 수 없다.

➡ _____

21 그러나 'tuskfish'는 포기하지 않는다.

➡ _____

22 'tuskfish'는 돌에 조개를 내리친다.

➡ _____

23 마침내 조개가 열리고 밥상이 차려진다.

➡ _____

24 하나, 둘, 셋, 뛰어라!

➡ _____

25 여러분은 아마 새가 물고기를 잡기 위해 바다로 날아 내려가는 것을 본 적이 있을 것이다.

➡ _____

26 그러나 물고기가 새를 잡기 위해 물 밖으로 뛰어오르는 것을 본 적이 있는가?

➡ _____

27 자, 새들은 'giant trevally'가 주변에 있을 때 조심해야 한다.

➡ _____

28 이 물고기는 170센티미터에 80킬로그램까지 자랄 수 있다.

➡ _____

29 그러나 그 크기에 속지 마라.

➡ _____

30 이 물고기는 빠르고 똑똑하다.

➡ _____

31 이것은 날고 있는 새를 발견하고 그 새의 속도와 거리를 계산할 수 있다.

➡ _____

32 새가 근처에 날고 있을 때, 'giant trevally'는 물 밖으로 뛰어올라 새를 잡는다.

➡ _____

[01~03] 다음 글을 읽고 물음에 답하시오.

ⓐTwo-thirds of our planet are covered by oceans. ⓑThey are full of wonder and are home to millions of species. Every day, we are learning new things about them. Let's find out about some interesting sea animals.

01 위 글의 밑줄 친 ⓐ에서 어법상 틀린 부분을 찾아 고치시오.

＿＿＿＿＿＿＿ ➡ ＿＿＿＿＿＿＿

서답형

02 위 글의 밑줄 친 ⓑThey가 가리키는 것을 본문에서 찾아 쓰시오.

➡ ＿＿＿＿＿＿＿＿＿＿

중요

03 위 글의 뒤에 올 내용으로 가장 알맞은 것을 고르시오.

① the oceans which cover two-thirds of our planet
② the stories about our planet which is full of wonder
③ millions of species living in oceans
④ the stories about some interesting sea animals
⑤ many new things we are learning about every day

[04~07] 다음 글을 읽고 물음에 답하시오.

Enjoy Your Meal

If you think fish are not smart, ①take a look at the tuskfish. This small fish whose favorite food is clams uses a tool to open them. Clams usually hide under the sand, so (A)they cannot be easily discovered. The tuskfish blows on the sand until a clam ② appears. The clam ＿ⓐ＿ tightly, so the fish cannot eat it. But the tuskfish doesn't give up. ③It smashes the clam against a rock. ④In the end, the clam opens and dinner ⑤is served.

*tuskfish: 놀래깃과의 물고기로 서태평양과 인도양에서 주로 서식한다.

서답형

04 위 글의 빈칸 ⓐ에 close를 알맞은 형태로 쓰시오.

➡ ＿＿＿＿＿＿＿＿＿＿

서답형

05 위 글의 밑줄 친 (A)they가 가리키는 것을 본문에서 찾아 쓰시오.

➡ ＿＿＿＿＿＿＿＿＿＿

서답형

06 다음 문장에서 위 글의 내용과 다른 부분을 찾아서 고치시오.

> When the clam is closed tightly and the tuskfish cannot eat it, the fish gives up eating it.

➡ ＿＿＿＿＿＿＿＿＿＿

07 다음 중 위 글의 밑줄 친 ①~⑤에 대한 설명이 옳지 않은 것을 고르시오.

① have a look at이나 look at으로 바꿔 쓸 수 있다.
② '조개가 나타날 때까지'라고 해야 하므로, is appeared로 고쳐야 한다.
③ the tuskfish를 가리킨다.
④ Finally로 바꿔 쓸 수 있다.
⑤ is ready로 바꿔 쓸 수 있다.

[08~10] 다음 글을 읽고 물음에 답하시오.

Enjoy Your Meal

If you think fish (A)[is / are] not smart, take a look at the tuskfish. This small fish whose favorite food is clams (B)[use / uses] ⓐa tool to open them. Clams usually hide under the sand, so they cannot be easily discovered. The tuskfish blows on the sand until a clam appears. ⓑThe clam is closed tightly, so the fish cannot eat it. But the tuskfish doesn't (C)[give up / keep trying]. It smashes the clam against a rock. In the end, the clam opens and dinner is served.

*tuskfish: 놀래깃과의 물고기로 서태평양과 인도양에서 주로 서식한다.

서답형

08 위 글의 괄호 (A)~(C)에서 문맥이나 어법상 알맞은 낱말을 골라 쓰시오.

(A) _____ (B) _____ (C) _____

서답형

09 위 글의 밑줄 친 ⓐa tool의 예에 해당하는 것을 본문에서 찾아 쓰시오.

➡ _____

서답형

10 위 글의 밑줄 친 ⓑ를 다음과 같이 바꿔 쓸 때 빈칸에 들어갈 알맞은 접속사를 쓰시오.

_____ the clam is closed tightly, the fish cannot eat it.

[11~13] 다음 글을 읽고 물음에 답하시오.

One, Two, Three, Jump!

You have probably seen a bird fly down to the sea to catch a fish. But have you ever seen a fish jump out of the water to catch a bird? Well, birds have to be careful when a giant trevally is around. This fish can grow up to 170cm and 80kg. But don't let its size fool you. This fish is quick and smart. It can spot a ⓐflying bird and calculate its speed and distance. When the bird flies nearby, the giant trevally jumps out of the water and catches it.

*giant trevally: 전갱잇과의 물고기로 서태평양과 인도양에서 서식한다.

11 위 글의 밑줄 친 ⓐflying과 문법적 쓰임이 같은 것을 모두 고르시오.

① I saw the smoke coming out of the house.
② Do you mind turning down the volume?
③ The boy sleeping under the tree is my brother.
④ She answered smiling at me.
⑤ Did you practice playing the cello?

중요

12 위 글의 주제로 알맞은 것을 고르시오.

① Birds can fly down to the sea to catch a fish.
② A giant trevally is a fish that jumps out of the water to catch a bird.
③ How big can a giant trevally grow?
④ How can a giant trevally spot a flying bird?
⑤ What can a giant trevally calculate?

13 Why do birds have to be careful when a giant trevally is around? Fill in the blanks (A) and (B) with suitable words.

Because the giant trevally (A)_____ out of the water and (B)_____ a bird when a bird flies nearby.

[14~16] 다음 글을 읽고 물음에 답하시오.

Enjoy Your Meal

If you think fish are not smart, take a look at the tuskfish. This small fish whose favorite food is clams uses a tool to open ⓐthem. Clams usually hide under the sand, so they cannot be easily discovered. The tuskfish blows on the sand until a clam appears. The clam is closed tightly, so the fish cannot eat it. But the tuskfish doesn't give up. ⓑ그것은 돌에 조개를 내리친다. In the end, the clam opens and dinner is served.

*tuskfish: 놀래깃과의 물고기로 서태평양과 인도양에서 주로 서식한다.

서답형

14 위 글의 밑줄 친 ⓐthem이 가리키는 것을 본문에서 찾아 쓰시오.

➡ _____

서답형

15 위 글의 밑줄 친 ⓑ의 우리말에 맞게 주어진 어휘를 이용하여 7 단어로 영작하시오.

smashes, rock

➡ _____

서답형

16 How does the tuskfish discover a clam in the sand? Answer in English in a full sentence beginning with "It". (9 words)

➡ _____

[17~19] 다음 글을 읽고 물음에 답하시오.

Sweet Dreams

Can you guess what these whales are doing in the picture? It looks like they are standing up ⓐ_____ a group. But they are actually sleeping! Humpback whales stand ⓑ_____ their tails while they sleep. They sleep near the surface. Since they are not fish, they need to come up ⓒto breathe. ⓓAlso, they don't fall sleepy completely. When they wake up, they come out of the water for a deep breath and dive back into the sea.

*humpback whale: 혹등고래라고 불리며, 북극해를 제외한 모든 대양에서 서식한다

17 위 글의 빈칸 ⓐ와 ⓑ에 들어갈 전치사가 바르게 짝지어진 것은?

| ⓐ ⓑ | ⓐ ⓑ |
① by – from   ② for – on
③ in – on   ④ for – to
⑤ in – from

18 위 글의 밑줄 친 ⓒto breathe와 to부정사의 용법이 같은 것을 모두 고르시오.

① He worked hard only to fail.
② She encouraged me to try once again.
③ She must be a fool to say like that.
④ There is no one to do it.
⑤ I want to be busy again.

서답형

19 위 글의 밑줄 친 ⓓ에서 어법상 틀린 부분을 찾아 고치시오.

_____ ➡ _____

[20~22] 다음 글을 읽고 물음에 답하시오.

ⓐ_____

You have probably seen a bird fly down to the sea to catch a fish. But have you ever seen a fish jump out of the water to catch a bird? Well, birds have to be careful when a giant trevally is around. This fish can grow

ⓑup to 170cm and 80kg. But don't let its size fool you. This fish is quick and smart. It can spot a flying bird and calculate its speed and distance. When the bird flies nearby, the giant trevally jumps out of the water and catches it.

*giant trevally: 전갱잇과의 물고기로 서태평양과 인도양에서 서식한다.

20 위 글의 빈칸 ⓐ에 들어갈 제목으로 가장 알맞은 것을 고르시오.

① Under the Sea
② Birds Flying Down to the Sea to Catch Fish
③ One, Two, Three, Jump!
④ Sweet Dreams
⑤ Don't Let the Great Speed Fool You!

21 위 글의 밑줄 친 ⓑup to와 같은 의미로 쓰인 것을 고르시오.

① What have you been up to?
② It's up to the manager to make the decision.
③ Are you up to this job?
④ Up to now, I believe he's innocent.
⑤ This room can hold up to 200 people.

22 Which question CANNOT be answered after reading the passage?

① Is there a bird which can fly down to the sea to catch a fish?
② How big can a giant trevally grow?
③ Is a giant trevally a quick and smart fish?
④ What can a giant trevally spot?
⑤ How can a giant trevally calculate the speed and distance of a flying bird?

[23~25] 다음 글을 읽고 물음에 답하시오.

_____ ⓐ _____

Can you guess what these whales are doing in the picture? (①) It looks like they are standing up in a group. (②) Humpback whales stand on their tails while they sleep. (③) They sleep near the surface. (④) Since they are not fish, they need to come up to breathe. (⑤) Also, they don't fall asleep completely. When they wake up, they come out of the water for a deep breath and dive back into the sea.

*humpback whale: 혹등고래라고 불리며, 북극해를 제외한 모든 대양에서 서식한다.

23 위 글의 빈칸 ⓐ에 들어갈 제목으로 가장 알맞은 것을 고르시오.

① One, Two, Three, Jump!
② Sweet Dreams
③ Under the Sea
④ Enjoy Your Meal
⑤ Don't Fall Asleep Completely

24 위 글의 흐름으로 보아, 주어진 문장이 들어가기에 가장 적절한 곳은?

But they are actually sleeping!

①   ②   ③   ④   ⑤

25 According to the passage, which is NOT true?

① Humpback whales stand on their tails while they sleep.
② Humpback whales sleep near the surface.
③ Humpback whales are not fish, so they need to come up to breathe.
④ Humpback whales fall asleep completely.
⑤ When humpback whales wake up, they come out of the water for a deep breath.

[01~03] 다음 글을 읽고 물음에 답하시오.

ⓐ우리 행성의 3분의 2는 is covered by oceans. ⓑThey are full of wonder and are home to millions of species. Every day, we are learning new things about ⓒthem. Let's find out about some interesting sea animals.

01 위 글의 밑줄 친 ⓐ의 우리말에 맞게 영작하시오.

➡ _____

02 위 글의 밑줄 친 ⓑ를 다음과 같이 바꿔 쓸 때 빈칸에 들어갈 알맞은 전치사를 쓰시오.

They are filled _____ wonder and are home to millions of species.

03 위 글의 밑줄 친 ⓒthem이 가리키는 것을 본문에서 찾아 쓰시오.

➡ _____

[04~06] 다음 글을 읽고 물음에 답하시오.

Sweet Dreams
ⓐ여러분은 그림 속 이 고래들이 무엇을 하고 있는지 추측할 수 있는가? It looks like they are standing up in a group. But they are actually sleeping! Humpback whales stand on their tails (A)[during / while] they sleep. They sleep (B)[near / nearby] the surface. Since they are not fish, they need to come up (C)[to breathe / breathing]. Also, they don't fall asleep completely. When they wake up, they come out of the water for a deep breath and dive back into the sea.

*humpback whale: 혹등고래라고 불리며, 북극해를 제외한 모든 대양에서 서식한다.

04 위 글의 밑줄 친 ⓐ의 우리말에 맞게 주어진 어휘를 알맞게 배열하시오.

what / can / in the picture / you / are doing / these whales / guess

➡ _____

_____

05 위 글의 괄호 (A)~(C)에서 어법상 알맞은 낱말을 골라 쓰시오.

(A) _____ (B) _____ (C) _____

06 본문의 내용과 일치하도록 다음 빈칸 (A)와 (B)에 알맞은 단어를 쓰시오.

Humpback whales are not fish, so they come (A)_____ _____ _____ _____ for a deep breath when they wake up, and (B)_____ _____ into the sea.

[07~10] 다음 글을 읽고 물음에 답하시오.

One, Two, Three, Jump!
ⓐYou have probably seen a bird fly down to the sea to catch a fish. ⓑBut have you ever seen a fish to jump out of the water to catch a bird? Well, birds have to be careful when a giant trevally is around. This fish can grow up to 170cm and 80kg. ⓒBut don't let its size fool you. This fish is quick and smart. It can spot a flying bird and calculate its speed and distance. When the bird flies nearby, the giant trevally jumps out of the

water and catches ⓓit.

*giant trevally: 전갱잇과의 물고기로 서태평양과 인도양에서 서식한다.

07 위 글의 밑줄 친 ⓐ를 복문으로 고칠 때 빈칸에 들어갈 알맞은 말을 (1)에는 세 단어로, (2)에는 두 단어로 각각 쓰시오.

(1) You have probably seen a bird fly down to the sea _____ _____ _____ it can catch a fish.

(2) You have probably seen a bird fly down to the sea _____ _____ it can catch a fish.

08 위 글의 밑줄 친 ⓑ에서 어법상 틀린 부분을 찾아 고치시오.

_____ ➡ _____

09 다음 빈칸 (A)와 (B)에 알맞은 단어를 넣어 위 글의 밑줄 친 ⓒ처럼 말한 이유를 완성하시오.

Though the giant trevally can grow up to 170cm and 80kg, it is (A)_____ _____ _____. So, you had better not be fooled by its (B)_____ because when a bird flies nearby, it spots the flying bird, calculates its speed and distance, and jumps out of the water to catch it.

*had better 동사원형: (~하는 것이) 좋을 것이다

10 위 글의 밑줄 친 ⓓit이 가리키는 것을 본문에서 찾아 쓰시오.

➡ _____

[11~14] 다음 글을 읽고 물음에 답하시오.

Enjoy Your Meal

If you think fish are not smart, take a look at the tuskfish. This small fish ___ⓐ___ favorite food is clams uses a tool to open them. Clams usually hide under the sand, so (A)they cannot be easily discovered. The tuskfish blows on the sand until a clam appears. The clam is closed tightly, so the fish cannot eat it. But the tuskfish doesn't give up. It smashes the clam against a rock. In the end, the clam opens and dinner ___ⓑ___.

*tuskfish: 놀래깃과의 물고기로 서태평양과 인도양에서 주로 서식한다.

11 위 글의 빈칸 ⓐ에 들어갈 알맞은 관계대명사를 쓰시오.

➡ _____

12 위 글의 빈칸 ⓑ에 serve를 알맞은 형태로 쓰시오.

➡ _____

13 위 글의 밑줄 친 (A)를 능동태로 고치시오.

➡ _____

14 다음 빈칸 (A)와 (B)에 알맞은 단어를 넣어, tuskfish가 자신이 가장 좋아하는 먹이인 조개를 열기 위해 도구를 사용하는 방법을 완성하시오.

When a clam appears from the sand, it is closed tightly. Then, the tuskfish (A)_____ the clam (B)_____ a rock to open it.

구석구석

After You Read A. Read and Correct

I learned about oceans today. Two-thirds of our planet is covered by oceans.

Two-thirds: '3분의 2'를 나타내는 분수 표현. 분자는 기수로, 분모는 서수로 씀.   be covered by: '~로 덮여 있다'(수동태)

They are home to millions of species. There are many interesting facts about
수많은

sea animals. For example, humpback whales stand on their tails while they

sleep, and they sleep near the surface.
수면 근처에서

구문해설 · millions of: 수많은   · species: (분류상의) 종   · whale: 고래   · surface: 수면, 표면

나는 오늘 바다에 대해 배웠다. 우리 행성의 3분의 2는 대양들로 덮여 있다. 그것들은 수많은 종의 서식지이다. 바다 동물들에 관한 많은 흥미로운 사실들이 있다. 예를 들어, 혹등고래들은 잠을 자는 동안 꼬리로 서 있고, 그들은 수면 근처에서 잠을 잔다.

Word Power

· He found a good spot to park the car.
to부정사의 형용사적 용법(앞의 명사 spot을 수식)

· I can spot you in the audience.

· Don't be fooled by his cute looks.
수동태

· Experience makes even fool wise.
make가 5형식 동사로 쓰여 fool이 목적어. wise가 목적격보어로 사용되고 있다.

구문해설 · spot: 장소, 위치, 발견하다, 찾아내다   · audience: 관중   · fool: 속이다; 바보
· look: 외모, 모습

· 그는 차를 주차하기 좋은 장소를 발견했다.
· 나는 관중 속에서 너를 발견할 수 있다.
· 그의 귀여운 외모에 속지 마라.
· 경험은 바보조차도 현명하게 만든다.

Think and Write Step 3

My Fun Animal: Beluga whale

I will introduce the beluga whale. It lives in the Arctic Ocean. It has a round

head. It usually eats fish and clams. An interesting fact about the beluga whale
감정동사: 감정을 유발할 때 현재분사

is that it is white all over. That's why people call it the white whale. When it is
보어절을 이끄는 접속사   그것이 ~한 이유이다.   call A B: A를 B라고 부르다   시간을 나타내는 접속사

born, it is gray. But when it grows up, its body becomes white! I want to see

this animal with my own eyes!
나 자신의

구문해설 · Arctic: 북극   · clam: 조개   · all over: 곳곳에

나의 재미있는 동물: 벨루가 고래

저는 벨루가 고래를 소개할게요. 벨루가 고래는 북극해에 살아요. 둥근 머리를 가졌어요. 벨루가 고래는 주로 물고기와 조개를 먹어요. 벨루가 고래에 관한 흥미로운 사실은 온몸이 하얗다는 거예요. 그것이 사람들이 벨루가 고래를 흰고래라고 부르는 이유예요. 벨루가 고래는 태어날 때, 회색이에요. 그러나 다 자라면, 몸은 하얀색이 돼! 저는 제 눈으로 이 동물을 보고 싶어요!

Words & Expressions

01 ⓐ~ⓔ에서 밑줄 친 spot이 같은 의미로 쓰인 것끼리 바르게 짝지어진 것을 <u>모두</u> 고르시오.

> ⓐ If you spot Mom and Dad coming, warn me.
> ⓑ It took me about twenty minutes to find a parking spot.
> ⓒ This looks like a good spot to stop and rest.
> ⓓ If you are lucky, you will also spot a deer or two.
> ⓔ These ants are often relatively easy to spot.

① ⓐ, ⓑ   ② ⓑ, ⓒ
③ ⓒ, ⓓ   ④ ⓓ, ⓔ
⑤ ⓐ, ⓔ

02 다음 빈칸에 공통으로 들어갈 말을 쓰시오.

> • Sometimes he _____ed why his father hated him.
> • The sight of the Taj Mahal filled us with _____.

03 빈칸에 가장 알맞은 말을 고르시오.

> The _____ of 3, 8, and 10 is 7.

① average   ② individual
③ standard   ④ usual
⑤ certain

04 빈칸 (A)와 (B)에 들어갈 말로 알맞은 것끼리 짝지어진 것을 고르시오.

> • The kitchen was full (A)_____ smoke.
> • Boston is so beautiful this time (B)_____ year.

  (A) (B)   (A) (B)
① with – of   ② with – in
③ of – of   ④ of – in
⑤ of – for

Conversation

[05~07] 다음 대화를 읽고 물음에 답하시오.

> B: We're almost at the top of the mountain. (①)
> G: _____(A)_____ (how, is, wonder, this, I, high, mountain) (②)
> B: It's _____(B)_____ 2,000m high. (③)
> G: Wow! (④)
> B: Yes, it is. (⑤) Let's keep going.

05 빈칸 (A)를 괄호 안에 주어진 단어를 알맞게 배열하여 채우시오.

➡ _____

06 빈칸 (B)에 알맞은 말을 고르시오.

① about   ② on   ③ in
④ for   ⑤ over

07 ①~⑤ 중 주어진 문장이 들어갈 곳은?

> This is a really high mountain.

①   ②   ③   ④   ⑤

[08~10] 다음 대화를 읽고 물음에 답하시오.

B: The weather is so nice outside. (①)

G: Yeah. (②) How about going on a picnic this afternoon?

B: Good idea. (③)

G: Oh, no! (④) The weather forecast says it'll be rainy in the afternoon. (⑤)

B: Let's go another time, then.

08 위 대화의 ①~⑤ 중 주어진 문장이 들어갈 곳은?

> Can you check the weather?

①   ②   ③   ④   ⑤

09 위 대화에서 다음 영영풀이에 해당하는 단어를 찾아 쓰시오.

> a statement about what you think is going to happen in the future

➡ _____

10 위 대화를 읽고 답할 수 있는 질문을 모두 고른 것은?

> ⓐ How is the weather this afternoon?
> ⓑ Who checked the weather forecast?
> ⓒ What day are they going to go on a picnic?
> ⓓ Is it nice outside now?
> ⓔ Who suggest going on a picnic?

① ⓐ, ⓑ
② ⓐ, ⓑ, ⓓ
③ ⓐ, ⓑ, ⓒ, ⓓ
④ ⓐ, ⓑ, ⓒ, ⓔ
⑤ ⓐ, ⓑ, ⓓ, ⓔ

[11~12] 다음 대화를 읽고 물음에 답하시오.

Suji: Check out this picture!

Tony: Wow! The camels are walking ___(A)___ a line ___(B)___ the desert.

Suji: Yeah. The desert looks very hot and dry.

Tony: I wonder how long camels can go without water in the desert.

Suji: Let's find out on the Internet.

Tony: Okay. 인터넷 정보에 따르면 낙타는 물 없이 2주 정도 갈 수 있대.

Suji: Wow, that's amazing! Camels are really interesting animals.

Tony: I want to travel with them in the desert someday.

11 위 대화의 빈칸 (A)와 (B)에 공통으로 들어갈 말을 쓰시오.

➡ _____

12 밑줄 친 우리말과 일치하도록 주어진 단어를 이용하여 영작하시오.

➡ _____
_____ (can, say)

Grammar

[13~14] 다음 중 밑줄 친 부분의 쓰임이 〈보기〉와 같은 것은?

13
> ┤ 보기 ├
> I drink a lot of water <u>when</u> I'm thirsty.

① Sunday is the only day <u>when</u> I can relax.
② He got interested in politics <u>when</u> he was in college.
③ <u>When</u> did she promise to meet him?
④ Since <u>when</u> did you get interested in collecting stamps?
⑤ He told me the <u>when</u> and the where of the event.

14

보기

> I like the girl <u>whose</u> hobby is playing the piano.

① The girl <u>whose</u> dog is very big is Ann.

② Do you know <u>whose</u> ball this is?

③ Kate asked me <u>whose</u> team I was on.

④ The detective was wondering <u>whose</u> fingerprint it was.

⑤ They have to decide <u>whose</u> computer they should use.

[15~16] 다음 주어진 두 문장을 관계대명사를 사용해서 하나의 문장으로 바르게 고친 것을 고르시오.

15

> • I have a friend.
> • Her father is a famous actor.

① I have a friend which father is a famous actor.

② I have a friend which of father is a famous actor.

③ I have a friend of which father is a famous actor.

④ I have a friend that father is a famous actor.

⑤ I have a friend whose father is a famous actor.

16

> • Look at the dog.
> • Its tail is very short.

① Look at the dog whom tail is very short.

② Look at the dog which tail is very short.

③ Look at the dog of which tail is very short.

④ Look at the dog of which the tail is very short.

⑤ Look at the dog that tail is very short.

17 다음 그림을 보고 빈칸에 맞는 단어를 채우시오.

> 시드니에는 밤의 경치가 아름다운 오페라 하우스가 있다.
>
> ➡ There is the Opera House _____ _____ _____ _____ in Sydney.
>
> (night view, wonderful, 5 단어)

18 다음 주어진 두 문장을 한 문장으로 가장 적절하게 바꾼 것은?

> • Let's wait here.
> • The rain stops.

① Let's wait here while the rain stops.

② Let's wait here when the rain stops.

③ Let's wait here until the rain stops.

④ Let's wait here as soon as the rain stops.

⑤ Let's wait here that the rain stops.

19 다음 중 어법상 <u>어색한</u> 문장은?

① After he had lunch, he played baseball with his friends.

② Linda lost her husband while she was 40.

③ She did a lot of acting when she was at college.

④ They didn't arrive at the hotel until very late.

⑤ As soon as he went to bed, he fell asleep.

20 빈칸 (A)~(C)에 들어갈 말로 알맞은 것끼리 짝지어진 것을 고르시오.

> • He wrote a book (A)_____ he was on his journey.
> • He ran away (B)_____ he saw me.
> • His mom put flowers on the table (C)_____ they finished cleaning.

(A)　　(B)　　(C)

① after – while – as soon as

② until – after – until

③ after – as soon as – until

④ while – as soon as – after

⑤ as soon as – while – after

Reading

[21~23] 다음 글을 읽고 물음에 답하시오.

Sweet Dreams

Can you guess what these whales are doing in the picture? It looks like they are standing up in a group. But they are actually sleeping! Humpback whales stand on their tails while they sleep. They sleep near the surface. (A) Since they are not fish, they need to come up to breathe. Also, they don't fall asleep completely. When they wake up, they come out of the water for a deep ⓐ and dive back into the sea.

*humpback whale: 혹등고래라고 불리며, 북극해를 제외한 모든 대양에서 서식한다.

21 본문의 한 단어를 변형하여 위 글의 빈칸 ⓐ에 들어갈 알맞은 단어를 쓰시오.

➡ _____

22 위 글의 밑줄 친 (A)Since와 같은 의미로 쓰인 것을 모두 고르시오.

① I have known her since she was a child.

② I have not seen him since.

③ Let's do our best, since we can expect no help from others.

④ Since we're not very busy now, we can get away from the office.

⑤ It has been two years since I left school.

23 Why do humpback whales sleep near the surface? Fill in the blanks with suitable words.

> They do so in order that they can come out of the water _____ _____ when they wake up.

[24~26] 다음 글을 읽고 물음에 답하시오.

> _____ⓐ_____
>
> If you think fish are not smart, take a look at the tuskfish. ⓑ가장 좋아하는 먹이가 조개인 이 작은 물고기는 조개를 열기 위해 도구를 사용한다. Clams usually hide under the sand, so they cannot be easily discovered. The tuskfish blows on the sand until a clam appears. The clam is closed tightly, so the fish cannot eat it. But the tuskfish doesn't give up. It smashes the clam against a rock. In the end, the clam opens and dinner is served.
>
> *tuskfish: 놀래깃과의 물고기로 서태평양과 인도양에서 주로 서식한다.

24 위 글의 빈칸 ⓐ에 들어갈 제목으로 알맞은 것을 고르시오.

① Under the Sea

② Clams Which Hide under the Sand

③ One, Two, Three, Jump!

④ Sweet Dreams

⑤ Enjoy Your Meal

25 위 글의 밑줄 친 ⓑ의 우리말에 맞게 주어진 어휘를 알맞게 배열하시오.

> a tool / this small fish / uses / clams / whose / is / them / favorite food / to open

➡ _____

_____

26 According to the passage, which is NOT true?

① The tuskfish's favorite food is clams.

② The tuskfish is a large fish.

③ Clams cannot be easily discovered because they usually hide under the sand.

④ The tuskfish discovers a clam in the sand by blowing on the sand until a clam appears.

⑤ The tuskfish smashes the clam against a rock.

[27~28] 다음 글을 읽고 물음에 답하시오.

One, Two, Three, Jump!

You have probably seen a bird fly down to the sea to catch a fish. But ⓐhave you ever seen a fish jump out of the water to catch a bird? Well, birds have to be careful when a giant trevally is around. ①This fish can grow up to 170cm and 80kg. But don't let ②its size fool you. This fish is quick and smart. ③It can spot a flying bird and calculate ④its speed and distance. When the bird flies nearby, ⑤ the giant trevally jumps out of the water and catches it.

*giant trevally: 전갱잇과의 물고기로 서태평양과 인도양에서 서식한다.

27 위 글의 밑줄 친 ⓐ의 현재완료와 용법이 같은 것을 모두 고르시오.

① I have played tennis three times.

② How long have you played the piano?

③ She has gone to Paris.

④ They have just finished it.

⑤ I have been to America before.

28 밑줄 친 ①~⑤ 중에서 가리키는 대상이 나머지 넷과 다른 것은?

①   ②   ③   ④   ⑤

[29~30] 다음 글을 읽고 물음에 답하시오.

My Fun Animal: Beluga whale

I will introduce the beluga whale. It lives in the Arctic Ocean. It has a round head. It usually eats fish and clams. An interesting fact about the beluga whale is that it is white all over. ⓐThat's because people call it the white whale. When it is born, it is gray. But when it grows up, its body becomes white! I want to see this animal with my own eyes!

29 위 글의 밑줄 친 ⓐ에서 흐름상 어색한 부분을 찾아 고치시오.

_____ ➡ _____

30 다음 빈칸 (A)와 (B)에 알맞은 단어를 넣어 벨루가 고래의 몸의 색깔 변화를 완성하시오.

> The beluga whale is born (A)_____, but when it grows up, its body becomes (B)_____.

01 ⓐ~ⓔ에서 밑줄 친 land의 의미가 같은 것끼리 짝지으시오.

> ⓐ It shows where the balls land.
> ⓑ Their journey took them to many foreign lands.
> ⓒ They moved to the country and bought some land.
> ⓓ He didn't hear the plane land.
> ⓔ It isn't clear whether the plane went down over land or sea.

➡ _____

02 밑줄 친 부분과 바꿔 쓸 수 있는 말을 고르시오.

> The front door is locked and all the windows are firmly shut.

① obviously　　② nearly
③ clearly　　　④ highly
⑤ tightly

03 다음 우리말에 맞도록 빈칸에 알맞은 말을 쓰시오.

(1) 북극 지방에서는 생물을 거의 볼 수 없다.
　➡ There is very little life to be seen in the _____.

(2) 공기가 너무 차서 우리는 숨을 쉬기도 어려웠다.
　➡ The air was so cold that we could hardly _____.

04 다음 빈칸에 공통으로 들어갈 말을 쓰시오.

> • Check _____ the prices at our new store!
> • Can you find _____ what time the meeting starts?
> • Don't lean _____ of the window.

[05~06] 다음 대화를 읽고 물음에 답하시오.

> A: Where is the coldest place on Earth?
> B: I thinks it's the South Pole.
> A: 그곳이 얼마나 추울지 궁금해.
> B: The book says the average ____(A)____ of the South Pole is about -49°C.
> A: That's amazing!

05 위 글의 빈칸 (A)에 알맞은 말을 고르시오.

① weather　　② temperature
③ amount　　 ④ surface
⑤ climate

06 밑줄 친 우리말과 일치하도록 주어진 단어를 이용해 영작하시오.

> (wonder, it)

➡ _____

[07~09] 다음 대화를 읽고 물음에 답하시오.

> B: Look at the baby penguins on TV. They're so cute.
> G: Yes, ____(A)____ they look very cold out there.
> B: Yeah, the South Pole is the coldest place on Earth.

G: I wonder how cold is it there.

B: The average temperature is about -58℃ in July and -26℃ in December.

G: Oh, then, ___ⓐ___ is colder than ___ⓑ___ there. Interesting!

B: Yes. ___(B)___ it's very cold there, it doesn't snow much.

G: That's interesting, too!

출제율 90%

07 빈칸 (A)와 (B)에 들어갈 말로 알맞은 것끼리 짝지어진 것을 <u>고르시오</u>.

① but – Therefore ② but – Unless
③ but – Although   ④ since – Unless
⑤ since – Although

출제율 95%

08 위 대화에 나온 단어를 이용해 빈칸 ⓐ, ⓑ에 알맞은 말을 쓰시오.

ⓐ _____ ⓑ _____

출제율 95%

09 밑줄 친 부분에서 어법상 <u>어색한</u> 것을 골라 바르게 고치시오.

➡ _____

[10~12] 다음 대화를 읽고 물음에 답하시오.

B: Sumin, what are you going to do on Sunday?

G: I'm going to go hiking. (①) Do you want to join me?

B: I'd love to. (②)

G: I'm thinking ___(A)___ going to Namsan.

B: Oh, the scenery there is so beautiful this time of year. (③)

G: Right. (④) I ___(B)___ that it's covered ___(C)___ red autumn leaves now. (⑤)

B: Great. How long does the shortest hiking course take?

G: 인터넷에 따르면 약 두 시간 정도 걸린대.

B: Okay, see you on Sunday!

출제율 100%

10 ①~⑤ 중 주어진 문장이 들어갈 곳은?

> Where do you want to go?

①   ②   ③   ④   ⑤

출제율 90%

11 빈칸 (A)~(C)에 들어갈 말로 알맞은 것끼리 짝지어진 것을 고르시오.

① of – heard – with   ② of – said – of
③ of – heard – of   ④ to – said – with
⑤ to – heard – with

출제율 90%

12 밑줄 친 우리말과 일치하도록 주어진 단어를 이용해 8 단어로 영작하시오. (say, it, about)

➡ _____

출제율 100%

13 다음 중 어법상 <u>어색한</u> 것을 고르시오.

① Tom sang a song while he washed the dishes.
② After Jenny mopped the floor, it looked very shiny.
③ He won't rest until he will find her.
④ Buy now before it's too late.
⑤ Call me when you arrive!

14 다음 빈칸에 들어갈 알맞은 말을 〈보기〉에서 골라 써 넣으시오.

> ┌── 보기 ──┐
> who   whose   which   of which

(1) I know a girl _____ favorite number is 7.

(2) Pinocchio is a cute doll _____ the wish is to become a boy.

(3) The people _____ called yesterday want to buy the house.

(4) Rapunzel is a beautiful princess _____ hair is very long.

(5) I have a piggy bank _____ the color is pink.

(6) I'm afraid the position for _____ you applied has been filled.

[15~16] 다음 글을 읽고 물음에 답하시오.

My Fun Animal: Octopus

I will introduce the octopus. It lives on the ocean floor. It has no bones so it can move around easily in the ocean. It usually eats small fish. An interesting fact about the octopus is ⓐthat it can change the color of its skin to hide from its enemies. When it meets an enemy, it shoots out dark black ink and swims away. I want to see this animal with my own eyes!

15 위 글의 밑줄 친 ⓐthat과 문법적 쓰임이 같은 것을 고르시오.

① What is that loud noise?

② Are you sure she's that young?

③ The trouble is that we are short of money.

④ This is my sister and that is my cousin.

⑤ He is the greatest novelist that has ever lived.

16 위 글을 읽고 문어에 대해서 알 수 없는 것을 고르시오.

① Where does it live?

② What does it usually eat?

③ What is an interesting fact about it?

④ How can it change the color of its skin?

⑤ When it meets an enemy, what does it do?

[17~18] 다음 글을 읽고 물음에 답하시오.

One, Two, Three, Jump!

You have probably seen a bird fly down to the sea to catch a fish. But have you ever seen a fish jump out of the water to catch a bird? Well, birds have to be careful when a giant trevally is around. This fish can grow up to 170cm and 80kg. But ⓐ그 크기에 속지 마라. This fish is quick and smart. It can spot a flying bird and calculate its speed and distance. When the bird flies nearby, the giant trevally jumps out of the water and catches it.

*giant trevally: 전갱잇과의 물고기로 서태평양과 인도양에서 서식한다.

17 위 글의 밑줄 친 ⓐ의 우리말에 맞게 주어진 어휘를 이용하여 6 단어로 영작하시오.

> its, fool

➡ _____

18 According to the passage, which is NOT true?

① It's impossible for a bird to fly down to the sea to catch a fish.

② There is a fish which can jump out of the water to catch a bird.

③ When a giant trevally is around, it will be better for birds to be careful.

④ A giant trevally can grow up to 170cm and 80kg.

⑤ A giant trevally is quick and smart.

[19~20] 다음 글을 읽고 물음에 답하시오.

Sweet Dreams

Can you guess what these whales are doing in the picture? It looks like they are standing up in a group. But they are actually sleeping! Humpback whales stand on their tails while they sleep. They sleep near the surface. Since they are not fish, they need to come up to breathe. Also, they don't fall asleep completely. When they wake up, they come ⓐ_____ the water for a deep breath and dive back ⓑ_____ the sea.

19 위 글의 빈칸 ⓐ와 ⓑ에 들어갈 전치사가 바르게 짝지어진 것은?

① out of – into   ② into – on

③ into – for   ④ out of – on

⑤ to – into

20 위 글의 주제로 알맞은 것을 고르시오.

① Why do humpback whales stand on their tails while they sleep?

② Where do humpback whales sleep?

③ When do humpback whales breathe?

④ How do humpback whales sleep and breathe?

⑤ Why do humpback whales dive back into the sea?

[21~23] 다음 글을 읽고 물음에 답하시오.

Enjoy Your Meal

If you think fish are not smart, take a look at the tuskfish. (①) This small fish whose favorite food is clams uses a tool ⓐto open them. (②) Clams usually hide under the sand, so they cannot be easily discovered. (③) The tuskfish blows on the sand until a clam appears. (④) The clam is closed tightly, so the fish cannot eat it. (⑤) It smashes the clam against a rock. In the end, the clam opens and dinner is served.

21 위 글의 흐름으로 보아, 주어진 문장이 들어가기에 가장 적절한 곳은?

But the tuskfish doesn't give up.

①   ②   ③   ④   ⑤

22 아래 〈보기〉에서 위 글의 밑줄 친 ⓐto open과 to부정사의 용법이 다른 것의 개수를 고르시오.

――― 보기 ―――

① I am happy to hear that.

② He has a few books to read.

③ His wealth enabled him to go abroad.

④ He can't be rich to ask me for some money.

⑤ His job is to sing a song.

① 1개   ② 2개   ③ 3개   ④ 4개   ⑤ 5개

23 Which question CANNOT be answered after reading the passage?

① What is the tuskfish's favorite food?

② Where do clams usually hide?

③ How does the tuskfish discover a clam in the sand?

④ How long does it take for the tuskfish to open the clam?

⑤ Why does the tuskfish smash the clam against a rock?

01 다음 문장을 주어진 〈조건〉에 맞춰 바꿔 쓰시오.

> How long does the shortest hiking course take?

조건
(1) wonder를 이용하여 궁금증을 표현할 것.
(2) curious를 이용하여 궁금증을 표현할 것.

(1) _____

_____

(2) _____

_____

02 밑줄 친 우리말과 일치하도록 주어진 단어를 사용하여 두 가지 문장으로 만드시오.

> A: Is there anything interesting?
> B: 이 기사에 따르면 과학자들이 새로운 행성을 발견했대.

(1) _____

_____

(say, 9 단어)

(2) _____

_____

(according, 10 단어)

03 다음 대화의 밑줄 친 문장 중 문맥상 또는 어법상 어색한 것을 찾아 바르게 고치시오.

> Suji: Check out this picture!
> Tony: Wow! The camels are walking in a line in the desert.
> Suji: Yeah. The desert looks very hot and dry.

Tony: I wonder how long can camels go without water in the desert.
Suji: Let's find out on the Internet.
Tony: Okay. The Internet says they can go about two weeks without water.
Suji: Wow, that's amazing! Camels are really interesting animals.
Tony: I want to travel with them in the desert someday.

➡ _____

_____

04 다음 주어진 두 문장을 관계대명사를 사용해서 하나의 문장으로 쓰시오.

(1) • I interviewed a man.
• His dream is to climb Baekdusan.

➡ _____

_____

(2) • The cat is sitting on the table.
• The name of the cat is Molly.

➡ _____

_____

05 다음 두 문장을 주어진 접속사를 사용해서 하나의 문장으로 쓰시오.

(1) • You have to finish your homework.
• You go to bed. (before)

➡ _____

_____

(2) • Tom waited in front of the door.
• Someone came out. (until)

➡ _____

_____

[06~08] 다음 글을 읽고 물음에 답하시오.

Sweet Dreams

Can you guess what these whales are doing in the picture? It looks like they are standing up in a group. But they are actually sleeping! Humpback whales stand on their tails while they sleep. They sleep near the surface. Since they are not fish, they need to come up to breathe. Also, ⓐ그들은 완전히 잠들지 않는다. When they wake up, they come out of the water for a deep breath and dive back into the sea.

*humpback whale: 혹등고래라고 불리며, 북극해를 제외한 모든 대양에서 서식한다.

06 위 글의 밑줄 친 ⓐ의 우리말에 맞게 주어진 어휘를 이용하여 5 단어로 영작하시오.

> fall, completely

➡ _____

07 다음 문장에서 위 글의 내용과 <u>다른</u> 부분을 찾아서 고치시오.

> Humpback whales sleep near the bottom of the sea.

_____ ➡ _____

08 Why do humpback whales need to come out of the water when they wake up? Fill in the blanks (A) and (B) with suitable words.

> Since they are not (A)_____, they need to come out of the water for (B)_____
> _____ _____.

[09~11] 다음 글을 읽고 물음에 답하시오.

One, Two, Three, Jump!

You have probably seen a bird (A)[fly / to fly] down to the sea to catch a fish. But have you ever seen a fish jump out of the water to catch a bird? Well, birds have to be careful when a giant trevally is around. This fish can grow up to 170cm and 80kg. ⓐBut don't let its size fool you. This fish is quick and smart. It can spot a flying bird and calculate its speed and distance. When the bird flies (B)[nearby / nearly], the giant trevally jumps (C)[into / out of] the water and catches it.

*giant trevally: 전갱잇과의 물고기로 서태평양과 인도양에서 서식한다.

09 위 글의 괄호 (A)~(C)에서 문맥이나 어법상 알맞은 낱말을 골라 쓰시오.

(A) _____ (B) _____ (C) _____

10 위 글의 밑줄 친 ⓐ를 다음과 같이 바꿔 쓸 때 빈칸에 들어갈 알맞은 말을 두 단어로 쓰시오.

> But don't allow its size _____ _____ you.

11 주어진 영영풀이에 해당하는 단어를 본문에서 찾아 쓰시오.

> to notice something or someone

➡ _____

창의사고력 서술형 문제

01 다음 사진을 보고, 〈조건〉에 맞게 대화를 완성하시오.

조건

- 궁금증 표현하기 2번, 보고하기의 표현을 1번 사용한다.
- 주어진 단어를 이용하여 문장을 만든다.

A: _____(wonder)
B: _____ Machu Picchu.(Internet)
A: _____(curious)
B: It is in Peru.

02 다음 내용을 바탕으로 바다 동물 보고서를 쓰시오.

- Animal: Beluga whale
- Where does it live?　　　It lives in the Arctic Ocean.
- What does it look like?　It has a round head.
- What does it eat?　　　It usually eats fish and clams.
- Interesting facts　　　It is white all over. When it is born, it is gray. But when it grows up, its body becomes white.

My Fun Animal: Beluga whale

I will introduce the beluga whale. It lives (A)_____. It has (B)_____. It usually eats (C)_____. An interesting fact about the beluga whale is that (D)_____. That's why people call it the white whale. When it is born, it is (E)_____. But when it grows up, its body becomes (F)_____! I want to see this animal with my own eyes!

단원별 모의고사

01 빈칸 (A)와 (B)에 들어갈 말로 알맞은 것끼리 짝지어진 것을 고르시오.

> • I drank a lot of coffee earlier and now I can't (A)_____ asleep.
> • The important thing is to (B)_____ trying.

   (A)   (B)   (A)   (B)
① go – take   ② turn – take
③ turn – keep   ④ fall – take
⑤ fall – keep

02 다음 빈칸을 〈보기〉에 있는 어휘를 이용하여 채우시오. (한 단어는 한 번만 사용)

> ┤ 보기 ├
> completely friendly nearby finally

(1) I went to a small store _____.
(2) The hotel staff were very _____ and helpful.
(3) I _____ forgot that it's his birthday today.
(4) We _____ arrived home at midnight.

03 다음 제시된 단어를 사용해서 자연스러운 문장을 만들 수 없는 것은? (형태 변화 가능)

> calculate hide surround take

① How long is this going to _____?
② You are _____! Put down your weapons!
③ He found it difficult to _____ his disappointment when she didn't arrive.

④ Several cups fell to the floor and _____ to pieces.
⑤ No matter how many times I _____, I'm missing 3,000 won.

04 다음 우리말에 맞도록 빈칸에 알맞은 말을 쓰시오. (철자가 주어진 경우 주어진 철자로 시작할 것.)

(1) 하늘에는 밝은 불꽃들이 가득했다.
➡ The sky _____ _____ of brightly colored fireworks.

(2) 내일 소풍 가지 않을래?
➡ Would you like to _____ _____ _____ _____ tomorrow?

(3) 비만아들은 어른이 되어서도 비만일 수 있습니다.
➡ Overweight children _____ _____ become overweight adults.

(4) 이번 지진으로 수백만 명의 이재민이 발생했다.
➡ The earthquake left _____ _____ people homeless.

05 대화가 자연스럽게 연결되도록 (A)~(D)를 순서대로 적절하게 배열하시오.

> (A) What are you doing?
> (B) This article says a whale family was seen in the East Sea.
> (C) I'm reading the newspaper.
> (D) Is there anything interesting?

➡ _____

[06~07] 다음 대화를 읽고 물음에 답하시오.

A: We're finally here.
B: Yes, I'm so excited. Let's look around.
A: _____ (A)
B: It's _____ (B) _____ the police station.
A: You're right. Let's go.

06 빈칸 (A)에 wonder를 이용해, 동그라미 친 부분의 위치에 대해 궁금증을 표현하는 문장을 쓰시오.

➡ _____

07 빈칸 (B)에 들어갈 말을 쓰시오.

➡ _____

[08~09] 다음 대화를 읽고 물음에 답하시오.

B: The weather is so nice outside.
G: Yeah. How about _____ (A) _____ (go) on a picnic this afternoon?
B: Good idea. Can you check the weather?
G: Oh, no! 일기 예보에 따르면 오후에 비가 올 거래.
B: Let's go another time, then.

08 다음 괄호 안의 단어를 문맥에 맞게 고쳐 빈칸 (A)를 채우시오.

➡ _____

09 밑줄 친 우리말과 일치하도록 주어진 단어를 사용하여 두 가지 문장으로 쓰시오.

(1) (say, rainy)

➡ _____
_____

(2) (according, rainy)

➡ _____
_____

[10~12] 다음 대화를 읽고 물음에 답하시오.

B: Sumin, what are you going to do on Sunday?
G: I'm going to go hiking. Do you want to join me?
B: I'd love to. Where do you want to go?
G: I'm thinking of going to Namsan.
B: Oh, _____ (A) _____. (is, of, the, so, year, scenery, this, time, beautiful)
G: Right. I heard that it's _____ (B) _____ with red autumn leaves now.
B: Great. How long does the shortest hiking course take?
G: The Internet says it takes about two hours.
B: Okay, see you on Sunday!

10 빈칸 (A)를 괄호 안에 주어진 단어를 알맞게 배열하여 채우시오.

➡ _____

11 빈칸 (B)에 들어갈 말을 고르시오.

① related   ② filled
③ covered   ④ located
⑤ contained

12 위 대화를 읽고 답할 수 있는 질문의 개수를 고르시오.

ⓐ Where are Sumin planning to go on Sunday?

ⓑ How many hiking courses are there in Namsan?

ⓒ Where does B find the information about the shortest course of the Han River?

ⓓ What day are they going to meet on?

ⓔ What is Sumin doing this Sunday?

① 1개　② 2개　③ 3개　④ 4개　⑤ 5개

13 다음 중 어법상 어색한 것을 고르시오.

① I took her classes for her during she was sick.

② Sue didn't stop practicing until she could play the instrument.

③ While you were out, you had two phone calls.

④ He didn't get married until he was well into his forties.

⑤ Turn the sweater inside out before you wash it.

14 다음 중 어법상 올바른 것을 고르시오.

① I have a friend who dog won the Fastest Dog contest.

② I met a girl of which mother writes novels.

③ The boy of whose hair is red is Mark.

④ She was in a large stone-chamber of which window was usually open.

⑤ The mountain of which the summit you can see over there is Mt. Namsan.

[15~16] 다음 우리말에 맞도록 괄호 안에 주어진 어휘를 이용하여 영작하시오.

15
나는 취미가 농구인 친구가 있다. (to play basketball, a friend, hobby, have, 10 단어)

➡ _____

16
그가 집에 돌아오면, 그는 아버지에게 전화할 것이다. (come back home, call his father, when)

➡ _____
_____

17 다음 문장에서 어법상 어색한 것을 찾아 바르게 고치시오.

(1) Charlotte is a wise spider which best friend is Wilbur.

➡ _____
_____

(2) The girl of which dress is yellow is Bora.

➡ _____

(3) I'll take care of your dog while you will be away.

➡ _____

18 다음 중 어법상 옳은 것을 고르시오.

① The boy whose the backpack is blue is Jinsu.

② I have a watch of which price is 9,000 won.

③ She will wait here until the contest will be over.

④ You should wait on the sidewalk as soon as the traffic light changes to green.

⑤ Mike called her back as soon as he saw her message.

[19~22] 다음 대화를 읽고 물음에 답하시오.

Sweet Dreams

Can you guess what these whales are doing in the picture? It looks like they are standing up in a group. But they are ⓐactually sleeping! Humpback whales stand on their tails while they sleep. They sleep near the surface. Since they are not fish, they need to come up to breathe. Also, they don't fall asleep completely. ⓑWhen they wake up, they come out of the water for a deep breathe and dive back into the sea.

*humpback whale: 혹등고래라고 불리며, 북극해를 제외한 모든 대양에서 서식한다.

19 위 글의 밑줄 친 ⓐactually와 바꿔 쓸 수 없는 말을 고르시오.

① in truth   ② in fact

③ exactly   ④ in reality

⑤ indeed

20 본문의 내용과 일치하도록 다음 빈칸 (A)~(C)에 알맞은 단어를 쓰시오.

Humpback whales sleep near (A)_____ _____ standing on (B)_____ _____, and they don't fall asleep (C)_____.

21 위 글의 밑줄 친 ⓑ에서 문맥상 어색한 단어를 고치시오.

_____ ➡ _____

22 위 글을 읽고 알 수 없는 것을 고르시오.

① Do humpback whales sleep on their side?

② Are humpback whales fish?

③ Why do humpback whales need to come up to breathe?

④ When humpback whales wake up, what do they do?

⑤ How often do humpback whales come out of the water for a deep breath?

[23~24] 다음 글을 읽고 물음에 답하시오.

Enjoy Your Meal

If you think fish are not smart, take a look at the tuskfish. This small fish whose favorite food is clams uses a tool to open them. Clams usually hide under the sand, so they cannot be easily discovered. The tuskfish blows on the sand until a clam appears. The clam is closed tightly, so the fish cannot eat ⓐit. But the tuskfish doesn't give up. It smashes the clam against a rock. In the end, the clam opens and dinner is served.

*tuskfish: 놀래깃과의 물고기로 서태평양과 인도양에서 주로 서식한다.

23 위 글의 주제로 알맞은 것을 고르시오.

① It's unclear why people think fish are not smart.
② The tuskfish is a smart fish which uses a tool to open clams.
③ The place where clams usually hide is under the sand.
④ It is not easy to discover clams.
⑤ The clams appear when the tuskfish blows on the sand.

24 위 글의 밑줄 친 ⓐit이 가리키는 것을 본문에서 찾아 쓰시오.

➡ _____

[25~27] 다음 글을 읽고 물음에 답하시오.

One, Two, Three, Jump!

You have probably seen a bird fly down to the sea to catch a fish. But ⓐ물고기가 새를 잡기 위해 물 밖으로 뛰어오르는 것을 본 적이 있는가? Well, birds have to be careful when a giant trevally is around. (①) This fish can grow up to ⓑ170cm and 80kg. (②) This fish is quick and smart. (③) It can spot a flying bird and calculate its speed and distance. (④) When the bird flies nearby, the giant trevally jumps out of the water and catches it. (⑤)

*giant trevally: 전갱잇과의 물고기로 서태평양과 인도양에서 서식한다.

25 위 글의 밑줄 친 ⓐ의 우리말에 맞게 주어진 어휘를 알맞게 배열하시오.

to catch / ever / a fish / jump / seen / you / out of the water / a bird / have

➡ _____
_____

26 위 글의 흐름으로 보아, 주어진 문장이 들어가기에 가장 적절한 곳은?

But don't let its size fool you.

①　　②　　③　　④　　⑤

27 위 글의 밑줄 친 ⓑ를 읽는 법을 영어로 쓰시오.

➡ _____
_____

MEMO

Up to You

🎙 의사소통 기능

- 후회 표현하기
  A: Oh, no! You got caught in the rain.
  B: I should have taken an umbrella.

- 기원하는 말 하기
  A: I'm going to sing in the school festival.
  B: I hope you move the audience.

🔧 언어 형식

- 분사구문
  Reading the article, he dropped his cup in surprise.

- 과거완료
  The article said Alfred Nobel **had died** in France from a heart attack.

Words & Expressions

Key Words

- **active** [ǽktiv] 휑 활동적인, 적극적인
- **actually** [ǽktʃuəli] 휌 사실
- **appreciate** [əprí:ʃièit] 동 고맙게 생각하다
- **article** [ɑ́:rtikl] 명 기사
- **audience** [ɔ́:diəns] 명 관객
- **award** [əwɔ́:rd] 명 상, 시상
- **chain** [tʃein] 동 사슬로 묶다(매다)
- **clothes** [klouz] 명 옷
- **contribute** [kəntríbju:t] 동 기여하다, 공헌하다
- **create** [kriéit] 동 창조하다, 만들어 내다
- **decide** [disáid] 동 결정하다
- **deeply** [dí:pli] 휌 몹시, 깊이, 매우
- **describe** [diskráib] 동 기술하다, 묘사하다
- **disappointed** [dìsəpɔ́intid] 휑 실망한, 낙담한
- **drop** [drɑp] 동 떨어뜨리다
- **due** [dju:] 휑 ~하기로 되어 있는, 예정된
- **dynamite** [dáinəmàit] 명 다이너마이트
- **even** [í:vən] 휌 훨씬
- **fault** [fɔ:lt] 명 잘못
- **graduate** [grǽdʒuet] 동 졸업하다
- **graduation** [grǽdʒuéiʃən] 명 졸업(식)
- **grandparents** [grǽndpɛərənts] 명 조부모
- **habit** [hǽbit] 명 습관
- **headline** [hédlain] 명 (신문 기사 등의) 표제
- **heart attack** 심장 마비
- **including** [inklú:diŋ] 전 ~을 포함해서
- **invention** [invénʃən] 명 발명품
- **inventor** [invéntər] 명 발명가
- **merchant** [mɔ́:rtʃənt] 명 상인
- **mistake** [mistéik] 명 실수, 잘못
- **mistakenly** [mistéikənli] 휌 실수로
- **moment** [móumənt] 명 (정확한 시점을 나타내는) 순간
- **move** [mu:v] 동 감동시키다
- **normal** [nɔ́:rməl] 휑 보통의, 정상적인
- **opinion** [əpínjən] 명 의견
- **originally** [ərídʒənəli] 휌 원래는, 처음에는
- **participate** [pɑ:rtísəpèit] 동 참가하다
- **perfect** [pɔ́:rfikt] 휑 완벽한
- **plan** [plæn] 명 계획 동 계획을 세우다
- **protect** [prətékt] 동 보호하다, 지키다
- **regret** [rigrét] 명 후회 동 후회하다
- **report** [ripɔ́:rt] 동 보도하다 명 기사, 보도
- **satisfied** [sǽtisfàid] 휑 만족한
- **score** [skɔ:r] 동 득점하다
- **shocked** 휑 충격을 받은
- **spill** [spil] 동 쏟아지다, 흐르다, 쏟다
- **step** [step] 동 밟다
- **stomachache** [stuhmuhkeik] 명 복통
- **trust** [trʌst] 동 신뢰하다, 믿다
- **unbelievable** [ʌnbilívəbəl] 휑 믿을 수 없는, 믿기 어려운
- **vacation** [veikéiʃən] 명 휴가, 방학
- **voice** [vɔis] 명 목소리

Key Expressions

- **be late for** ~에 지각하다
- **be over** 끝나다
- **catch one's breath** 숨을 고르다
- **catch one's eye** 눈길을 끌다
- **describe A as B** A를 B로 기술하다, 묘사하다
- **get caught** 잡히다
- **give it a try** 시도하다
- **give up** 포기하다
- **hang out** 많은 시간을 보내다
- **in surprise** 놀라서
- **keep in touch** 연락하고 지내다
- **keep -ing** 계속해서 ~하다
- **make a mistake** 실수하다
- **put off** 미루다, 연기하다
- **rather than** ~보다는
- **stay up** 안 자다, 깨어 있다
- **take eyes off** 눈을 떼다
- **take part in** ~에 참가하다
- **thanks to** ~ 덕분에
- **think of A as B** A를 B라고 생각하다

Word Power

※ 서로 비슷한 뜻을 가진 어휘

- □ **active** 활동적인 – **dynamic** 역동적인
- □ **decide** 결정하다 – **determine** 결정하다
- □ **merchant** 상인 – **trader** 무역상
- □ **normal** 보통의 – **ordinary** 보통의
- □ **protect** 보호하다 – **defend** 방어하다

- □ **appreciate** 감사하다 – **be grateful** 감사하다
- □ **fault** 잘못 – **blunder** 잘못, 실수
- □ **move** 감동시키다 – **touch** 감동을 주다
- □ **participate** 참가하다 – **engage in** 참가하다
- □ **trust** 신뢰하다, 믿다 – **rely on** 의존하다

※ 서로 반대의 뜻을 가진 어휘

- □ **active** 활동적인 ↔ **inactive** 활동이 없는
- □ **normal** 정상적인 ↔ **abnormal** 비정상인
- □ **perfect** 완벽한 ↔ **imperfect** 불완전한
- □ **trust** 신뢰하다, 믿다 ↔ **distrust** 불신하다

- □ **including** 포함해서 ↔ **excluding** 제외하고
- □ **opinion** 의견 ↔ **fact** 사실
- □ **satisfied** 만족한 ↔ **dissatisfied** 불만족한

※ 동사 – 명사

- □ **appreciate** 감사하다 – **appreciation** 감사
- □ **describe** 묘사하다 – **description** 묘사
- □ **participate** 참가하다 – **participation** 참가

- □ **decide** 결정하다 – **decision** 결정
- □ **graduate** 졸업하다 – **graduation** 졸업(식)

※ 동사 – 명사 – 행위자

- □ **contribute** 기여하다 – **contribution** 기여 – **contributor** 기여자
- □ **create** 창조하다 – **creation** 창조 – **creator** 창조자
- □ **educate** 교육하다 – **education** 교육 – **educator** 교육자
- □ **invent** 발명하다 – **invention** 발명품 – **inventor** 발명가
- □ **protect** 보호하다 – **protection** 보호 – **protector** 보호자

English Dictionary

- □ **appreciate** 고맙게 생각하다
  → to be grateful for something
  어떤 것에 대해 감사하다

- □ **contribute** 기여하다, 공헌하다
  → to help to cause something to happen
  어떤 일이 발생하도록 돕다

- □ **describe** 기술하다, 묘사하다
  → to explain about something
  어떤 것에 관하여 설명하다

- □ **due** ~하기로 되어 있는, 예정된
  → expected at or planned for a certain time
  어떤 시간에 예정되어 있거나 계획된

- □ **dynamite** 다이너마이트
  → a powerful explosive
  강력한 폭약, 폭발물

- □ **graduation** 졸업(식)
  → a ceremony at which degrees or diplomas are given out
  학위나 졸업장이 주어지는 의식

- □ **headline** (신문 기사 등의) 표제
  → the title written in large letters over a story in a newspaper
  신문 기사에 큰 글씨로 쓰여진 제목

- □ **merchant** 상인
  → a person who sells products in large amounts
  대량으로 상품을 파는 사람

- □ **regret** 후회하다
  → to feel sorry or unhappy about something
  무엇인가에 대하여 유감스럽거나 불행하다고 느끼다

- □ **report** 보도하다
  → to give information about something via newspaper, TV or radio
  신문, TV 또는 라디오를 통해서 무언가에 관한 정보를 주다

- □ **score** 득점하다
  → to gain a goal or point in a sport or game
  운동 또는 경기에서 점수를 얻다

- □ **spill** 쏟아지다, 흐르다, 쏟다
  → to flow over the edge of a container
  용기의 가장자리 너머로 흐르다

- □ **unbelievable** 믿을 수 없는, 믿기 어려운
  → difficult or impossible to believe
  믿기 어렵거나 불가능한

01 접미사 -or를 붙여 명사로 만들 수 <u>없는</u> 것을 <u>모두</u> 고르시오.

① produce   ② invent   ③ protect

④ educate   ⑤ collect

02 다음 밑줄 친 부분의 의미로 알맞지 <u>않은</u> 것은?

① We hope everyone will <u>contribute</u> to the discussion. (기여하다)

② He <u>should have been</u> more careful. (~해야 한다)

③ The cost is $150 per night, <u>including</u> buffet breakfast. (포함해서)

④ She plays an <u>active</u> part in local politics. (적극적인)

⑤ It would be hard to <u>describe</u> my feelings. (묘사하다)

03 다음 영영풀이가 나타내는 말을 고르시오.

> to give information about something via newspaper, TV or radio

① research   ② inspect   ③ report

④ review   ⑤ examine

04 다음 〈보기〉의 밑줄 친 단어와 같은 의미로 쓰인 것을 <u>모두</u> 고르시오.

> ┌─ 보기 ─┐
> I'm deeply <u>moved</u> by such kindness.

① They <u>move</u> house fairly frequently.

② She <u>moved</u> quickly towards the door.

③ Could you <u>move</u> your car, please?

④ These stories surprised and <u>moved</u> me.

⑤ His speech <u>moved</u> the audience to tears.

05 다음 밑줄 친 부분과 의미가 가장 가까운 것을 고르시오.

> I <u>am grateful for</u> all your help.

① enjoy   ② increase

③ appreciate   ④ am aware of

⑤ deal with

[06~07] 다음 빈칸에 알맞은 것을 고르시오.

06
> They arrived early, _____ good weather.

① such as   ② in spite of

③ thanks to   ④ depending on

⑤ by means of

07
> He decided to quit _____ accept the new rules.

① as if   ② as well as

③ in addition to   ④ rather than

⑤ by the time

01 다음 짝지어진 단어의 관계가 같도록 빈칸에 알맞은 말을 쓰시오.

> act : actor = win : _____

02 밑줄 친 부분과 바꿔 쓸 수 있는 말을 주어진 철자로 시작하여 쓰시오.

> All the students at the school must <u>engage</u> in volunteer work.

➡ p_____

[03~04] 다음 빈칸에 공통으로 들어갈 말을 쓰시오.

03
> • Clark had to sit down to _____ his breath.
> • There are some paintings that _____ my eye.

04
> • Do you _____ in touch with him?
> • Why do you _____ talking that way?

05 다음 제시된 의미에 맞는 단어를 주어진 철자로 시작하여 빈칸에 쓰고, 알맞은 것을 골라 문장을 완성하시오.

> • d_____ : a powerful explosive
> • h_____ : the title written in large letters over a story in a newspaper
> • m_____ : a person who sells products in large amounts

(1) Have you seen the _____ in today's paper?

(2) The _____ paid customs on what he had bought in China.

(3) They used _____ to break big stones.

06 다음 우리말에 맞게 주어진 단어를 바르게 배열하시오.

(1) 그의 새 책은 내년에 출판될 예정이다.
(next, new, year, his, published, is, book, be, to, due)

➡ _____

(2) 그 영화는 매우 자극적인 스릴러물로 묘사되고 있다.
(film, a, thriller, charged, the, described, highly, is, as)

➡ _____

(3) 나는 같은 실수를 다시 하지 않을 거야.
(make, the, mistake, won't, I, again, same)

➡ _____

(4) 소풍에서 비를 만나기 전까지는 좋았지.
(until, the, the, at, was, in, fine, picnic, we, caught, it, rain, got)

➡ _____

Conversation

① 후회 표현하기

> **A** Oh, no! You got caught in the rain. 오, 저런! 너 비를 맞았구나.
>
> **B** I should have taken an umbrella. 나는 우산을 가져갔어야 했어.

- 'I should have+과거분사 ~.'는 '나는 ~했어야 했는데 (하지 못해 유감이다)'의 의미로 과거 사실에 대한 후회, 안타까움, 유감 등을 나타낼 때 사용하는 표현이다. 'I should not/shouldn't have+과거분사 ~.'는 '나는 ~하지 말았어야 했다.'라는 뜻을 나타낸다. 이 표현에서는 'should'를 'ought to'로 바꾸어 'I ought to have+과거분사'로 표현할 수 있다. '~하지 말았어야 했는데 (했다)'는 의미의 'I should not have+과거분사'는 'I ought not to have+과거분사'로 나타낼 수 있다.

- 안타까움, 후회를 나타내는 비슷한 표현으로 'I had to ~, but I didn't.', 'I (really) regret ~.' 등이 있고, sorry를 사용하여 'I'm sorry that 주어+과거동사 ~.'로 나타내기도 한다. 'should have+과거분사'는 과거 사실에 대한 가정의 표현으로 '~했어야 했는데 (하지 않았다)'의 의미를 나타내는 과거에 하지 않은 일에 대해 후회하는 표현이다. should 대신 could를 사용하여 'could have+과거분사'가 되면 '~할 수 있었는데'의 의미가 될 수 있다.

- 'should have p.p.'는 과거에 했어야 하는 일 또는 하지 못한 일에 대한 후회, 유감, 안타까움을 표현하며 '~했어야 했는데 (못했다)'의 의미로 사용되고, 'could/would have p.p.'는 과거의 일에 대한 유감을 의미하여 '~할 수 있었는데 (못했다), ~했어야 했는데 (못했다)'의 의미로 가정법에 주로 사용된다. 'must have p.p.'는 과거에 대한 강한 추측을 나타내어 '~이었음에 틀림없다'의 의미로 사용되고, 'can not have p.p.'는 과거에 대한 강한 부정의 추측을 나타내어 '~이었을 리가 없다'의 의미로 사용되며, 'may have p.p.'는 과거에 대한 약한 추측을 나타내어 '~했을지도 모른다'의 의미로 사용된다.

후회 표현하기

- I should[shouldn't] have 과거분사 나는 ~했어야[하지 말았어야] 했는데
- I ought(not) to have 과거분사 나는 ~했어야(하지 말았어야) 했는데
- I (really) regret (that) 주어+과거동사 ~한 것이 유감이다/후회한다
- I'm sorry that 주어+과거동사 ~한 것이 유감이다

핵심 Check

1. 우리말에 맞게 괄호 안의 단어들을 바르게 배열하시오.

    (1) 나는 열심히 공부했어야 했다. (should, I, hard, studied, have)
    ➡ _____

    (2) 나는 학교에 늦지 말았어야 했다. (have, I, school, for, should, not, late, been)
    ➡ _____

2 기원하는 말 하기

> **A** I'm going to sing in the school festival. 나는 학교 축제에서 노래를 할 예정이야.
>
> **B** I hope you move the audience. 네가 관객들을 감동시키기를 바라.

■ 상대에게 좋은 일이 생기도록 기원하는 표현은 'I hope ~.'를 사용한다. I hope 뒤에 접속사 that은 보통 생략하고, 기원하고자 하는 내용의 '주어+동사 ~'를 넣어 'I hope you succeed.(네가 성공하기를 기원해.)'처럼 말한다. hope 이외에도 wish, pray 등을 사용하여 'I wish ~.' 또는 'I pray ~.'라고 하기도 한다.

■ 상대가 하는 일이 잘 되기를 기원하면서 '행운을 빌어!'라고 할 때 'I'll keep my fingers crossed (for you)!'라고 한다. 'keep one's fingers crossed'란 집게손가락 위에 가운데 손가락을 교차시켜서 소원이 이루어지도록(= hope for something) 행운을 비는 동작을 묘사한 말로 'I'll keep my fingers crossed (for you).(행운을 빌어.)'처럼 사용한다.

■ 상대의 구체적인 행동을 언급하지 않고 단순히 상대에게 행운이 깃들기를 기원하는 의미로 '행운을 빌어.'와 같은 표현으로 'Good luck to you.(행운을 빌어.)', 'I hope everything goes well with you.(다 잘되기를 희망해.)' 등을 사용하기도 한다. 'Have a nice ~!'도 상대에게 행운을 기원하는 말이다. 'Break a leg!(행운을 빌어!)'라는 표현은 주로 공연이나, 행사, 경기 등을 앞두고 있는 사람에게 '행운을 빌어!'라고 격려할 때 자주 쓰인다.

기원하기

- I hope ~. ~하기를 희망한다.
- I would like you to ~. 나는 네가 ~하기를 원한다.
- What I really want is ~. 내가 정말로 원하는 것은 ~하는 것이다.
- I really want you to ~. 나는 정말로 네가 ~하기를 원한다.
- I hope everything goes well with you. 다 잘되기를 희망해.
- I'll keep my fingers crossed (for you). 행운을 빌어.
- Good luck to you. / Break a leg. 행운을 빌어.

핵심 Check

2. 다음 대화의 빈칸에 알맞은 것을 고르시오.

A: I'm planning to visit my grandparents in Busan.

B: Sounds great. I _____ you have a wonderful vacation.

① try   ② hope   ③ decide

④ remember   ⑤ break

Listen and Speak 1 A

G: Mike, why ❶were you late for class?

B: I had a bad ❷stomachache.

G: Oh, no! Are you okay now?

B: Yeah. ❸I should have eaten ❹less last night.

G: Mike, 왜 수업에 늦었니?
B: 배가 많이 아팠어.
G: 오, 저런! 지금은 괜찮니?
B: 응. 어젯밤 덜 먹었어야 했어.

❶ be late for ~: ~에 늦다
❷ stomachache: 복통, 위통
❸ 'I should have+과거분사 ~.'는 '나는 ~했어야 했다.'라는 뜻으로 과거 사실에 대한 후회를 표현할 때 사용하는 표현이다.
❹ less: 더 적게, 덜하게

Check(√) True or False

(1) Mike ate less last night. T ☐ F ☐

(2) Mike was late for class due to a bad stomachache. T ☐ F ☐

Listen and Speak 2 B

G: Jaemin, ❶are you ready for the singing contest?

B: Well, ❷I'm thinking of giving up, Tina.

G: Why? I thought you really wanted to ❸take part in the contest.

B: I don't think I'm a good singer.

G: Come on. You're ❹the best singer I know.

B: ❺Do you really think so?

G: Of course. You have a really nice voice.

B: ❻Thank you for saying so. I'll ❼do my best.

G: ❽I hope you win the contest.

G: 재민아, 노래 경연 대회에 나갈 준비는 됐니?
B: 음, 포기할까 생각 중이야, Tina.
G: 왜? 나는 네가 그 대회에 정말로 참가하고 싶어 한다고 생각했어.
B: 나는 내가 노래를 잘하는 것 같지 않아.
G: 그러지 말고. 너는 내가 아는 가장 노래를 잘하는 사람이야.
B: 정말로 그렇게 생각하니?
G: 물론이지. 너는 정말 멋진 목소리를 가졌어.
B: 그렇게 말해 줘서 고마워. 최선을 다해 볼게.
G: 네가 대회에서 우승하기를 바라.

❶ be ready for ~: ~할 준비가 되다
❷ 'I'm thinking of ~.'는 '나는 ~을 할까 생각 중이다.'라는 뜻으로 of 뒤에 동명사를 취해 의도나 계획을 나타낼 때 쓰는 표현이며 'I'm considering ~ing' 또는 'I intend to 동사원형 ~.'과 바꿔 쓸 수 있다. 전치사 of 대신 about을 사용하여 'I'm thinking about ~.'으로도 표현한다.
❸ take part in: ~에 참가하다
❹ the best singer와 I know 사이에 목적격 관계대명사 who(m)나 that이 생략되어 있다.
❺ 'Do you really think so?'는 상대방의 말이 확실한지를 묻는 표현으로 'Are you sure?'로 바꿔 말할 수 있다.
❻ thank you 다음에 전치사 for를 사용해서 감사의 이유를 덧붙여 말할 수 있다.
❼ do one's best: 최선을 다하다
❽ 'I hope you ~.'는 '나는 네가 ~하기를 바란다[희망한다].'라는 뜻으로 상대방에게 기원하는 말을 할 때 쓸 수 있는 표현이다.

Check(√) True or False

(3) Tina hopes Jaemin wins the contest. T ☐ F ☐

(4) Jaemin will take part in the singing contest. T ☐ F ☐

Listen and Speak 1 B

G: Jiho, what's up? You look tired.

B: Yeah. I ❶stayed up ❷late last night.

G: Did you play computer games again?

B: No, not this time. I ❸had to finish my history project.

G: Is it ❹due today?

B: Yeah. I ❺shouldn't have ❻put it off until the last moment.

G: Hmm, I understand. I often have the same problem.

B: Really? Well, ❼let's try to change our bad habits.

G: 지호야. 무슨 일이니? 너 피곤해 보여.

B: 응. 어젯밤에 늦게까지 깨어 있었어.

G: 너 또 컴퓨터 게임을 했니?

B: 아니, 이번엔 아니야. 나는 역사 과제를 끝내야 했어.

G: 그 과제가 오늘까지니?

B: 응. 나는 마지막 순간까지 미루지 말았어야 했어.

G: 음, 이해해. 나도 종종 같은 문제를 겪어.

B: 정말? 음. 우리의 나쁜 습관을 바꾸도록 노력하자.

❶ stay up: 안 자다, 깨어 있다
❷ late는 동사인 stay up을 꾸며주고 있으므로 부사로 '늦게'의 의미로 사용되었다.
❸ had to는 'have to(~해야 한다)'의 과거형으로 '~해야만 했다'로 해석한다.
❹ due: ~하기로 되어 있는, 예정된
❺ 'should not have+과거분사'는 '~하지 말았어야 했는데 (했다)'의 의미로, 말하는 시점보다 과거의 일에 대한 유감이나 후회를 나타낼 때 사용한다.
❻ put off: 미루다, 연기하다 until은 전치사로 '~까지'의 뜻이다.
❼ Let's+동사원형: ~하자 try to 동사원형: ~하는 것을 노력하다

Check(√) True or False

(5) Jiho doesn't know the due date of the history project.　　T ☐　F ☐

(6) Jiho stayed up late last night playing computer games.　　T ☐　F ☐

Listen and Speak 2 C

A: ❶What are you going to do tomorrow?

B: I'm going to sing in the school festival.

A: Great! ❷I hope you ❸move the audience.

B: Thanks. I hope so, too.

A: 너는 내일 무엇을 할 계획이니?
B: 학교 축제에서 노래 부를 거야.
A: 멋지네! 나는 네가 청중을 감동시키기를 바라.
B: 고마워. 나도 그러길 바라.

❶ 상대방에게 무엇을 할 계획인지(또는 어떤 계획이 있는지) 물어볼 때 'What are you planning[going] to+동사원형?'을 사용할 수 있다.
❷ 'I hope you ~.'는 '나는 네가 ~하기를 바란다[희망한다].'라는 뜻으로 상대방에게 기원하는 말을 할 때 쓸 수 있는 표현이다.
❸ move: (남을) 감동시키다 audience: 청중

Check(√) True or False

(7) B is planning to sing in the school festival.　　T ☐　F ☐

(8) A hopes to move the audience.　　T ☐　F ☐

Listen and Speak 1 C

A: ❶What's wrong?

B: I ❷got caught in the rain.

A: Oh, ❸I'm sorry to hear that.

B: ❹I should have taken an umbrella.

❶ 상대방이 뭔가에 불만족하거나 실망하고 있는 것을 보고 그 원인을 물을 때 'What's wrong?'이라고 물을 수 있다. 비슷한 표현으로 'What's the matter?' 혹은 'What's the problem?'도 있다.

❷ get caught in the rain: 비를 만나다

❸ 슬픔, 불만족, 실망에 대해 위로할 때 'I'm sorry to hear that.'을 사용하며 '안 됐구나.'로 해석한다.

❹ 'I should have+과거분사 ~.'는 '나는 ~했어야 했다.'라는 뜻으로 과거 사실에 대한 후회를 표현할 때 사용하는 표현이다. should 대신에 ought to를 사용하기도 한다.

Listen and Speak 2 A

G: Jinsu, what are you going to do ❶during the vacation?

B: I'm going to read ❷lots of books. What about you?

G: I'm planning to visit my grandparents in Busan.

B: Sounds great. ❸I hope you have a wonderful vacation.

❶ during+명사: ~ 동안에

❷ lots of: 많은

❸ 'I hope that 주어+동사 ~.'는 기원하고자 할 때 사용하는 표현으로 'I hope' 뒤에 기원하고자 하는 내용을 넣어 말한다.

Real Life Talk Watch a Video

Minho: Linda, what are you reading?

Linda: I'm reading ❶graduation messages from my classmates.

Minho: Oh, it looks like they had ❷a lot to say to you.

Linda: Many of them wrote ❸that they like my smile.

Minho: That's nice. What else?

Linda: Some of them said I didn't ❹hang out enough with them.

Minho: That's not your fault. You were always busy.

Linda: Yeah, but ❺I should have spent more time with my classmates.

Minho: ❻You still have time after graduation.

Linda: You're right.

Minho: ❼I hope you ❽keep in touch with your classmates ❾after graduation.

Linda: Thanks. I hope so, too.

❶ graduation: 졸업

❷ lot이 '많음'이라는 뜻의 명사로 사용되고 있다. to say to you는 명사 lot을 수식하는 형용사적 용법이다.

❸ that은 wrote의 목적어(명사절)를 이끄는 접속사이다.

❹ hang out: 많은 시간을 보내다

❺ 'should have 과거분사'는 '~했어야 했는데 (하지 못했다.)'의 의미로 후회를 표현할 때 사용하는 표현이다. 비슷한 표현으로 'I regret that 주어+과거동사 ~.', 'I feel sorry that 주어+과거동사 ~.', 'I ought to have 과거분사 ~.', 'I wish I had 과거분사 ~.'가 있다.

❻ still: 아직(도) graduation: 졸업

❼ 'I hope you ~.'는 '나는 네가 ~하기를 바란다[희망한다].'라는 뜻으로 상대방에게 기원하는 말을 할 때 쓸 수 있는 표현이다. 바꿔 쓸 수 있는 표현으로 'I would like you to 동사원형 ~.', 'I really want you to 동사원형 ~.', 'What I really want is for you to 동사원형 ~.' 등이 있다.

❽ keep in touch with: ~와 연락하고 지내다

❾ 'after'는 전치사로 '~ 후에'의 뜻이며 뒤에 명사가 올 수 있다.

Real Life Talk Step 2

A: ❶I can't believe we're ❷graduating soon.

B: Yeah. Is there anything ❸you regret about your middle school life?

A: Yes. ❹I should have been active in classes.

B: Well, you have a second ❺chance in high school.

A: ❻I guess you're right.

B: ❼I hope you are active in classes in high school.

❶ 어떤 사실에 대해 놀라움을 나타낼 때에는 'I can't believe 주어+동사 ~.', 'I was surprised that 주어+동사 ~.' 등과 같은 표현을 이용해 말할 수 있다.

❷ graduate: 졸업하다

❸ anything과 you regret about your middle school life 사이에 목적격 관계대명사 that이 생략되어 있다. regret: 후회하다

❹ 'I should have+과거분사 ~.'는 '나는 ~했어야 했다.'라는 뜻으로 과거 사실에 대한 후회를 표현할 때 사용하는 표현이다. active: 적극적인

❺ chance: 기회

❻ 'I guess you're right.'는 '네 말이 맞는 것 같아.'의 의미로, 상대방의 말에 동의하는 표현이다.

❼ 'I hope that 주어+동사 ~.'는 기원하고자 할 때 사용하는 표현으로 'I hope' 뒤에 기원하고자 하는 내용을 넣어 말한다.

● 다음 우리말과 일치하도록 빈칸에 알맞은 말을 쓰시오.

Listen and Speak 1 A

G: Mike, why _____ _____ _____ _____ class?

B: I had a bad _____.

G: Oh, no! _____ you okay now?

B: Yeah. I _____ _____ _____ less last night.

해석

G: Mike, 왜 수업에 늦었니?
B: 배가 많이 아팠어.
G: 오, 저런! 지금은 괜찮니?
B: 응. 어젯밤 덜 먹었어야 했어.

Listen and Speak 1 B

G: Jiho, what's _____? You look _____.

B: Yeah. I _____ _____ _____ last night.

G: Did you play computer games _____?

B: No, _____ this time. I _____ _____ finish my history project.

G: Is it _____ today?

B: Yeah. I _____ _____ _____ _____ _____ _____ the last moment.

G: Hmm, I understand. I often have _____ _____ problem.

B: Really? Well, let's _____ _____ _____ our bad _____.

G: 지호야, 무슨 일이니? 너 피곤해 보여.
B: 응. 어젯밤에 늦게까지 깨어 있었어.
G: 너 또 컴퓨터 게임을 했니?
B: 아니, 이번엔 아니야. 나는 역사 과제를 끝내야 했어.
G: 그 과제가 오늘까지니?
B: 응. 나는 마지막 순간까지 미루지 말았어야 했어.
G: 음, 이해해. 나도 종종 같은 문제를 겪어.
B: 정말? 음, 우리의 나쁜 습관을 바꾸도록 노력하자.

Listen and Speak 1 C

1. A: What's _____?

   B: I _____ _____ _____ the rain.

   A: Oh, I'm _____ _____ hear that.

   B: I should _____ _____ an umbrella.

2. A: _____ wrong?

   B: I _____ the test.

   A: Oh, I'm sorry to _____ _____.

   B: I _____ _____ _____ _____ _____.

3. A: What's wrong?

   B: I _____ my bike.

   A: Oh, I'm sorry to hear that.

   B: _____ _____ _____ _____ it.

4. A: What's wrong?

   B: I _____ _____ _____ school.

   A: Oh, I'm sorry to hear that.

   B: I _____ _____ _____ _____ _____.

1. A: 무슨 일 있니?
   B: 오, 비를 맞았어.
   A: 오, 안됐구나.
   B: 나는 우산을 가져왔어야 했어.

2. A: 무슨 일 있니?
   B: 시험에 떨어졌어.
   A: 오, 안됐구나.
   B: 나는 공부를 열심히 했어야 했어.

3. A: 무슨 일 있니?
   B: 자전거를 잃어버렸어.
   A: 오, 안됐구나.
   B: 나는 사슬로 묶어놨어야 했어.

4. A: 무슨 일 있니?
   B: 학교에 늦었어.
   A: 오, 안됐구나.
   B: 나는 일찍 일어났어야 했어.

Listen and Speak 2 A

G: Jinsu, what are you _____ _____ _____ _____ the vacation?

B: I'm going to read _____ _____ books. What _____ you?

G: I'm planning to _____ my grandparents in Busan.

B: Sounds great. I _____ _____ _____ a wonderful vacation.

Listen and Speak 2 B

G: Jaemin, are you _____ _____ the singing contest?

B: Well, _____ _____ _____ _____ _____ _____, Tina.

G: Why? I thought you really _____ _____ _____ _____ _____ the contest.

B: I don't think I'm a _____ _____.

G: Come on. You're _____ _____ _____ _____ _____.

B: Do you really _____ _____?

G: Of course. You have a really nice _____.

B: Thank _____ _____ _____ so, I'll _____ _____ _____.

B: _____ _____ _____ _____ the contest.

Listen and Speak 2 C

1. A: What are you going to do tomorrow?
   B: I'm _____ _____ _____ in the school festival.
   A: Great! I _____ _____ _____ the _____.
   B: Thanks. I _____ _____, too.

2. A: What are you going to do tomorrow?
   B: I'm going to play soccer.
   A: Great! I _____ _____ _____ _____ _____.
   B: Thanks. I hope so, too.

3. A: What are you going to do tomorrow?
   B: I'm going to _____ _____ the speech contest.
   A: Great! _____ _____ _____ _____ the contest.
   B: Thanks. _____ _____ _____, too.

해석

G: 진수야, 방학 동안 무엇을 할 거니?
B: 나는 책을 많이 읽을 거야. 너는 어떠니?
G: 나는 부산에 계신 조부모님을 방문할 계획이야.
B: 좋구나. 멋진 방학을 보내길 바라.

G: 재민아, 노래 경연 대회에 나갈 준비는 됐니?
B: 음, 포기할까 생각 중이야, Tina.
G: 왜? 나는 네가 그 대회에 정말로 참가하고 싶어 한다고 생각했어.
B: 나는 내가 노래를 잘하는 것 같지 않아.
G: 그러지 말고. 너는 내가 아는 노래를 가장 잘하는 사람이야.
B: 정말로 그렇게 생각하니?
G: 물론이지. 너는 정말 멋진 목소리를 가졌어.
B: 그렇게 말해 줘서 고마워. 최선을 다해 볼게.
G: 네가 대회에서 우승하기를 바라.

1. A: 너는 내일 무엇을 할 계획이니?
   B: 학교 축제에서 노래 부를 거야.
   A: 멋지네! 나는 네가 청중을 감동시키기를 바라.
   B: 고마워. 나도 그러길 바라.

2. A: 너는 내일 무엇을 할 계획이니?
   B: 축구를 할 거야.
   A: 멋지네! 나는 네가 득점하기를 바라.
   B: 고마워. 나도 그러길 바라.

3. A: 너는 내일 무엇을 할 계획이니?
   B: 연설 대회에 참가할 거야.
   A: 멋지네! 나는 네가 대회에서 우승하기를 바라.
   B: 고마워. 나도 그러길 바라.

Real Life Talk Watch a Video

Minho: Linda, what are you reading?

Linda: I'm reading _____ messages from my classmates.

Minho: Oh, it _____ _____ they had _____ _____ _____ to you.

Linda: Many of them _____ _____ they like my smile.

Minho: That's nice. What _____?

Linda: _____ _____ _____ said I didn't _____ _____ _____ them.

Minho: That's not your _____. You were always busy.

Linda: Yeah, but I _____ _____ _____ _____ my classmates.

Minho: You still have time _____ _____.

Linda: You're right.

Minho: I _____ _____ _____ _____ _____ _____ _____ your classmates after graduation.

Linda: Thanks. _____ _____ _____, too.

Real Life Talk Step 2

1. A: I _____ _____ we're graduating soon.

   B: Yeah. Is _____ _____ you _____ about your middle school life?

   A: Yes. I _____ _____ _____ _____ in classes.

   B: Well, you _____ _____ _____ _____ _____ _____ in high school.

   A: I _____ you're right.

   B: I _____ _____ _____ _____ _____ in classes in high school.

2. A: I can't _____ _____ _____ soon.

   B: Yeah. Is there _____ _____ _____ _____ your middle school life?

   A: Yes. I _____ _____ _____ part in many school events.

   B: Well, you have a second chance in high school.

   A: I _____ you're _____.

   B: I _____ _____ _____ _____ _____ _____ many school events in high school.

Conversation 시험대비 기본평가

01 다음 대화의 빈칸에 알맞은 것을 고르시오.

> A: What are you going to do tomorrow?
> B: I'm going to sing in the school festival.
> A: Great! I hope _____.
> B: Thanks. I hope so, too.

① you do better next time
② you move the audience
③ you have a chance to visit the school festival
④ you take part in the school festival
⑤ you read the book about the festival

02 다음 대화의 밑줄 친 문장과 같은 의미의 문장을 고르시오.

> G: Mike, why were you late for class?
> B: I had a bad stomachache.
> G: Oh, no! Are you okay now?
> B: Yeah. I should have eaten less last night.

① I regret that I didn't eat less last night.
② I forgot not to eat less last night.
③ I feel sorry that I ate less last night.
④ I didn't know if I ate less last night.
⑤ I don't think that I had to eat less last night.

03 대화가 자연스럽게 연결되도록 (A)~(D)를 순서대로 적절하게 배열한 것은?

> (A) I'm going to participate in the speech contest.
> (B) Great! I hope you win the contest.
> (C) What are you going to do tomorrow?
> (D) Thanks. I hope so, too.

① (B) – (A) – (C) – (D)
② (B) – (C) – (A) – (D)
③ (C) – (A) – (B) – (D)
④ (C) – (B) – (A) – (D)
⑤ (C) – (D) – (B) – (A)

[01~03] 다음 대화를 읽고 물음에 답하시오.

G: Jiho, what's up? You look tired.

B: Yeah. I stayed up late last night. (①)

G: (②) Did you play computer games again?

B: No, not this time. (③)

G: Is it due today?

B: Yeah. I _____(A)_____ until the last moment. (④)

G: Hmm, I understand. I often have the same problem. (⑤)

B: Really? Well, _____(B)_____ .

01 ①~⑤ 중 주어진 문장이 들어갈 곳으로 가장 알맞은 것은?

| I had to finish my history project. |

①   ②   ③   ④   ⑤

02 위 대화의 빈칸 (A)에 알맞은 말을 고르시오.

① should have put it off

② shouldn't have put it off

③ must have put it off

④ must not have put it off

⑤ may not have put it off

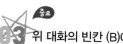
03 위 대화의 빈칸 (B)에 알맞은 말을 고르시오.

① let's get up early in the morning

② let's prepare the midterm exam

③ let's play the computer games

④ let's finish the history project

⑤ let's try to change our bad habits

04 다음 대화의 빈칸에 들어갈 말을 〈보기〉에서 골라 바르게 배열한 것은?

A: I can't believe we're graduating soon.

B: _____

A: _____

B: _____

A: _____

B: I hope you are active in classes in high school.

(A) Yes. I should have been active in classes.

(B) Well, you have a second chance in high school.

(C) Yeah. Is there anything you regret about your middle school life?

(D) I guess you're right.

① (B) – (A) – (C) – (D)

② (B) – (C) – (A) – (D)

③ (C) – (A) – (B) – (D)

④ (C) – (B) – (A) – (D)

⑤ (C) – (D) – (B) – (A)

[05~06] 다음 대화를 읽고 물음에 답하시오.

G: Jaemin, are you ready for the singing contest? (①)

B: Well, I'm thinking of giving ____(A)____, Tina. (②)

G: Why? I thought you really wanted to take part in the contest.

B: I don't think I'm a good singer. (③)

G: Come on. (④)

B: Do you really think so?

G: Of course. You have a really nice voice.

B: Thank you for saying so. (⑤) I'll do my best.

G: I hope you win the contest.

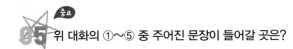

05 위 대화의 ①~⑤ 중 주어진 문장이 들어갈 곳은?

> You're the best singer I know.

①　　　　②　　　　③　　　　④　　　　⑤

06 빈칸 (A)에 알맞은 말을 고르시오.

① on　　　② up　　　③ in
④ for　　　⑤ with

07 다음 중 짝지어진 대화가 어색한 것은?

① A: This is my first visit to Busan.
　 B: Oh, really? I hope you have a good time in Busan.
② A: I've practiced a lot, but I lost the game.
　 B: I'm sorry to hear that. I hope you will win next time.
③ A: My grandmother is sick in bed with a cold.
　 B: That's too bad. I hope she'll get well soon.
④ A: I have been to Sydney many times.
　 B: Oh, I hope you can visit there sometime.
⑤ A: My bag is too heavy.
　 B: You shouldn't have bought too much.

[08~10] 다음 대화를 읽고 물음에 답하시오.

Minho: Linda, what are you reading?
Linda: I'm reading graduation messages from my classmates. (①)
Minho: Oh, it looks like they had a lot to say to you.

Linda: Many of (A)them wrote that they like my smile.
Minho: That's nice. What else?
Linda: Some of them said I didn't hang out enough with them. (②)
Minho: (③) You were always busy.
Linda: Yeah, but I should have spent more time with my classmates. (④)
Minho: You still have time after graduation.
Linda: You're right.
Minho: I hope you keep in touch with your classmates after graduation. (⑤)
Linda: Thanks. I hope so, too.

08 위 대화의 ①~⑤ 중 주어진 문장이 들어갈 곳은?

> That's not your fault.

①　　　　②　　　　③　　　　④　　　　⑤

서답형

09 밑줄 친 (A)them이 가리키는 것을 두 단어로 쓰시오.

➡ _____

10 위 대화의 내용과 일치하지 않는 것을 고르시오.

① Linda의 친구들은 Linda의 미소를 좋아한다.
② Linda는 졸업 후에도 친구들과 계속 연락하기를 바란다.
③ Linda는 항상 바빴다.
④ Linda는 지금 학급 친구들에게 받은 졸업 메시지를 읽고 있는 중이다.
⑤ Linda의 친구들은 Linda가 그들과 많은 시간을 보냈다고 생각한다.

01 밑줄 친 문장과 같은 의미가 되도록 주어진 단어를 이용하여 쓰시오.

> B: Mike, why were you late for class?
> B: I had a bad stomachache.
> G: Oh, no! Are you okay now?
> B: Yeah. I should have eaten less last night.

➡ _____ (not)

[02~03] 다음 대화를 읽고 물음에 답하시오.

> G: Jaemin, are you ready ___(A)___ the singing contest?
> B: Well, I'm thinking ___(B)___ giving up, Tina.
> G: Why? I thought you really wanted to take part in the contest.
> B: I don't think I'm a good singer.
> G: Come on. You're the best singer I know.
> B: Do you really think so?
> G: Of course. You have a really nice voice.
> B: Thank you for saying so. I'll do my best.
> G: (C)네가 대회에서 우승하기를 바라.

02 위 대화의 빈칸 (A)와 (B)에 들어갈 말을 〈보기〉에서 골라 쓰시오.

> ┤ 보기 ├
> as   for   from   in   of   to

(A) _____ (B) _____

03 밑줄 친 (C)의 우리말을 주어진 단어를 이용하여 영작하시오. (6 words)

➡ _____ (hope)

[04~05] 다음 대화를 읽고 물음에 답하시오.

> G: Jiho, what's up? You look tired.
> B: Yeah. I stayed ___(A)___ late last night.
> G: ⓐDid you play computer games again?
> B: No, not this time. ⓑI had to finish my history project.
> G: ⓒIs it due today?
> B: Yeah. ⓓI shouldn't put it off until the last moment.
> G: Hmm, I understand. I often have the same problem.
> B: Really? ⓔWell, let's try to change our bad habits.

04 빈칸 (A)에 알맞은 말을 쓰시오.

➡ _____

05 밑줄 친 ⓐ~ⓔ 중 흐름상 또는 어법상 어색한 것을 고르고 바르게 고치시오.

➡ _____

_____

06 후회하는 표현과 대화에 나오는 단어를 이용하여 빈칸을 채우시오. (7 words)

> A: I can't believe we're graduating soon.
> B: Yeah. Is there anything you regret about your middle school life?
> A: Yes. _____
> B: Well, you have a second chance in high school.
> A: I guess you're right.
> B: I hope you are active in classes in high school.

➡ _____

Grammar

① 분사구문

> • **Reading the article**, he dropped his cup in surprise.
> 기사를 읽으며 그는 놀라서 컵을 떨어뜨렸다.

■ 분사가 이끄는 구를 분사구문이라고 하며, 이유, 조건, 시간, 동시동작, 양보 등의 뜻을 나타낸다. 분사구문은 '접속사+주어+동사'로 이루어진 부사절의 주어가 주절의 주어와 일치할 때 접속사와 주어를 생략하고 동사를 분사로 만들어 부사구로 표현한 것이다. 이때 생략되는 접속사에 따라 뜻이 달라진다.

 • I panicked when I saw smoke coming out of the engine.
  → I panicked **seeing** smoke coming out of the engine. (시간)
   나는 엔진에서 연기가 나는 것을 보고 겁에 질렸다.

■ 부사절과 주절의 주어가 다를 때는 부사절의 주어를 생략하지 않고 사용하며 이것을 독립분사구문이라고 한다. 일반인이 주어일 경우에는 생략한다. (비인칭 독립분사구문)

 • As it was dark, we quickened our pace.
  → It **being** dark, we quickened our pace. 날이 어두웠기 때문에 우리는 발걸음을 재촉했다.

■ 분사구문의 부정은 분사 앞에 'not'이나 'never'를 쓴다.

 • Because he didn't pass the exam, he is feeling down.
  → Not **passing** the exam, he is feeling down. 그는 시험에 떨어져서 기분이 우울하다.

■ 분사구문의 의미를 분명히 하기 위해 분사 앞에 접속사를 쓰는 경우도 있다. 이 경우는 부사절에서 '주어+be동사'를 생략한 것과 같은 형태가 된다.

 • I have just dropped in while **taking** a walk. 산책하다가 잠깐 들렀습니다.

■ 부사절의 시제가 주절보다 앞선 경우에는 완료분사구문(having+과거분사)으로 쓴다.

 • After I had finished the work, I went home directly.
  = **Having finished** the work, I went home directly. 일을 끝내고 바로 집으로 갔다.

■ 분사구문에서 Being이나 Having been은 대부분 생략하지만, 보어가 명사일 경우나 분사가 아닌 경우에 보통 접속사 없이 being을 생략하지 않는다.

 • Though she was nervous, she said it was a good experience.
  → Though (**being**) nervous, she said it was a good experience.
   그녀는 긴장되기는 했지만, 좋은 경험이었다고 말했다.

■ 과거분사로 시작되는 분사구문은 being이 생략된 것으로 수동의 의미를 갖는다.

 • (Being) **Seen** from above, the cars looked tiny. 위에서 보니 차들이 아주 조그마했다.

핵심 Check

1. 다음 괄호 안에서 알맞은 단어를 고르시오.

 (1) (Live / Living) next door, I seldom see her.

 (2) (Feeling / Felt) tired, he took a nap.

② 과거완료

> • The article said Alfred Nobel **had died** in France from a heart attack.
> 기사에는 Alfred Nobel이 심장 마비로 프랑스에서 죽었다고 쓰여 있었다.

■ 과거완료는 'had+과거분사'의 형태로, 과거 이전에 일어난 일이 과거의 어느 시점까지 영향을 미칠 때 쓴다. 과거완료도 현재완료처럼 경험, 계속, 완료, 결과의 용법이 있다. 또한 과거의 어느 시점보다 먼저 일어난 일이나 상태를 나타낼 때도 쓰이며 이것을 보통 '대과거'라고 한다.

- She **had** never **been** greatly concerned about her appearance. (경험)
  그녀는 생전 자기 외모에 크게 신경을 쓰지 않았었다.
- He **had been** fat since he was in elementary school. (계속) 그는 초등학교 때부터 뚱뚱했었습니다.
- The child **had** just **wakened**. (완료) 아이는 방금 잠을 깬 참이었다.
- He **had gone** to America leaving his family in Korea. (결과) 그는 가족을 한국에 남겨 두고 미국으로 가버렸다.
- She remembered everything that **had happened** long before. (대과거)
  그녀는 오래 전의 일들을 모두 기억하고 있었다.

■ 한 문장에 두 가지 과거의 일이 나올 때, 두 동작이 거의 동시에 일어났거나 시간차가 거의 없이 연속적으로 일어났을 경우에는 단순과거로 표현한다. 또, 접속사 after나 before가 쓰여 두 동작의 전후 관계가 명백할 때도 단순과거로 표현할 수 있다.

- She **smiled** at him and he **smiled** back. (시간차가 거의 없는 연속 동작)
  그녀가 그를 보고 웃자 그도 마주 보고 웃어 주었다.
- **Did** she leave a message before she **went**? (전후 관계가 명백함)
  그녀가 가기 전에 전갈을 남겼어요?

핵심 Check

2. 다음 괄호 안에서 알맞은 말을 고르시오.

(1) I asked him whether he (had done / does) it all himself.

(2) Later, Terry found that she (had not turned / did not turn) off the light.

(3) The airplane (has / had) just taken off when she arrived at the airport.

01 다음 빈칸에 들어갈 말로 알맞은 것은?

> _____ late, I had to hurry.

① Being   ② Been   ③ Am

④ Was   ⑤ Be

02 다음 괄호 안에서 알맞은 말을 고르시오.

(1) (Read / Reading) the article, he dropped his cup in surprise.

(2) (Knowing not / Not knowing) the library was closed, I made the trip in vain.

(3) When you arrived, he (has / had) only just left.

(4) I had never (visiting / visited) there before.

03 다음 우리말에 맞게 빈칸에 알맞은 것은?

> 그가 그 돈을 가져갔다고 나에게 실토했다.
> = He confessed to me that he _____ the money.

① takes   ② taking   ③ took

④ has taken   ⑤ had taken

04 다음 우리말에 맞게 주어진 어휘를 바르게 배열하시오.

(1) 텔레비전을 보면서 그녀는 저녁을 먹었다.

    (ate, watching, she, dinner, TV)

    ➡ _____

(2) 기사에는 Alfred Nobel이 심장 마비로 프랑스에서 죽었다고 쓰여 있었다.

    (a heart attack, Alfred Nobel, France, the article, said, died, had, from, in)

    ➡ _____

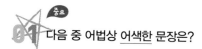
01 다음 중 어법상 어색한 문장은?

① Talking on the phone, she watched TV.
② Turning to the right, you will find the post office.
③ She washes away the fatigue of the day listens to music.
④ While walking home from work, I found this bakery.
⑤ Catching his breath, Nobel kept reading.

02 다음 주어진 문장의 밑줄 친 부분과 용법이 같은 것은?

Lucy had gone to Seattle when I reached Boston.

① Jacob had studied on the subject for two months.
② Mary had been on a diet since last month.
③ Howard had met her several times.
④ I knew someone had stolen my purse on the subway.
⑤ I had finished my homework when my friend came to my house.

03 다음 문장의 밑줄 친 부분 중 어법상 어색한 것은?

Alfred, ⓐthought ⓑthat he shouldn't be ⓒacting ⓓthis way, ⓔquickly left the place.

① ⓐ　　② ⓑ　　③ ⓒ　　④ ⓓ　　⑤ ⓔ

04 다음 빈칸에 알맞은 말이 바르게 짝지어진 것은?

• Not _____ tired, she took out her book and read until 2:00 A.M.
• The roads were wet because it _____ during the night.

① feeling – has rained
② feeling – had rained
③ feel – has rained
④ felt – had rained
⑤ felt – rained

서답형

05 다음 괄호 안에서 알맞은 말을 고르시오.

(1) When I arrived at the station, the train (already left / had already left).
(2) He begged forgiveness for what he (did / had done).
(3) Until last week, Emily (never went / had never been) to a soccer match.
(4) (Run / Running) to the bus stop, we sat down to catch our breath.
(5) While (talk / talking) on the phone, he cleaned his room.
(6) I felt so awkward, (knowing not / not knowing) where to look.

06 다음 주어진 두 문장을 한 문장으로 바꿀 때 어색한 것은?

> • The thief saw the police.
> • He ran away.

① When the thief saw the police, he ran away.
② Seeing the police, the thief ran away.
③ As the thief saw the police, he ran away.
④ As soon as the thief saw the police, he ran away.
⑤ When saw the police, the thief ran away.

07 다음 중 어법상 어색한 것은?

① When I woke up this morning, the snow had already stopped.
② We talked about what happened the previous week.
③ I watched TV after I did my science homework.
④ The team found thousands of interesting creatures that had never been seen before.
⑤ My family had lived in Baghdad for several generations.

서답형

08 다음 두 문장을 한 문장으로 바꿔 쓸 때 빈칸에 들어갈 한 단어를 쓰시오.

> • I was nervous.
> • I forgot my lines at the school musical.
> ➡ _____ nervous, I forgot my lines at the school musical.

➡ _____

[09~10] 다음 우리말을 바르게 영작한 것을 고르시오.

09

> Sam이 공원에 도착했을 때, Kate는 집에 가고 없었다.

① When Sam arrives at the park, Kate goes home.
② When Sam arrived at the park, Kate went home.
③ When Sam arrived at the park, Kate had gone home.
④ When Sam had arrived at the park, Kate went home.
⑤ When Sam had arrived at the park, Kate had gone home.

10

> 피곤했기 때문에 그녀는 일찍 집에 돌아왔다.

① Because tired, she came back home early.
② Because she tired, she came back home early.
③ Being she tired, she came back home early.
④ Being tired, she came back home early.
⑤ Being she was tired, she came back home early.

서답형

11 시간 흐름에 따른 사건 전개에 맞게 빈칸을 채워 문장을 완성하시오.

> • Mom bought a cellphone for me last week.
> ➡ I lost the cellphone.
> ➡ I don't have the cellphone now.
> ➡ I lost the cellphone that _____.

➡ _____

[12~13] 다음 밑줄 친 부분의 쓰임이 주어진 문장과 같은 것은?

12

> <u>Being</u> sick, I went to see a doctor.

① <u>Having</u> no partner, he danced with grace.
② <u>Being</u> honest, she was liked by many people.
③ <u>Walking</u> along the street, I met Jake's sister.
④ He kept on reading while <u>eating</u>.
⑤ <u>Going</u> out now, you'll get wet.

13

> When David arrived at the station, the train <u>had</u> already <u>left</u>.

① She <u>had</u> never <u>been</u> greatly concerned about her appearance.
② Mike <u>had lost</u> the power of speech because of the operation.
③ I <u>had visited</u> Madrid three times until then.
④ I was in a hotel, and I <u>had</u> just <u>finished</u> shaving.
⑤ My grandmother <u>had lived</u> on the farm for two years when I was born.

서답형
[14~15] 다음 문장에서 생략할 수 있는 것을 찾아 쓰시오.

14

> (1) While he was listening to music, he did his homework.
> (2) Though she was lonely, Maryanne was good-humored.

➡ (1) _____ (2) _____

15

> He had lived in Alabama before he moved to Texas.

➡ _____

[16~17] 다음 밑줄 친 우리말을 참고하여 주어진 문장의 틀린 부분을 찾아 바르게 고친 것을 고르시오.

16

> <u>어제만큼 해가 빛나지는 않지만 그리 쌀쌀하지는 않다.</u> Not shining as much as it did yesterday, it isn't that chilly.

① Shining not as much as it did yesterday, it isn't that chilly.
② Not shining the sun as much as it did yesterday, it isn't that chilly.
③ The sun not shining as much as it did yesterday, it isn't that chilly.
④ Though not shining as much as it did yesterday, it isn't that chilly.
⑤ The sun didn't shining as much as it did yesterday, it isn't that chilly.

17

> <u>그 소녀는 열쇠를 집에 두고 온 것을 알아차렸다.</u> The girl had found that she left her key at home.

① The girl found that she had left her key at home.
② The girl found that she left her key at home.
③ The girl had found that she had left her key at home.
④ The girl finds that she had left her key at home.
⑤ The girl found that she leaves her key at home.

Grammar **83**

 주어진 문장을 분사구문으로 바꿔 쓰시오.

(1) Because I got up too late, I missed the school bus.

➡ _____

(2) As he was talking on the phone, he watered the plants.

➡ _____

(3) If you have a problem, ask the teacher.

➡ _____

(4) Although she knew it was wrong, she wouldn't change it.

➡ _____

(5) Because I didn't have any money, I couldn't buy a bike.

➡ _____

(6) If the weather is good, we'll eat out.

➡ _____

02 적절한 접속사와 과거완료를 이용하여 다음 두 문장을 한 문장으로 바꿔 쓰시오.

(1) • They couldn't find the treasure.
 • Mr. Joe hid it under the sea.

➡ _____

_____

(2) • I arrived at home.
 • Lucky already fell asleep.

➡ _____

_____

03 다음 우리말에 맞게 주어진 어구를 바르게 배열하시오.

(1) 산에서 바라보니 경치는 푸르고 아름답다.
(the landscape, the mountains, green and beautiful, seen, is, from)

➡ _____

_____

(2) 아파서 나는 하루 종일 집에 있어야 했다.
(I, home, all day, had, being, stay, sick, to)

➡ _____

(3) 선생님이 들어왔을 때 그녀는 일을 막 끝마쳤다.
(she, her task, the teacher, when, finished, came, had, just, in)

➡ _____

(4) 그들이 플랫폼으로 달려갔지만 기차는 막 출발해 버렸다. (the train, the platform, they, had, ran, gone, but, just, to)

➡ _____

_____

04 다음 문장에서 어법상 어색한 부분을 분사구문을 이용하여 바르게 고치시오. (생략하지 말 것.)

(1) Deeply disappointing at the news, Nobel decided to change people's opinions about him.

_____ ➡ _____

(2) Taking his holiday, he came back refreshed.

_____ ➡ _____

[05~06] 그림을 보고 주어진 어휘를 이용하여 빈칸을 알맞게 채우시오.

05

Emma _____ to the sea up to last week. It was her first visit. (be, never)

06

_____ at the station, David found that the train had already left. (arrive)

07 다음 우리말을 괄호 안의 지시대로 영작하시오.

(1) 지금 곧 떠나면, 그 기차를 놓치지 않을 겁니다.
(right, leave, miss)

➡ _____

(분사구문을 써서)

➡ _____

(접속사를 써서)

(2) 그녀는 내게 뛰어오면서 그녀의 손을 흔들었다.
(as, wave)

➡ _____

(분사구문을 써서)

➡ _____

(접속사를 써서)

(3) 그는 중국에 가기 전에 2년 동안 중국어를 공부했다. (study)

➡ _____

_____

08 다음 문장에서 어법상 어색한 것을 바르게 고쳐 다시 쓰시오.

(1) My grandmother was ill for five days when I visited her.

➡ _____

(2) The ground had been covered with snow because it snowed during the night.

➡ _____

_____

(3) Walked in the park, he met an old friend.

➡ _____

(4) Getting so cold outside, the rain changed into snow.

➡ _____

_____

(5) Making of thick trees, the doors looked unbreakable.

➡ _____

_____

(6) Eaten dinner, he was not hungry.

➡ _____

How Will You Be Remembered?

It was just a normal morning. Alfred Nobel sat in his chair to read
시간을 나타내는 비인칭 주어   부사적 용법의 to부정사(목적): ~하기 위해서
the newspaper. While he was drinking his coffee, a headline caught his
                    ~하는 동안(접속사)   catch one's eye: 눈길을 끌다
eye: *The Merchant of Death, Alfred Nobel, Is Dead.*

"What? What is this?"
앞 문장의 'The Merchant of Death, Alfred Nobel, Is Dead'라고 적힌 headline을 가리킨다.
Reading the article, he dropped his cup in surprise. His coffee spilled
= As he read the article   놀라서
all over his clothes and desk, but he couldn't take his eyes off the
                                            can't take one's eyes off: ~에서 눈을 뗄 수 없다
newspaper.

↓ The article
The article was about his own death! It said Nobel had died in France
                                                        기사가 쓰인 것보다 죽음이 더 먼저 일어난 일이므로 과거완료 had died로 표현
from a heart attack.

"Oh my goodness! Am I dead?"
어머나!, 아이고!, 놀람을 나타낼 때 사용하는 표현
Catching his breath, Nobel kept reading. Soon, he became even
= After he caught his breath   keep+동사-ing: 계속 ~하다   훨씬(비교급 강조)
more shocked. The article described him as the inventor of dynamite
                        describe A as B: A를 B로 기술하다(묘사하다)
and other dangerous objects for war. It said that he had become rich
                        It = The article / 기사가 쓰여진 것보다 부유해진 것이 더 먼저 일어난 일이므로 과거완료 시제로 표현
from the deaths of others. He couldn't believe his eyes. It was true that
                                                                                                    가주어   that 이하: 진주어
dynamite was one of his many inventions. But he never imagined that
                        one of+복수 명사: ~ 중 하나
the world would think of him as "the merchant of death."
                        think of A as B: A를 B로 생각하다

---

headline (신문 기사 등의) 표제

catch one's eye 눈길을 끌다

merchant 상인

spill 쏟아지다, 흐르다, 쏟다

heart attack 심장 마비

catch one's breath 숨을 고르다

shocked 충격을 받은

describe 기술하다, 묘사하다

dynamite 다이너마이트

📎 **확인문제**

• 다음 문장이 본문의 내용과 일치하면 T, 일치하지 <u>않으면</u> F를 쓰시오.

1 Alfred Nobel sat in his chair to read the newspaper. ☐

2 Alfred Nobel couldn't continue reading the article in surprise. ☐

3 The article said that Alfred Nobel had become rich from the deaths of others. ☐

4 Alfred Nobel expected that the world would think of him as "the merchant of death." ☐

Nobel was deeply disappointed.
몹시, 깊이, 매우

"How could this be? This is unbelievable! I'm not a merchant of death. I want to be remembered in a different way. I want to be
to부정사의 수동태
remembered as a person who made the world better."
~로 기억되다   주격 관계대명사

He decided to change people's opinions about him.

In 1888, a French newspaper mistakenly reported Alfred Nobel's death. The person who had actually died was his brother, Ludvig.
주격 관계대명사

Thanks to the report, however, Nobel decided to do something to
~ 덕분에. 다음에 명사(구)가 이어짐   decide: to부정사를 목적어로 취하는 동사
contribute to the world. In 1895, he decided to use his money to create
부사적 용법의 to부정사(목적): ~하기 위해서
the Nobel Prize. Originally, there were only five awards. A sixth award was added in 1968. Today, when we think of Alfred Nobel, we think of
수동태
the Nobel Prize, rather than dynamite.

deeply 몹시, 깊이, 매우

disappointed 실망한, 낙담한

unbelievable 믿을 수 없는, 믿기 어려운

mistakenly 실수로

thanks to ~ 덕분에

contribute 기여하다, 공헌하다

rather than ~보다는

📎 **확인문제**

● 다음 문장이 본문의 내용과 일치하면 T, 일치하지 <u>않으면</u> F를 쓰시오.

1 Nobel wanted to be remembered as a person who made the world better. ☐

2 In 1888, a French newspaper reported Alfred Nobel's death on purpose. ☐

3 It was Nobel's brother, Ludvig, who had actually died. ☐

4 Nobel had already decided to do something to contribute to the world before reading the report. ☐

5 In 1895, Nobel decided to use his money to create the Nobel Prize. ☐

6 Today, when we think of Alfred Nobel, we think of dynamite, rather than the Nobel Prize. ☐

● 우리말을 참고하여 빈칸에 알맞은 말을 쓰시오.

1 _____ Will You _____ _____?

2 It was just a _____ _____.

3 Alfred Nobel _____ _____ _____ _____ to read the newspaper.

4 While he was drinking his coffee, a headline _____ _____ _____: *The Merchant of Death, Alfred Nobel, Is Dead.*

5 "What? What is this?"

6 Reading the article, he dropped his cup _____ _____.

7 His coffee spilled all over his clothes and desk, but he couldn't _____ _____ _____ _____ the newspaper.

8 The article was about _____ _____ _____!

9 It said Nobel had died in France _____ _____ _____ _____.

10 "Oh _____ _____! Am I dead?"

11 _____ _____ _____, Nobel kept reading.

12 Soon, he became _____ _____ _____.

13 The article _____ him _____ the inventor of dynamite and other dangerous objects for war.

14 It said that he _____ _____ _____ from the deaths of others.

15 He _____ _____ his eyes.

16 It was true that dynamite was _____ _____ _____ _____ _____.

1 당신은 어떻게 기억될까요?

2 그저 평범한 아침이었다.

3 Alfred Nobel은 신문을 읽기 위해 의자에 앉았다.

4 커피를 마시는 동안 한 기사 제목이 그의 눈길을 끌었다. "죽음의 상인, Alfred Nobel 사망하다"

5 "뭐라고? 이게 뭐지?"

6 기사를 읽으며 그는 놀라서 컵을 떨어뜨렸다.

7 커피가 그의 옷과 책상 온 곳에 쏟아졌지만 그는 신문에서 눈을 뗄 수 없었다.

8 기사는 그 자신의 죽음에 관한 것이었다!

9 기사에는 Nobel이 심장 마비로 프랑스에서 죽었다고 쓰여 있었다.

10 "오, 이럴 수가! 내가 죽었다고?"

11 숨을 고른 후, Nobel은 계속 읽었다.

12 곧, 그는 훨씬 더 충격을 받게 되었다.

13 기사는 그를 전쟁에 쓰이는 다이너마이트와 다른 위험한 물건의 발명가로 기술했다.

14 기사에는 그가 다른 사람들의 죽음으로 인해 부유해졌다고 쓰여 있었다.

15 그는 자신의 눈을 믿을 수 없었다.

16 다이너마이트가 그의 많은 발명품 중 하나인 것은 사실이었다.

17 But he never imagined that the world would _____ _____ him _____ "the merchant of death."

18 Nobel was deeply _____.

19 "_____ could this be?

20 This is _____!

21 I'm not a _____ _____ _____.

22 I want to be remembered _____ _____ _____ _____.

23 I want to _____ _____ as a person who made _____ _____ _____."

24 He decided _____ _____ _____ _____ about him.

25 In 1888, a French newspaper _____ reported Alfred Nobel's death.

26 The person _____ _____ _____ was his brother, Ludvig.

27 _____ _____ the report, however, Nobel decided to do something to _____ _____ the world.

28 In 1895, he decided to use his money _____ _____ the Nobel Prize.

29 Originally, there were _____ _____ _____.

30 A _____ _____ was added in 1968.

31 Today, when we think of Alfred Nobel, we think of the Nobel Prize, _____ _____ dynamite.

---

17 하지만 그는 세상이 그를 '죽음의 상인'으로 생각할 거라고는 결코 상상하지 못했다.

18 Nobel은 몹시 실망했다.

19 "어떻게 이럴 수가 있지?

20 이건 믿을 수 없어!

21 나는 죽음의 상인이 아니야.

22 나는 다르게 기억되고 싶어.

23 나는 세상을 더 좋게 만든 사람으로 기억되고 싶어."

24 그는 자신에 대한 사람들의 견해를 바꾸기로 결심했다.

25 1888년에, 한 프랑스 신문에서 실수로 Alfred Nobel의 죽음을 보도했다.

26 실제로 죽은 사람은 Alfred Nobel의 형인 Ludvig였다.

27 하지만 그 보도 덕분에, Nobel은 세상에 공헌하기 위해 무언가를 하기로 결심했다.

28 1895년에, 그는 자신의 돈을 노벨상을 만드는 데 사용하기로 결정했다.

29 원래 다섯 종류의 상만 있었다.

30 여섯 번째 상은 1968년에 추가되었다.

31 오늘날 우리가 Alfred Nobel을 생각할 때, 우리는 다이너마이트보다는 노벨상을 떠올린다.

● 우리말을 참고하여 본문을 영작하시오.

1 당신은 어떻게 기억될까요?

➡ _____

2 그저 평범한 아침이었다.

➡ _____

3 Alfred Nobel은 신문을 읽기 위해 의자에 앉았다.

➡ _____

4 커피를 마시는 동안 한 기사 제목이 그의 눈길을 끌었다. "죽음의 상인, Alfred Nobel 사망하다"

➡ _____

_____

5 "뭐라고? 이게 뭐지?"

➡ _____

6 기사를 읽으며 그는 놀라서 컵을 떨어뜨렸다.

➡ _____

7 커피가 그의 옷과 책상 온 곳에 쏟아졌지만 그는 신문에서 눈을 뗄 수 없었다.

➡ _____

8 기사는 그 자신의 죽음에 관한 것이었다!

➡ _____

9 기사에는 Nobel이 심장 마비로 프랑스에서 죽었다고 쓰여 있었다.

➡ _____

10 "오, 이럴 수가! 내가 죽었다고?"

➡ _____

11 숨을 고른 후, Nobel은 계속 읽었다.

➡ _____

12 곧, 그는 훨씬 더 충격을 받게 되었다.

➡ _____

13 기사는 그를 전쟁에 쓰이는 다이너마이트와 다른 위험한 물건의 발명가로 기술했다.

➡ _____

14 기사에는 그가 다른 사람들의 죽음으로 인해 부유해졌다고 쓰여 있었다.

➡ _____

15 그는 자신의 눈을 믿을 수 없었다.

➡ _____

16 다이너마이트가 그의 많은 발명품 중 하나인 것은 사실이었다.

➡ _____

17 하지만 그는 세상이 그를 '죽음의 상인'으로 생각할 거라고는 결코 상상하지 못했다.

➡ _____

18 Nobel은 몹시 실망했다.

➡ _____

19 "어떻게 이럴 수가 있지?

➡ _____

20 이건 믿을 수 없어!

➡ _____

21 나는 죽음의 상인이 아니야.

➡ _____

22 나는 다르게 기억되고 싶어.

➡ _____

23 나는 세상을 더 좋게 만든 사람으로 기억되고 싶어."

➡ _____

24 그는 자신에 대한 사람들의 견해를 바꾸기로 결심했다.

➡ _____

25 1888년에, 한 프랑스 신문에서 실수로 Alfred Nobel의 죽음을 보도했다.

➡ _____

26 실제로 죽은 사람은 Alfred Nobel의 형인 Ludvig였다.

➡ _____

27 하지만 그 보도 덕분에, Nobel은 세상에 공헌하기 위해 무언가를 하기로 결심했다.

➡ _____

28 1895년에, 그는 자신의 돈을 노벨상을 만드는 데 사용하기로 결정했다.

➡ _____

29 원래 다섯 종류의 상만 있었다.

➡ _____

30 여섯 번째 상은 1968년에 추가되었다.

➡ _____

31 오늘날 우리가 Alfred Nobel을 생각할 때, 우리는 다이너마이트보다는 노벨상을 떠올린다.

➡ _____

[01~03] 다음 글을 읽고 물음에 답하시오.

It was just a normal morning. Alfred Nobel sat in his chair to read the newspaper. ⓐWhile he was drinking his coffee, a headline caught his eye: *The Merchant of Death, Alfred Nobel, Is Dead.*

"What? What is this?"

Reading the article, he dropped his cup in surprise. His coffee spilled all over his clothes and desk, but he couldn't take his eyes off the newspaper.

01 위 글의 밑줄 친 ⓐWhile과 같은 의미로 쓰인 것을 고르시오.

① It took him a while to calm down.
② I've read fifty pages, while he's read only twenty.
③ He didn't while away his holidays on the beach.
④ She came to the door while I was ringing the bell.
⑤ Some are rich, while others are poor.

02 위 글에서 알 수 있는 Alfred Nobel의 심경으로 가장 알맞은 것을 고르시오.

① nervous and anxious
② embarrassed and confused
③ disappointed and depressed
④ excited and satisfied
⑤ surprised and ashamed

03 According to the passage, which is NOT true?

① It was just like any other morning.
② Alfred Nobel sat in his chair to read the newspaper drinking his coffee.
③ A headline attracted the attention of Alfred Nobel.
④ The article was about Alfred Nobel's own death.
⑤ Alfred Nobel ignored the article about his own death.

[04~07] 다음 글을 읽고 물음에 답하시오.

The article was about his own death! ⓐIt said Nobel had died in France from a heart attack.

"Oh my goodness! Am I dead?"

Catching his breath, Nobel kept reading. Soon, he became ⓑeven more shocked. The article described him as the inventor of dynamite and other dangerous objects for war. It said that he ⓒhad become rich from the deaths of others. He couldn't believe his eyes. It was true that dynamite was one of his many inventions. But he never imagined that the world would think of him as "the merchant of death."

04 위 글의 밑줄 친 ⓐIt이 가리키는 것을 본문에서 찾아 쓰시오.

➡ _____

05 위 글의 밑줄 친 ⓑeven과 바꿔 쓸 수 없는 말을 고르시오.

① much   ② very
③ far   ④ still
⑤ a lot

06 위 글의 밑줄 친 ⓒhad become과 과거완료의 용법이 같은 것을 고르시오.

① I recognized him well because I had often seen him before.

② He had lived there for ten years when his father died.

③ I lost the book which I had bought the day before.

④ When we called on her, she had been ill in bed for a week.

⑤ I had never seen such a strange animal before.

서답형

07 본문의 내용과 일치하도록 다음 빈칸 (A)와 (B)에 알맞은 단어를 쓰시오.

> Nobel became rich by inventing (A)_____ and other dangerous objects for war, but they could kill lots of people, so the article described him as "(B)_____ _____ _____ _____."

[08~10] 다음 글을 읽고 물음에 답하시오.

> Nobel was deeply disappointed.
> "How could this be? This is unbelievable! I'm not a merchant of death. I want to be remembered ⓐin a different way. I want to be remembered as a person who made the world better."
> ⓑ그는 자신에 대한 사람들의 견해를 바꾸기로 결심했다.

서답형

08 위 글의 밑줄 친 ⓐin a different way가 구체적으로 가리키는 것을 본문에서 찾아 쓰시오.

➡ _____

서답형

09 위 글의 밑줄 친 ⓑ의 우리말에 맞게 주어진 어휘를 이용하여 8 단어로 영작하시오.

> decided, people's opinions

➡ _____
_____

10 According to the passage, which is NOT true?

① Nobel was extremely disappointed.

② Nobel couldn't believe that he was a merchant of a death.

③ Nobel didn't think he was a merchant of death.

④ Nobel wanted to be remembered as a person who made the world better, not as a merchant of death.

⑤ People remembered Nobel as a person who made the world better.

[11~12] 다음 글을 읽고 물음에 답하시오.

> In 1888, a French newspaper mistakenly reported Alfred Nobel's death. The person who had actually died was his brother, Ludvig. Thanks to the report, however, Nobel decided to do something to contribute to the world. In 1895, he decided to use his money to create the Nobel Prize. Originally, there were only five awards. A sixth award ___ⓐ___ in 1968. Today, when we think of Alfred Nobel, we think of the Nobel Prize, rather than dynamite.

서답형

11 위 글의 빈칸 ⓐ에 add를 알맞은 형태로 쓰시오.

➡ _____

12 위 글의 제목으로 가장 알맞은 것을 고르시오.

① A Mistaken Report about Alfred Nobel's Death
② A Mistake Led to the Precious Result!
③ Actually Alfred Nobel Was Not Dead!
④ Originally, There Were Only Five Awards!
⑤ What Do You think of Alfred Nobel?

[13~15] 다음 글을 읽고 물음에 답하시오.

The article was about his own death! It said Nobel had died in France ____ⓐ____ a heart attack.

"Oh my goodness! Am I dead?"

(A)Catching his breath, Nobel kept reading. Soon, he became even more shocked. The article described him as the inventor of dynamite and other dangerous objects for war. It said that he had become rich ____ⓑ____ the deaths of others. He couldn't believe his eyes. It was true that dynamite was one of his many inventions. But he never imagined that the world would (B)think of him as "the merchant of death."

서답형

13 위 글의 빈칸 ⓐ와 ⓑ에 공통으로 들어갈 전치사를 쓰시오.

➡ _____

14 위 글의 밑줄 친 (A)Catching과 문법적 쓰임이 같은 것을 모두 고르시오.

① My hobby is reading books.
② The girl sat by the window, listening to music.
③ Smiling brightly, he welcomed her.
④ Being healthy is the most important.
⑤ John answered the phone, watching TV.

15 위 글의 밑줄 친 (B)think of와 바꿔 쓸 수 없는 말을 고르시오. (2개)

① regard
② respect
③ discuss
④ look upon
⑤ see

[16~19] 다음 글을 읽고 물음에 답하시오.

(A)Nobel was deeply disappointing.

"How could this be? This is unbelievable! I'm not a merchant of death. I want to be remembered in a different way. I want to be remembered (B)as a person ____ⓐ____ made the world better."

He decided to change people's opinions about him.

서답형

16 위 글의 빈칸 ⓐ에 들어갈 알맞은 관계대명사를 쓰시오.

➡ _____

서답형

17 위 글의 밑줄 친 (A)에서 어법상 틀린 부분을 찾아 고치시오.

_____ ➡ _____

18 위 글의 밑줄 친 (B)as와 의미가 다른 것을 고르시오.

① He lives as a saint.
② I don't like a position as an assistant music teacher.
③ This can be used as a knife.
④ He was famous as a statesman.
⑤ Some animals, as the fox and the squirrel, have bushy tails.

19 위 글의 앞에 올 내용으로 가장 알맞은 것을 고르시오.

① People deeply respected Nobel.

② Nobel expected to be remembered as a person who made the world better.

③ Nobel tried to change people's opinions about him.

④ Nobel was mentioned as a merchant of death.

⑤ People changed their opinions about Nobel.

[20~21] 다음 글을 읽고 물음에 답하시오.

It was just a normal morning. (①) While he was drinking his coffee, a headline caught his eye: The Merchant of Death, Alfred Nobel, Is Dead. (②)

"What? What is this?" (③)

Reading the article, he dropped his cup _____ ⓐ surprise. (④) His coffee spilled all over his clothes and desk, but he couldn't take his eyes _____ ⓑ the newspaper. (⑤)

20 위 글의 빈칸 ⓐ와 ⓑ에 들어갈 전치사가 바르게 짝지어진 것은?

     ⓐ   ⓑ   ⓐ   ⓑ

① at – from   ② at – off

③ in – off   ④ to – from

⑤ in – for

21 위 글의 흐름으로 보아, 주어진 문장이 들어가기에 가장 적절한 곳은?

Alfred Nobel sat in his chair to read the newspaper.

①   ②   ③   ④   ⑤

[22~24] 다음 글을 읽고 물음에 답하시오.

In 1888, a French newspaper (A)[mistakenly / purposely] reported Alfred Nobel's death. The person who had (B)[accidentally / actually] died was his brother, Ludvig. Thanks to the report, _____ ⓐ , Nobel decided to do something to contribute to the world. In 1895, he decided to use his money to create the Nobel Prize. Originally, there were only five awards. (C)[A sixth award was added / Six awards were added] in 1968. Today, when we think of Alfred Nobel, we think of the Nobel Prize, rather than dynamite.

22 위 글의 빈칸 ⓐ에 들어갈 알맞은 말을 고르시오.

① therefore   ② as a result

③ however   ④ that is

⑤ in addition

23 위 글의 괄호 (A)~(C)에서 문맥이나 어법상 알맞은 낱말을 골라 쓰시오.

(A) _____ (B) _____

(C) _____

24 위 글을 읽고 알 수 없는 것을 고르시오.

① When did a French newspaper report Alfred Nobel's death?

② Was the article that the French newspaper reported true?

③ What did Nobel decide to do in 1895?

④ Originally, how many awards were there?

⑤ Why did they add one more award?

[01~04] 다음 글을 읽고 물음에 답하시오.

It was just a normal morning. Alfred Nobel sat in his chair to read the newspaper. While he was drinking his coffee, a headline caught his eye: ⓐ*The Merchant of Death, Alfred Nobel, Are Dead.*

"What? What is ⓑthis?"

ⓒReading the article, he dropped his cup in surprise. His coffee spilled all over his clothes and desk, but he couldn't take his eyes off the newspaper.

01 위 글의 밑줄 친 ⓐ에서 어법상 틀린 부분을 찾아 고치시오.

_____ ➡ _____

02 위 글의 밑줄 친 ⓑthis가 가리키는 것을 우리말로 쓰시오.

➡ _____

03 위 글의 밑줄 친 분사구문 ⓒ를 부사절로 고치시오.

➡ _____

04 Why did Alfred Nobel drop his cup while reading the article? Fill in the blank with a suitable word.

Because he was surprised to read the _____ of the newspaper.

[05~07] 다음 글을 읽고 물음에 답하시오.

The article was about his own death! It said Nobel had died in France from a heart attack. "Oh my goodness! Am I dead?"

Catching his breath, Nobel kept reading. Soon, he became even more shocked. The article described him as the inventor of dynamite and other dangerous objects for war. It said that he had become rich from the deaths of others. He couldn't believe his eyes. It was true that dynamite was one of his many inventions. But he never imagined that ⓐ세상이 그를 '죽음의 상인'으로 생각할 거라고는."

05 위 글의 밑줄 친 ⓐ의 우리말에 맞게 주어진 어휘를 이용하여 11 단어로 영작하시오.

think of, the merchant

➡ _____
_____

06 다음 문장에서 위 글의 내용과 다른 부분을 찾아서 고치시오.

The article said Nobel's brother had died in France from a heart attack.

_____ ➡ _____

07 본문의 내용과 일치하도록 다음 빈칸 (A)와 (B)에 알맞은 단어를 쓰시오.

Nobel became even (A)_____ _____ because the article described him as the inventor of dynamite and other dangerous objects for war saying that he had become rich from (B)_____ _____ _____.

[08~11] 다음 글을 읽고 물음에 답하시오.

Nobel was (A)[deep / deeply] disappointed. "How could this be? This is (B)[reasonable / unbelievable]! I'm not a merchant of death. I want to ___ⓐ___ in a different way. I want to ___ⓑ___ as a person who made the world better."

He decided (C)[changing / to change] people's opinions about him.

08 위 글의 빈칸 ⓐ와 ⓑ에 공통으로 들어갈 remember의 알맞은 형태를 쓰시오.

➡ _____

09 위 글의 괄호 (A)~(C)에서 문맥이나 어법상 알맞은 낱말을 골라 쓰시오.

(A) _____ (B) _____ (C) _____

10 주어진 영영풀이에 해당하는 단어를 본문에서 찾아 쓰시오.

a person who buys or sells goods in large quantities, especially one who imports and exports them

➡ _____

11 본문의 내용과 일치하도록 다음 빈칸 (A)와 (B)에 알맞은 단어를 쓰시오.

Nobel was extremely (A)_____ because he was mentioned as a merchant of death. So he wanted people to remember him as a person who made (B)_____ _____ _____.

[12~14] 다음 글을 읽고 물음에 답하시오.

In ⓐ1888, a French newspaper mistakenly reported Alfred Nobel's death. The person who had actually died was his brother, Ludvig. Thanks to the report, however, Nobel decided to do something to contribute to the world. In ⓑ1895, he decided to use his money to create the Nobel Prize. Originally, there were only five awards. A sixth award was added in ⓒ1968. ⓓToday, when we think of Alfred Nobel, we think of the Nobel Prize, rather than dynamite.

12 위 글의 밑줄 친 ⓐ~ⓒ를 읽는 법을 영어로 쓰시오.

ⓐ _____
ⓑ _____
ⓒ _____

13 위 글의 밑줄 친 ⓓ를 다음과 같이 바꿔 쓸 때 빈칸 (A)~(B)에 들어갈 알맞은 단어를 쓰시오.

Today, when we think of Alfred Nobel, we think of (A)_____ _____ _____ more than (B)_____.

14 Who had actually died? Fill in the blank with a suitable word.

It was Alfred Nobel's brother, _____, who had actually died.

해석

After You Read A. Read and Correct

WORLD NEWS

APRIL 13, 1888

The Merchant of Death, Alfred Nobel, Is Dead
The Merchant of Death와 Alfred Nobel은 동격

Alfred Nobel died yesterday in France from a heart attack. He invented
die from: ~으로 죽다

dynamite and other dangerous objects for war. He became rich from the deaths
다른   물건들   [원인·이유] ~으로 인해

of others. He is responsible for the deaths of thousands of people. The world
다른 사람들

will remember him as "the merchant of death."
[역할·자격·기능·성질 따위를 나타내어] ~으로

구문해설 • heart attack: 심장마비 • invent: 발명하다 • dynamite: 다이너마이트
• be responsible for: ~에 대해 책임이 있다, ~의 원인이 되다 • thousands of: 수천의
• merchant: 상인

세계 뉴스
1888년 4월 13일
죽음의 상인, Alfred Nobel 사망하다

Alfred Nobel이 어제 프랑스에서 심장마비로 사망했다. 그는 전쟁에 쓰이는 다이너마이트와 다른 위험한 물건들을 발명했다. 그는 다른 사람들의 죽음으로 인해 부유해졌다. 그는 수천 명의 사람들의 죽음에 대해 책임이 있다. 세상은 그를 "죽음의 상인"으로 기억할 것이다.

Word Power

• Tim invented special shoes for the beach.
'-ion'과 '-or'은 명사형 접미사로 특정 동사 뒤에 붙이면 해당 동사가 명사로 품사와 뜻이 바뀐다.
'-or'은 '~하는 사람(행위자)'이라는 의미를 만들어 주는 접미사이다. 동사가 'e'로 끝나는 경우 'e'를 빼고 접미사를 붙인다.

• Thomas Edison made over 1,000 inventions in his life.
= more than

• Who is the inventor of the plane?
발명품 앞에는 정관사 the를 붙인다.

구문해설 • invent: 발명하다 • invention: 발명, 발명품 • inventor: 발명가

• Tim은 특별한 해변용 신발을 발명했다.
• Thomas Edison은 일생 동안 천 개 이상의 발명품을 만들었다.
• 비행기의 발명가는 누구인가?

Think and Write Step 2

Looking back this year, I'm glad that I donated money to children in Africa.
분사구문 (= When I look back this year)

I did this because I wanted to make a difference for children in need. To save
아프리카의 아이들에게 돈을 기부한 것   부사적 용법(목적)

money, I didn't buy snacks for a month. I donated the money to UNICEF.
~ 동안

Before I donated, I sometimes left food on my plate. Now I really appreciate

my meals. I'm proud of myself.
주어와 목적어가 같은 대상일 때 쓰인 재귀대명사

구문해설 • donate: 기부하다 • make a difference: 변화를 가져오다, 차이를 낳다, 영향을 주다, 중요하다
• in need: 어려움에 처한[하여], 궁핍한[하여] • appreciate: 고맙게 여기다

올해를 뒤돌아보니, 나는 아프리카의 아이들에게 돈을 기부해서 기쁘다. 나는 어려움에 처한 아이들의 상황을 변화시키고 싶었기 때문에 기부를 했다. 돈을 모으기 위해, 나는 한 달 동안 간식을 사지 않았다. 나는 그 돈을 유니세프에 기부했다. 나는 기부하기 전에는 가끔 접시에 음식을 남겼다. 이제 나는 내 음식을 정말 고맙게 여긴다. 나는 내 자신이 자랑스럽다.

[01~02] 다음 빈칸에 가장 알맞은 단어를 고르시오.

01

| I am _____ that I am negative. |

① disappointed   ② satisfied

③ excited   ④ proud

⑤ confident

02

| The new factory is expected to _____ more than 400 new jobs. |

① describe   ② reduce   ③ prevent

④ create   ⑤ complete

03 다음 빈칸 (A)와 (B)에 들어갈 말로 알맞게 짝지어진 것은?

- It seems difficult, but I'll (A)_____ it a try.
- The match has been (B)_____ off until tomorrow because of bad weather.

① give – got   ② give – put

③ give – done   ④ put – got

⑤ put – put

04 다음 괄호 안의 단어를 문맥에 맞게 고쳐 쓰시오.

| We had an _____ time in Paris. (believe) |

[05~07] 다음 대화를 읽고 물음에 답하시오.

G: Jaemin, are you ready for the singing contest?

B: Well, 포기할까 생각 중이야, Tina.

G: Why? I thought you really wanted to ___(A)___ part in the contest.

B: I don't think I'm a good singer.

G: Come on. You're the best singer I know.

B: Do you really think so?

G: Of course. You have a really nice voice.

B: Thank you for saying so. I'll ___(B)___ my best.

G: _____(C)_____

05 밑줄 친 우리말과 일치하도록 주어진 단어를 이용해 영작하시오.

➡ _____ (give, of, 5 단어)

06 빈칸 (A)와 (B)에 알맞은 말을 〈보기〉에서 골라 쓰시오.

| 보기 |
| do   get   keep   put   take |

(A) _____ (B) _____

07 빈칸 (C)에 알맞은 말을 고르시오.

① I hope I participate in the singing contest.

② I hope you put off the contest.

③ I hope you win the contest.

④ I hope you'll join the contest again.

⑤ I hope I have the chance to win.

[08~10] 다음 대화를 읽고 물음에 답하시오.

G: Jiho, what's up? You look tired.

B: Yeah. I stayed up (A)[late / lately] last night.

G: Did you play computer games again?

B: No, not this time. I had to finish my history project.

G: Is it due today?

B: Yeah. 나는 마지막 순간까지 미루지 말았어야 했어.

G: Hmm, I understand. I often have the same problem.

B: Really? Well, let's try (B)[changing / to change] our bad habits.

08 위 대화의 괄호 (A)와 (B)에서 적절한 것을 골라 쓰시오.

(A) _____ (B) _____

09 위 대화에서 다음 영영풀이에 해당하는 단어를 찾아 쓰시오.

> expected at or planned for a certain time

➡ _____

10 위 대화의 밑줄 친 우리말과 일치하도록 괄호 안에 주어진 단어를 알맞게 배열하여 영작하시오.

> (put, until, off, shouldn't, moment, the, I, last, have, it)

➡ _____

[11~12] 다음 대화를 읽고 물음에 답하시오.

Minho: Linda, what are you reading?

Linda: I'm reading graduation messages from my classmates. (①)

Minho: Oh, it looks like they had a lot to say to you. (②)

Linda: Many of them wrote that they like my smile.

Minho: That's nice. (③)

Linda: Some of them said I didn't hang out enough with them.

Minho: That's not your fault. (④) You were always busy.

Linda: Yeah, but 나는 학급 친구들과 더 많은 시간을 보냈어야 했어. (⑤)

Minho: You still have time after graduation.

Linda: You're right.

Minho: I hope you keep in touch with your classmates after graduation.

Linda: Thanks. I hope so, too.

11 위 대화의 ①~⑤ 중 주어진 문장이 들어갈 곳은?

> What else?

① ② ③ ④ ⑤

12 위 대화의 밑줄 친 우리말을 영작하시오.

➡ _____

_____ (9 단어)

Grammar

13 다음 중 어법상 어색한 문장을 고르시오.

① She had lived in Busan for 15 years before she got married.

② Mike had stayed up until his dad returned.

③ When I had got up, she already went to work.

④ Nathalie lost the cell phone that her mom had bought for her.

⑤ When Tom opened the door, Kate had already eaten an apple.

14 다음 문장을 바꾸어 쓸 때 가장 적절한 것은?

> Being late for school, Ann ran to catch the school bus.

① She was late for school, Ann ran to catch the school bus.
② If she was late for school, Ann ran to catch the school bus.
③ Though she was late for school, Ann ran to catch the school bus.
④ Ann ran to catch the school bus, and she was late for school.
⑤ Because she was late for school, Ann ran to catch the school bus.

15 그림을 보고 주어진 어휘를 이용하여 빈칸을 알맞게 채우시오.

_____ _____ sunny, I decided to go hiking. (be)

16 다음 중 어법상 어색한 문장을 고르시오.

① Not knowing where he was, Helen just wanted to know how to get to him.
② Looking back this year, I'm glad that I donated money to children in Africa.
③ Doing this work every day, you will soon improve.
④ Being very tall, she became a basketball player.
⑤ Not telling the truth the previous day, he fell in danger.

17 다음 두 문장을 when으로 시작하여 한 문장으로 연결하되, 두 사건의 시간차가 드러나도록 고쳐 쓰시오.

(1) • Mina returned home.
　　• Her brother ate all her cookies.
　　➡ _____
　　_____

(2) • The waiter finally arrived with the food.
　　• The guests already left the restaurant.
　　➡ _____
　　_____

18 다음 문장을 바꿔 쓸 때 빈칸에 알맞은 말을 쓰시오.

(1) Being a thrilling movie, it lacks reality.
　　➡ _____, it lacks reality.
(2) Feeling hungry, I ate some cookies.
　　➡ _____, I ate some cookies.
(3) Turning left, you will find the police station on your right.
　　➡ _____, you will find the police station on your right.

19 다음 ⓐ~ⓖ 중 어법상 옳은 것을 모두 고르시오.

> ⓐ Read the book, I drank a cup of tea.
> ⓑ Being not late for school, Amy walked to school.
> ⓒ Seeing from a distance, it has a beautiful rainbow design.
> ⓓ Not knowing what to do, she asked him for help.
> ⓔ Using a saw, you should wear gloves.
> ⓕ When I arrived there, the meeting has

already begun.

ⓖ He stayed up late until his mom had returned.

ⓗ Mina couldn't buy the book because she had spent all her money.

➡ _____

Reading

[20~21] 다음 글을 읽고 물음에 답하시오.

WORLD NEWS

APRIL 13, 1888

The Merchant of Death, Alfred Nobel, Is Dead

Alfred Nobel died yesterday in France from a heart attack. He invented dynamite and other dangerous objects for war. He became rich from the deaths of others. He is responsible for the ___ⓐ___ of thousands of people. The world will remember him as "the merchant of death."

20 위 글의 빈칸 ⓐ에 들어갈 알맞은 말을 본문에서 찾아 쓰시오.

➡ _____

21 위 글의 종류로 알맞은 것을 고르시오.

① e-mail ② article
③ essay ④ diary
⑤ review

[22~24] 다음 글을 읽고 물음에 답하시오.

In 1888, a French newspaper mistakenly reported Alfred Nobel's death. ⓐ실제로 죽은 사람은 Alfred Nobel의 형인 Ludvig였다. Thanks to the report, however, Nobel decided ⓑto do something to contribute to the world. In 1895, he decided to use his money to create the Nobel Prize. Originally, there were only five awards. A sixth award was added in 1968. Today, when we think of Alfred Nobel, we think of the Nobel Prize, rather than dynamite.

22 위 글의 밑줄 친 ⓐ의 우리말에 맞게 주어진 어휘를 알맞게 배열하시오.

who / was / Ludvig / the person / his brother / had actually died / , /

➡ _____
_____

23 위 글의 밑줄 친 ⓑto do와 to부정사의 용법이 같은 것을 모두 고르시오.

① It's time to go home.
② It is not difficult to read this book.
③ They came here to see you.
④ Give me something to eat.
⑤ My hobby is to collect stamps.

24 위 글의 내용을 다음과 같이 정리하고자 한다. 빈칸 (A)와 (B)에 들어갈 알맞은 단어를 본문에서 찾아 쓰시오.

Thanks to the incorrect report of a French newspaper, Nobel decided to do something to (A)_____ _____ the world and decided to use his money to create (B)_____ _____ _____.

[25~26] 다음 글을 읽고 물음에 답하시오.

ⓐLooking back this year, I'm glad that I donated money to children in Africa. I did this because I wanted to make a difference for children in need. To save money, I didn't buy snacks for a month. I donated the money to UNICEF. Before I donated, I sometimes left food on my plate. Now I really appreciate my meals. I'm proud of myself.

25 위 글의 밑줄 친 ⓐ와 분사구문의 용법이 같은 것을 고르시오.

① Drinking lots of water, you will get healthier.

② Feeling sick, I couldn't take a rest.

③ Having no money, I had to go home on foot.

④ Living near the sea, I cannot swim.

⑤ Walking down the street, I happened to meet Tony.

26 Which question CANNOT be answered after reading the passage?

① What did the writer do?

② Why did the writer do it?

③ How did the writer do it?

④ How much money did the writer donate to UNICEF?

⑤ How did it make the writer different?

[27~29] 다음 글을 읽고 물음에 답하시오.

The article was about his own death! It said Nobel had died in France from a heart attack.

"Oh my goodness! Am I dead?"

Catching his breath, Nobel kept reading.

(①) Soon, he became even more shocked. (②) The article described him as the inventor of dynamite and other dangerous objects for war. (③) He couldn't believe his eyes. (④) It was true that dynamite was one of his many inventions. (⑤) But he never imagined that the world would think of him as "the merchant of death."

27 위 글의 흐름으로 보아, 주어진 문장이 들어가기에 가장 적절한 곳은?

> It said that he had become rich from the deaths of others.

①　　　②　　　③　　　④　　　⑤

28 위 글의 제목으로 알맞은 것을 고르시오.

① Nobel Died in France from a Heart Attack

② Oh My Goodness! Am I "the Merchant of Death?"

③ A Man Who Became Rich from the Deaths of Others

④ Nobel, the Inventor of Dynamite

⑤ Dynamite, One of Nobel's Many Inventions

29 According to the passage, which is NOT true?

① The article said Nobel had died in France from a heart attack.

② Because of the shocking news, Nobel couldn't read the article any more.

③ The article said that Nobel had become rich from the deaths of others.

④ Dynamite was one of Nobel's many inventions.

⑤ Nobel never imagined that the world would think of him as "the merchant of death."

단원별 예상문제

01 다음 짝지어진 단어의 관계가 〈보기〉와 같은 것끼리 짝지어
진 것을 고르시오.

출제율 90%

┌─ 보기 ─┐

move – touch

ⓐ active – inactive
ⓑ including – excluding
ⓒ normal – ordinary
ⓓ decide – determine
ⓔ satisfied – dissatisfied

① ⓐ, ⓑ ② ⓑ, ⓒ ③ ⓒ, ⓓ
④ ⓓ, ⓔ ⑤ ⓐ, ⓔ

02 다음 빈칸 (A)와 (B)에 들어갈 말로 알맞은 것끼리 짝지어진
것을 고르시오.

출제율 95%

• By the time we arrived, the meeting
was (A)_____.
• If we get caught (B)_____ a traffic
jam, it'll take 3 hours.

   (A) (B)   (A) (B)
① on – in   ② on – on
③ over – in   ④ over – on
⑤ in – in

03 빈칸에 공통으로 들어갈 말을 쓰시오. (주어진 철자로 시작
할 것.)

출제율 95%

• She t_____ her eyes off the road to
glance at me.
• About 24,000 people t_____ part in
the marathon.

04 다음 괄호 안의 단어를 문맥에 맞게 고쳐 빈칸을 채우시오.

출제율 90%

(1) It was my first job after _____ from
Oxford in 2019. (graduate)
(2) He's the art _____ of this movie.
(direct)

05 밑줄 친 문장과 같은 의미가 되도록 빈칸을 채우시오.

출제율 90%

A: What's wrong?
B: I was late for school.
A: Oh, I'm sorry to hear that.
B: I should have got up early.

➡ I _____ late.

06 대화가 자연스럽게 연결되도록 (A)~(D)를 순서대로 적절하
게 배열한 것은?

출제율 100%

(A) Sounds great. I hope you have a
wonderful vacation.
(B) I'm planning to visit my grandparents
in Busan.
(C) Jinsu, what are you going to do
during the vacation?
(D) I'm going to read lots of books. What
about you?

① (B) – (A) – (C) – (D)
② (B) – (C) – (A) – (D)
③ (C) – (A) – (B) – (D)
④ (C) – (B) – (A) – (D)
⑤ (C) – (D) – (B) – (A)

Minho: Linda, what are you reading?

Linda: I'm reading graduation messages from my classmates.

Minho: Oh, it looks like they had a lot to say to you.

Linda: Many of them wrote (A)[that / what] they like my smile.

Minho: That's nice. What else?

Minho: Some of them said I didn't hang ____ⓐ____ enough with them.

Minho: That's not your fault. You were always busy.

Linda: Yeah, but I ____ⓑ____ more time with my classmates.

Minho: You still have time (B)[after / before] graduation.

Linda: You're right.

Minho: I hope you keep in touch with your classmates after graduation.

Linda: Thanks. I hope so, too.

출제율 90%

07 위 대화의 빈칸 ⓐ에 알맞은 말을 쓰시오.

➡ _____

출제율 95%

08 위 대화의 빈칸 ⓑ에 알맞은 말을 고르시오.

① shouldn't have taken
② should have left
③ shouldn't have left
④ should have spent
⑤ shouldn't have spent

출제율 95%

09 위 대화의 괄호 (A)와 (B)에서 적절한 것을 골라 쓰시오.

(A) _____ (B) _____

G: Jiho, what's up? You look tired.

B: Yeah. (①) I stayed up late last night.

G: Did you play computer games again? (②)

B: No, not this time. (③) I had ____(A)____ (finish) my history project.

G: Is it due today?

B: Yeah. I shouldn't ____(B)____ (put off, it) until the last moment. (④)

G: Hmm, I understand. (⑤)

B: Really? Well, let's try to change our bad habits.

출제율 100%

10 위 대화의 ①~⑤ 중 주어진 문장이 들어갈 곳은?

I often have the same problem.

①   ②   ③   ④   ⑤

출제율 95%

11 주어진 괄호 안의 단어를 문맥에 맞게 고쳐 빈칸 (A)와 (B)를 채우시오.

(A) _____ (B) _____

출제율 100%

12 위 대화를 읽고 답할 수 없는 질문을 고르시오.

① How will they change their habits?
② When is the due date of the history project?
③ How does Jiho look like?
④ What is the bad habit which they have to change?
⑤ What did Jiho do last night?

13 다음 중 어법상 <u>어색한</u> 문장을 고르시오. (2개)

① While I was walking on the street, I saw a famous movie star.
② Walked on the street, I saw a famous movie star.
③ Walking on the street, I saw a famous movie star.
④ I walking on the street, I saw a famous movie star.
⑤ While walking on the street, I saw a famous movie star.

14 그림을 보고 주어진 어휘를 이용하여 빈칸을 알맞게 채우시오.

When Ann ran to the bus stop, the bus _____ _____ _____. (just, leave)

15 다음 중 어법상 <u>어색한</u> 문장을 고르시오.

① She came earlier than I had expected.
② When Tom had opened the door, Alex already watered the plants.
③ I watched TV after I did my homework.
④ An article said that he had died!
⑤ The person who had actually died was his brother, Ludvig.

[16~18] 다음 글을 읽고 물음에 답하시오.

The article was about his own death! It said Nobel had died in France from a heart attack.

"Oh my goodness! Am I (A)[died / dead]?"

Catching his breath, Nobel kept reading. Soon, he became even more (B)[shocking / shocked]. The article described him as the inventor of dynamite and other dangerous (C)[objects / subjects] for war. It said that he ____@____ rich from the deaths of others. He couldn't believe his eyes. ⓑIt was true that dynamite was one of his many inventions. But he never imagined that the world would think of him as "the merchant of death."

16 위 글의 빈칸 ⓐ에 become을 알맞은 형태로 쓰시오.

➡ _____

17 위 글의 괄호 (A)~(C)에서 문맥이나 어법상 알맞은 낱말을 골라 쓰시오.

(A) _____ (B) _____ (C) _____

18 위 글의 밑줄 친 ⓑIt과 문법적 쓰임이 같은 것을 고르시오.

① I make it a rule to get up early.
② It is 2 miles from here to the airport.
③ Did you see it?
④ It is important for you to choose good friends.
⑤ How's it going with you?

[19~21] 다음 글을 읽고 물음에 답하시오.

The Man Behind the Nobel Prize
ⓐAlfred Nobel decided to use his money to create the Nobel Prize. He wanted to honor people who made the world better. The Nobel Prize is given to people for great work in physics, chemistry, medicine, literature and the promotion of peace.

[출제율 90%]

19 위 글의 밑줄 친 ⓐ를 복문으로 고칠 때 빈칸에 들어갈 알맞은 말을 쓰시오.

> Alfred Nobel decided to use his money
> _____ _____ _____ he _____
> _____ the Nobel Prize.

[출제율 95%]

20 Why did Alfred Nobel create the Nobel Prize? Answer in English beginning with "Because".

➡ _____

_____

[출제율 100%]

21 다음 중 위 글에서 설명한 노벨상 수상 부문에 해당하지 않는 것을 고르시오.

① 물리학   ② 경제학   ③ 의학

④ 문학   ⑤ 평화

[22~24] 다음 글을 읽고 물음에 답하시오.

In 1888, a French newspaper mistakenly reported Alfred Nobel's death. The person who had actually died was his brother, Ludvig. _____ⓐ_____ the report, however, Nobel decided to do something to contribute to the world. In 1895, he decided to use his money to create the Nobel Prize. Originally, there were only five awards. A sixth award was added in 1968. Today, when we think of Alfred Nobel, we think of the Nobel Prize, rather than dynamite.

[출제율 95%]

22 위 글의 빈칸 ⓐ에 들어갈 알맞은 말을 모두 고르시오.

① Instead of   ② In spite of

③ Thanks to   ④ In addition to

⑤ Because of

[출제율 100%]

23 위 글의 주제로 알맞은 것을 고르시오.

① A French newspaper mistakenly reported Alfred Nobel's death.

② The incorrect report made Nobel decide to contribute to the world.

③ The person who had actually died was not Nobel but his brother, Ludvig.

④ The incorrect report can cause the harmful effect.

⑤ We should think of the Nobel Prize, rather than dynamite.

[출제율 95%]

24 According to the passage, which is NOT true?

① In 1888, a French newspaper reported Alfred Nobel's death on purpose.

② It was Alfred Nobel's brother, Ludvig, who had actually died.

③ Nobel decided to use his money to create the Nobel Prize.

④ In 1968, the number of the awards increased to six.

⑤ Today, when we think of Alfred Nobel, the Nobel Prize rather than dynamite comes to our mind first.

01 다음 대화의 흐름상 빈칸에 들어갈 말을 주어진 〈조건〉에 맞춰 쓰시오.

┌─ 조건 ─┐
- 기원하는 말 하기
- 대화에 나와 있는 어휘 이용하기
- 9 단어

A: I can't believe we're graduating soon.
B: Yeah. Is there anything you regret about your middle school life?
A: Yes. I should have taken part in many school events.
B: Well, you have a second chance in high school.
A: I guess you're right.
B: _____ in high school.

➡ _____

02 다음 문장과 바꿔 쓸 수 있는 문장을 주어진 단어를 이용하여 바꿔 쓰시오.

I should have eaten less last night.

(1) _____ (ought)
(2) _____ (regret)
(3) _____ (sorry)

03 다음 대화의 밑줄 친 문장 중 문맥상 또는 어법상 어색한 것을 찾아 바르게 고치시오.

Minho: Linda, what are you reading?
Linda: ①I'm reading graduation messages from my classmates.
Minho: Oh, it looks like they had a lot to say to you.

Linda: ②Many of them wrote that they like my smile.
Minho: That's nice. What else?
Linda: ③Some of them said I didn't hang out enough with them.
Minho: That's not your fault. You were always busy.
Linda: Yeah, but ④I must have spent more time with my classmates.
Minho: You still have time after graduation.
Linda: You're right.
Minho: ⑤I hope you keep in touch with your classmates after graduation.
Linda: Thanks. I hope so, too.

➡ _____

04 분사구문은 부사절로, 부사절은 분사구문으로 바꿔 쓰시오.

(1) Being sick, he went to see a doctor.
   ➡ _____

(2) You will get a perfect result, following these instructions.
   ➡ _____
   _____

(3) As there was no bus left, I had to walk home.
   ➡ _____

(4) He goes to work by train every morning and comes home the same way.
   ➡ _____
   _____

05 다음 두 문장을 that을 이용하여 한 문장으로 연결할 때 두 사건의 시간차가 드러나도록 빈칸을 알맞게 채우시오.

(1) • The article said.

• He became rich from the deaths of others.

= The article said that he _____ rich from the deaths of others.

(2) • When he returned to Korea after twenty years' absence, he found it.

• Everything changed completely.

= When he returned to Korea after twenty years' absence, he found that everything _____ completely.

[06~08] 다음 글을 읽고 물음에 답하시오.

The article was about his own death! It said Nobel ____ⓐ____ in France from a heart attack. "Oh my goodness! Am I dead?"

ⓑCatching his breath, Nobel kept reading. Soon, he became even more shocked. The article described him as the inventor of dynamite and other dangerous objects for war. It said that he had become rich from the deaths of others. He couldn't believe his eyes. It was true that dynamite was one of his many inventions. But he never imagined that the world would think of ⓒhim as "the merchant of death."

06 위 글의 빈칸 ⓐ에 die를 알맞은 형태로 쓰시오.

➡ _____

07 위 글의 밑줄 친 분사구문 ⓑ를 부사절로 고치시오.

➡ _____

08 위 글의 밑줄 친 ⓒhim이 가리키는 것을 본문에서 찾아 쓰시오.

➡ _____

[09~11] 다음 글을 읽고 물음에 답하시오.

In 1888, a French newspaper mistakenly reported Alfred Nobel's death. The person who had actually died was his brother, Ludvig. Thanks to the report, however, ⓐ Nobel decided to do something to contribute to the world. In 1895, he decided to use his money to create the Nobel Prize. Originally, there were only five awards. A sixth award was added in 1968. Today, when we think of Alfred Nobel, ⓑ우리는 다이너마이트보다는 노벨상을 떠올린다.

09 위 글의 밑줄 친 ⓐ를 다음과 같이 바꿔 쓸 때 빈칸에 들어갈 알맞은 말을 세 단어로 쓰시오.

Nobel _____ _____ _____ to do something to contribute to the world.

10 위 글의 밑줄 친 ⓑ의 우리말에 맞게 주어진 어휘를 알맞게 배열하시오.

rather than / think of / dynamite / the Nobel Prize / we / , /

➡ _____

11 본문의 내용과 일치하도록 다음 빈칸 (A)와 (B)에 알맞은 단어를 쓰시오.

In 1888, a French newspaper mistakenly reported that _____ _____ died, but the person who had actually died was his brother, Ludvig.

01 〈보기〉에 주어진 표현과 분사구문을 이용하여 3 문장 이상 쓰시오.

> 보기
>
> have nothing to do / go for a walk
> tired / come back home early
> they are not fish / they need to come up to breathe
> walk on the street / saw a famous movie star

(1) _____
(2) _____
(3) _____

02 다음 내용을 바탕으로 보람을 느꼈던 일에 관해 쓰시오.

> • What did you do?
>   I donated money to children in Africa.
> • Why did you do it?
>   I wanted to make a difference for children in need.
> • How did you do it?
>   I didn't buy snacks for a month.
> • How did it make you different?
>   Now I really appreciate my meals.
> • How do you feel about yourself?
>   I'm proud of myself.

> Looking back this year, I'm glad that I (A)_____. I did this because I wanted to (B)_____. To save money, I didn't (C)_____. I donated the money to UNICEF. Before I donated, I sometimes left food on my plate. Now I really appreciate (D)_____. I'm proud of (E)_____.

단원별 모의고사

01 다음 빈칸에 공통으로 들어갈 말을 고르시오.

> • She's late _____ work every day.
> • After the long walk, we were all ready _____ a drink.

① to   ② for   ③ of

④ from   ⑤ on

02 다음 괄호 안의 단어를 문맥에 맞게 고쳐 쓰시오.

> They were equally amazed at her. It was _____(believe) that she was only the same age as many of them.

03 다음 빈칸을 〈보기〉에 있는 어휘를 이용하여 채우시오.

> ┌── 보기 ──────────────────┐
> catch   get   give   hang
> keep   stay   spend
> └────────────────────────┘

(1) We _____ half an hour looking for the keys, but eventually _____ up and went home.

(2) I often _____ out in coffee shops.

(3) Josh could _____ up all night without getting tired.

04 다음 우리말에 맞도록 빈칸에 알맞은 말을 쓰시오. (철자가 주어진 경우 주어진 철자로 시작할 것)

(1) 그녀는 기대하지 못했다는 듯 놀라서 외쳤다.
➡ She shouted _____ surprise as if she weren't expecting it.

(2) 우리가 계속 연락하고 지내기를 바라.
➡ I h_____ we'll _____ in _____.

(3) 그들에게 나의 전화번호를 주는 바보 같은 실수를 저질렀다.
➡ I stupidly _____ the _____ of giving them my phone number.

(4) 나는 이곳을 나의 고향으로 생각한다.
➡ I t_____ _____ this place _____ my home.

[05~06] 다음 대화를 읽고 물음에 답하시오.

> G: Jiho, what's up? You look (A)[angry / excited / tired].
> B: Yeah. I stayed up late last night.
> G: Did you play computer games again?
> B: No, not this time. I had to finish my history project.
> G: Is it (B)[due / plan / work] today?
> B: Yeah. 나는 마지막 순간까지 미루지 말았어야 했어.
> G: Hmm, I understand. I often have the same problem.
> B: Really? Well, let's try to (C)[change / keep / make] our bad habits.

05 위 대화의 괄호 (A)~(C)에서 적절한 것을 골라 쓰시오.

(A) _____ (B) _____ (C) _____

06 위 글의 밑줄 친 우리말과 일치하도록 주어진 단어를 이용해 영작하시오.

> put, should, it, until, 10 단어

➡ _____

[07~09] 다음 대화를 읽고 물음에 답하시오.

G: Jaemin, are you ready ___ⓐ___ the singing contest?

B: Well, I'm thinking ___ⓑ___ giving ___ⓒ___ , Tina.

G: Why? I thought you really wanted to take part ___ⓓ___ the contest.

B: ①I don't think I'm a good singer.

G: Come on. ②You're the best singer I know.

B: ③Do you really think so?

G: ④Of course not. You have a really nice voice.

B: Thank you ___ⓔ___ saying so. I'll do my best.

G: ⑤I hope you win the contest.

07 위 대화의 빈칸 ⓐ~ⓔ에 들어가지 <u>않는</u> 말을 고르시오.

① for ② in ③ of ④ on ⑤ up

08 위 대화의 밑줄 친 ①~⑤ 중 흐름상 또는 어법상 어색한 것을 고르시오.

①　　　②　　　③　　　④　　　⑤

09 질문에 답할 수 <u>없는</u> 것을 <u>모두</u> 고르시오.

① 재민이는 무슨 종류의 노래를 잘하는가?

② Tina는 재민이가 대회에서 무엇을 하기를 바라는가?

③ 노래 대회는 언제 있는가?

④ 왜 재민이는 대회를 포기할까 생각 중이었는가?

⑤ 재민이는 노래 대회에 나갈 것인가?

[10~12] 다음 대화를 읽고 물음에 답하시오.

Minho: Linda, what are you reading?

Linda: _____

Minho: _____

Linda: _____

Minho: _____

Linda: Some of them said I didn't hang out enough with them.

Minho: That's not your fault. You were always busy.

Linda: Yeah, but I should have spent more time with my classmates.

Minho: You still have time after graduation.

Linda: You're right.

Minho: 네가 졸업 후에도 학급 친구들과 계속 연락하기를 바라.

Linda: Thanks. I hope so, too.

10 위 대화의 빈칸에 들어갈 말을 바르게 배열하시오.

(A) Oh, it looks like they had a lot to say to you.

(B) Many of them wrote that they like my smile.

(C) I'm reading graduation messages from my classmates.

(D) That's nice. What else?

➡ _____

11 위 대화에서 다음 영영풀이에 해당하는 단어를 찾아 쓰시오.

a ceremony at which degrees or diplomas are given out

➡ _____

12 밑줄 친 우리말과 일치하도록 주어진 단어를 이용해 영작하시오. (hope, touch, after) (11 words)

➡ _____

_____

13 다음 문장에서 어법상 <u>어색한</u> 것을 바르게 고쳐 다시 쓰시오.

(1) When I woke up this morning, the rain already stopped.

➡ _____

_____

(2) The article said Alfred Nobel died in France from a heart attack.

➡ _____

_____

(3) Ann was late for school, Ann ran to catch the school bus.

➡ _____

_____

14 다음 우리말을 주어진 어휘를 이용하여 영작하시오.

(1) 내가 집에 갔을 때, 나는 누군가 우리 집에 침입했었다는 것을 알았다. (got, found, break into, someone, 12 단어)

➡ _____

_____

(2) 그들은 친구들이 도착하기 전에 피자를 다 먹었다. (the pizza, their friends, arrive, finish, 9 단어)

➡ _____

_____

(3) 팝콘을 먹으면서 그는 TV를 보았다. (eat, watch, popcorn, 5 단어)

➡ _____

(4) 오른쪽으로 돌면, 너는 꽃 가게를 발견할 수 있을 것이다. (the flower shop, to the right, find, turn, 10 단어)

➡ _____

15 Which is grammatically wrong? Select ALL.

① Be nervous on the stage, the actor forgot his lines.

② While listening to music, he washed the dishes.

③ Losing the game, she felt disappointed.

④ Jimmy had borrowed some money because he lost his bag.

⑤ I went to bed after I watched my favorite TV show.

[16~18] 다음 글을 읽고 물음에 답하시오.

The article was about his own death! It said Nobel had died in France from a heart attack. "Oh my goodness! Am I dead?"

ⓐ숨을 고른 후, Nobel은 계속 읽었다. Soon, he became even more shocked. The article described him as the inventor of dynamite and other dangerous objects for war. It said that he had become rich from the deaths of others. He couldn't believe his eyes. It was true ⓑthat dynamite was one of his many inventions. But he never imagined that the world would think of him as "the merchant of death."

16 위 글의 밑줄 친 ⓐ의 우리말에 맞게 주어진 어휘를 이용하여 6 단어로 영작하시오. (분사구문을 사용하시오.)

kept

➡ _____

17 위 글의 밑줄 친 ⓑthat과 문법적 쓰임이 같은 것을 고르시오.

① The trouble is that we are short of money.
② She warned me that I should be more careful.
③ It's true that we were a little late.
④ I heard that you've been abroad.
⑤ There was no hope that she would recover her health.

18 Why did Nobel become even more shocked as he continued to read the article? Fill in the blanks (A) and (B) with suitable words.

> Because he realized that the world would think of him as "the merchant of (A)_____" after he died and he never (B)_____ it.

[19~21] 다음 글을 읽고 물음에 답하시오.

> In 1888, a French newspaper mistakenly reported Alfred Nobel's death. (①) Thanks to the report, however, Nobel decided to do something to contribute to the world. (②) In 1895, he decided to use his money ⓐto create the Nobel Prize. (③) Originally, there were only five awards. (④) A sixth award was added in 1968. (⑤) Today, when we think of Alfred Nobel, we think of the Nobel Prize, rather than dynamite.

19 위 글의 흐름으로 보아, 주어진 문장이 들어가기에 가장 적절한 곳은?

> The person who had actually died was his brother, Ludvig.

①   ②   ③   ④   ⑤

20 다음 〈보기〉에서 위 글의 밑줄 친 ⓐto create와 to부정사의 용법이 다른 것의 개수를 고르시오.

> ┤ 보기 ├
> ① He promised never to be late again.
> ② He grew up to be a cook.
> ③ I don't have any friends to talk with.
> ④ All he can do is to support himself.
> ⑤ I'm glad to meet you.

① 1개   ② 2개   ③ 3개   ④ 4개   ⑤ 5개

21 When was a sixth award added? Answer in English in a full sentence beginning with "It". (5 words)

➡ _____

[22~23] 다음 글을 읽고 물음에 답하시오.

> Looking back this year, I'm glad that I participated in the tree planting program. I ⓐdid this because I wanted to do something for the environment. To get more people to join this program, I put up some posters and encouraged my friends to join. I didn't care about trees before I participated in this program. Now I know they are really important for us. I feel proud of myself.

22 위 글의 밑줄 친 ⓐdid this가 가리키는 것을 본문에서 찾아 쓰시오.

➡ _____

23 According to the passage, which is NOT true?

① This year, the writer participated in the tree planting program.
② The writer wanted to do something for the environment.
③ The writer put up some posters.
④ The writer encouraged his or her friends to join the program.
⑤ The writer doesn't care about trees.

Lesson Special

Picture the Future

Words & Expressions

Key Words

- **after** [金ftər] 전 ~ 후에
- **appear** [əpíər] 동 나타나다
- **bathroom** [bǽθrùːm] 명 욕실
- **brightly** [bráitli] 부 밝게
- **clear** [kliər] 동 맑게[투명하게] 하다 형 투명한, 맑은
- **comfortable** [kʌ́mfərtəbl] 형 편안한, 안락한
- **drawer** [drɔːr] 명 서랍
- **driverless** [dráivərlis] 형 운전자가 필요 없는
- **future** [fjúːtʃər] 명 미래
- **grocery** [gróusəri] 명 식료품 및 잡화
- **health condition** 건강 상태
- **land** [lænd] 동 내려앉다, 착륙하다 명 육지, 땅
- **press** [pres] 동 누르다
- **remind** [rimáind] 동 상기시키다

- **rub** [rʌb] 동 문지르다, 비비다
- **scan** [skæn] 동 정밀 검사[촬영]하다
- **select** [silékt] 동 선택하다
- **sensor** [sénsər] 명 센서, 감지기
- **shake** [ʃeik] 동 흔들리다, 흔들다
- **shine** [ʃain] 동 빛나다, 비추다
- **shower** [ʃáuər] 명 샤워실, 샤워
- **solution** [səlúːʃən] 명 해결책
- **special** [spéʃəl] 형 특별한
- **story** [stɔ́ːri] 명 (건물의) 층
- **usual** [júːʒuəl] 형 일상의, 늘 하는 명 늘 먹던 것
- **whisper** [hwíspər] 동 속삭이다
- **yell** [jel] 동 소리치다, 외치다

Key Expressions

- **be tired of** ~에 싫증이 나다
- **by 동사ing** ~함으로써
- **come back** 돌아오다
- **don't have to 동사원형** ~할 필요가 없다
- **feel like** ~인 것처럼 느끼다
- **give a presentation** 발표를 하다
- **on top of** ~의 꼭대기에

- **pay for** ~의 값을 지불하다
- **print out** (프린트로) 출력하다
- **remind A to 동사원형** A에게 ~할 것을 상기시키다
- **send A to B** A를 B에게 보내다
- **step in** ~에 발을 디디다
- **stop 동명사** ~하기를 멈추다
- **thanks to 명사** ~ 덕분에

Word Power

※ 명사+less: ~이 없는

☐ **careless** 부주의한

☐ **driverless** 운전자가 필요 없는

☐ **endless** 끝없는

☐ **harmless** 해롭지 않은

☐ **homeless** 집 없는

☐ **useless** 쓸모없는

☐ **wireless** 선이 없는

※ 서로 비슷한 뜻을 가진 어휘

☐ **press** 누르다 – **push down** ~을 꽉 누르다

☐ **rub** 문지르다, 비비다 – **stroke** 쓰다듬다

☐ **select** 선택하다 – **choose** 고르다, 선택하다

☐ **story** (건물의) 층 – **floor** 층

※ 서로 반대의 뜻을 가진 어휘

☐ **appear** 나타나다 ↔ **disappear** 사라지다

☐ **comfortable** 편안한 ↔ **uncomfortable** 불편한

☐ **future** 미래 ↔ **past** 과거

☐ **usual** 일상의 ↔ **unusual** 특이한, 흔치 않은

☐ **special** 특별한 ↔ **general** 일반적인

English Dictionary

☐ **appear** 나타나다
→ to start to be seen, to arrive, or to exist in a place, especially suddenly
특히 갑자기 보이거나, 도착하거나, 어느 장소에 존재하기 시작하다

☐ **press** 누르다
→ to push a button, switch, etc. to make a machine start, a bell ring, etc.
기계가 시작하거나, 종이 울리도록 하기 위해서 버튼이나 스위치 등을 누르다

☐ **remind** 상기시키다
→ to make someone remember something that they must do
누군가가 그들이 해야만 하는 것을 기억하게 만들다

☐ **rub** 문지르다, 비비다
→ to move your hand, or something such as a cloth, backwards and forwards over a surface while pressing firmly
꽉 누른 채 손이나 천 같은 어떤 것을 표면 위로 앞뒤로 움직이다

☐ **select** 선택하다
→ to choose something or someone by thinking carefully about which is the best, most suitable, etc.
어떤 것을 또는 누군가를 무엇이 최선인지, 가장 적절한지 등에 관해 조심스러운 생각으로 고르다

☐ **shake** 흔들리다, 흔들다
→ to move suddenly from side to side or up and down usually with a lot of force, or to make something or someone do this
보통 큰 힘으로 위아래나 옆으로 갑자기 움직이거나 어떤 것이나 누군가를 이렇게 하도록 만들다

☐ **shine** 빛나다, 비추다
→ to produce bright light
밝은 빛이 생기게 하다

☐ **whisper** 속삭이다
→ to speak or say something very quietly, using your breath rather than your voice
목소리보다는 숨을 사용해서 매우 조용하게 말하다

☐ **yell** 소리치다, 외치다
→ to shout or say something very loudly, especially because you are frightened, angry, or excited
특히 겁이 나거나, 화가 나거나, 흥분해서 매우 크게 소리치거나 말하다

Reading

Picture the Future

It's 7 a.m. The bed <u>shakes</u> and Minji Kim yells, "Five more minutes!"
흔들리다'(자동사)
The bed <u>stops shaking</u>. Suddenly, Minji's mom appears on a screen on
stop ~ing: ~하기를 그만두다. stop+to부정사: ~하기 위해 멈추다(부사적 용법 목적)
the wall and says, "You're going to be late for school!" Minji rubs her
eyes and says, "Clear the windows." The dark windows become clear
and the sun shines brightly through them.

In the bathroom, a red light scans Minji's body. A voice says, "54
kilograms. Your health condition is excellent." When she steps in the
shower, water comes out from the top and sides. <u>After</u> her shower,
~ 후에(전치사)+명사(구)
warm air comes out and dries her. When she gets out, <u>a drawer opens</u>
서랍이 열리며 그 안에 오늘 입을 옷이 들어 있다
<u>with today's clothes</u>.

In the kitchen, her father says, "Good morning, Honey. What do you
want for breakfast?" Minji says, "The usual, please." Mr. Kim presses
a few buttons on the cooking machine. <u>The machine</u> prints out some
문맥상 음식을 찍어 내는 삼차원 프린터(3-D printer)를 의미
bacon, eggs and bread. Mr. Kim says goodbye and rushes out the door.

A few minutes <u>later</u>, Minji's father appears on a screen and shouts,
후에
"I forgot my glasses!" Ms. Kim smiles and answers, "No problem. I'll
send a drone to your office." Mr. Kim says, "Thanks a million!"

shake 흔들리다, 흔들다
yell 소리치다, 외치다
appear 나타나다
rub 문지르다, 비비다
clear 맑게[투명하게] 하다; 투명한, 맑은
shine 빛나다, 비추다
brightly 밝게
bathroom 욕실
scan 정밀 검사[촬영]하다
health condition 건강 상태
step in ~에 발을 디디다
shower 샤워실, 샤워
drawer 서랍
usual 일상의, 늘 하는; 늘 먹던 것
press 누르다
print out (프린터로) 출력하다

확인문제

● 다음 문장이 본문의 내용과 일치하면 T, 일치하지 <u>않으면</u> F를 쓰시오.

1 Minji's mom appears on a screen on the wall and says, "You're going to be late for school!" ☐

2 When Minji steps in the shower, water comes out from the bottom. ☐

3 The cooking machine prints out some bacon, eggs and bread. ☐

4 Mr. Kim will send a drone to Ms. Kim's office. ☐

Ms. Kim and Minji get into a driverless flying car. They sit in
~을 타다

comfortable chairs around a table. Ms. Kim touches the car window

to select the groceries for this week. She pays for them by putting her
~하기 위해서(부사적 용법-목적)   앞 문장에서 Ms. Kim이 선택한 식료품 by+동사-ing: ~함으로써

finger on a sensor. They will be delivered to her house.
                Ms. Kim이 선택한 식료품 조동사 수동태(조동사+be+과거분사)

The car lands at Minji's school on top of a 150-story building. Today
                                    150층의, 150층짜리(숫자 150과 '층'을 나타내는 명사 story가 하이픈으로 연결된 복합 형용사)

Minji will give a presentation with Dona, a student in America. But
                                    Dona와 a student in America는 동격

Minji doesn't have to go to America. Thanks to a VR classroom, they
    don't have to+동사원형: ~할 필요가 없다   thanks to+명사(구): ~ 덕분에 virtual reality(컴퓨터를 이용해서 만들어진 가상 현실)

will feel like they are in the same classroom.
    ~인 것처럼 느끼다

When Minji's family comes back home, dinner is ready. They eat and

talk about their day. After a delicious dinner, the cleaning robot clears
                        a+형용사+식사명

the table and washes the dishes. Minji says, "I learned a game called
                                    = (which is) called chess. a game을 뒤에서 수식하는 과거분사구

chess today. Do you want to play?" Everyone agrees.

A 3-D chess board appears on the table. They have lots of fun.
                                            = much

Right before Minji goes to bed, she whispers to her watch.
                                    문맥상 단순한 손목시계가 아니라 스마트폰을 대체하는 미래의 아이템임을 알 수 있다.

"Remind Daddy to take his glasses tomorrow."
remind A+to부정사: A에게 ~할 것을 상기시키다

---

driverless 운전자가 필요 없는

comfortable 편안한, 안락한

select 선택하다

grocery 식료품 및 잡화

pay for ~의 값을 지불하다

sensor 센서, 감지기

land 내려앉다, 착륙하다

story (건물의) 층

give a presentation 발표를 하다

whisper 속삭이다

확인문제

● 다음 문장이 본문의 내용과 일치하면 T, 일치하지 않으면 F를 쓰시오.

1 Ms. Kim and Minji get into a driverless flying car. ☐

2 Ms. Kim touches the smartphone to select the groceries for this week. ☐

3 Ms. Kim and Minji's flying car lands on the playground of Minji's school. ☐

4 Minji's school is located on top of a 150-story building. ☐

5 After a delicious dinner, Minji clears the table and washes the dishes. ☐

● 우리말을 참고하여 빈칸에 알맞은 말을 쓰시오.

1 _____ the Future

2 _____ 7 a.m.

3 The bed _____ and Minji Kim yells, "_____ _____ _____!"

4 The bed _____ _____.

5 Suddenly, Minji's mom _____ on a screen on the wall and says, "You're going to _____ _____ _____ school!"

6 Minji rubs her eyes and says, "_____ the windows."

7 The dark windows _____ _____ and the sun shines brightly through them.

8 In the bathroom, a red light _____ _____ _____.

9 A voice says, "54 kilograms. Your _____ _____ is excellent."

10 When she steps in the shower, water _____ _____ _____ the top and sides.

11 After her shower, warm air _____ out and _____ her.

12 When she gets out, a drawer opens _____ _____ _____.

13 In the kitchen, her father says, "Good morning, Honey. What do you want _____ _____?"

14 Minji says, "_____ _____, please."

15 Mr. Kim _____ a few buttons _____ the cooking machine.

16 The machine _____ _____ some bacon, eggs and bread.

17 Mr. Kim says goodbye and _____ _____ the door.

1 미래를 상상하다

2 오전 7시이다.

3 침대가 흔들리고 김민지가 "5분만 더!"라고 소리를 지른다.

4 침대가 흔들기를 멈춘다.

5 갑자기, 민지의 엄마가 벽 스크린에 나타나 말한다. "학교에 늦겠구나!"

6 민지는 눈을 비비며 "창문을 투명하게 해 줘."라고 말한다.

7 어두운 창문이 투명해지며 창문으로 햇살이 밝게 비춘다.

8 욕실에서 빨간 빛이 민지의 몸을 정밀 검사한다.

9 목소리가 "54킬로그램. 건강 상태가 매우 좋습니다."라고 말한다.

10 그녀가 샤워실 안에 발을 디디자, 물이 위와 양측에서 나온다.

11 샤워 후에, 따뜻한 공기가 나와 그녀를 말린다.

12 그녀가 나가자, 서랍이 열리며 오늘의 옷이 나타난다.

13 부엌에서 민지의 아빠가 "좋은 아침이구나. 얘야. 아침으로 무엇을 먹고 싶니?"라고 말한다.

14 민지는 "늘 먹던 걸로 주세요."라고 말한다.

15 아빠가 요리 기계의 버튼 몇 개를 누른다.

16 기계는 베이컨, 달걀, 빵을 만들어 낸다.

17 아빠는 작별 인사를 하고 문 밖으로 급히 나간다.

18 _____ _____ _____ _____, Minji's father appears on a screen and shouts, "I forgot my glasses!"

19 Ms. Kim smiles and answers, "No problem. I'll _____ _____ _____ _____ your office."

20 Mr. Kim says, "Thanks _____ _____!"

21 Ms. Kim and Minji get into a _____ _____ _____.

22 They sit _____ _____ _____ around a table.

23 Ms. Kim touches the car window _____ _____ the groceries for this week.

24 She pays for them _____ _____ her finger _____ _____ _____.

25 They _____ _____ _____ to her house.

26 The car lands at Minji's school on top of a _____ building.

27 Today Minji will _____ _____ _____ _____ _____ Dona, a student in America.

28 But Minji _____ _____ _____ go to America.

29 _____ _____ a VR classroom, they will _____ _____ they are in the same classroom.

30 When Minji's family comes back home, dinner _____ _____.

31 They eat and _____ _____ their day.

32 After a delicious dinner, the cleaning robot clears the table and _____ _____ _____.

33 Minji says, "I learned a game _____ _____ today. Do you want to play?"

34 Everyone _____.

35 A _____ _____ _____ appears on the table.

36 They have _____ _____ _____.

37 Right before Minji goes to bed, she _____ _____ her watch.

38 "_____ Daddy _____ _____ his glasses tomorrow."

---

18 몇 분 후에. 민지의 아빠가 스크린에 나타나 소리친다. "안경을 깜빡했어요!"

19 민지의 엄마가 미소 지으며 답한다. "괜찮아요. 드론을 당신의 사무실로 보낼게요."

20 민지의 아빠가 "정말 고마워요!"라고 말한다.

21 민지의 엄마와 민지는 운전자가 필요 없는 비행 자동차에 탄다.

22 두 사람은 탁자 주변의 편안한 의자에 앉는다.

23 민지의 엄마가 이번 주 식료품을 선택하기 위해 자동차 창문을 터치한다.

24 그녀는 센서에 손가락을 대서 식료품 값을 지불한다.

25 식료품은 집으로 배달될 것이다.

26 자동차는 150층 빌딩의 꼭대기에 있는 민지의 학교에 내린다.

27 오늘 민지는 미국에 있는 학생 Dona와 함께 발표를 할 것이다.

28 하지만 민지가 미국에 갈 필요는 없다.

29 VR(가상 현실) 교실 덕분에, 그들은 같은 교실에 있는 것처럼 느낄 것이다.

30 민지의 가족이 집에 돌아오자 저녁이 준비된다.

31 그들은 식사를 하며 그 날에 관해 이야기한다.

32 맛있는 저녁 식사 후에. 청소 로봇이 식탁을 치우고 설거지를 한다.

33 민지가 "오늘 체스라고 불리는 놀이를 배웠어요. 해 보실래요?"라고 말한다.

34 모두가 동의한다.

35 탁자 위에 삼차원 체스판이 나타난다.

36 그들은 아주 즐거운 시간을 보낸다.

37 민지는 자러 가기 직전에, 자신의 손목시계에 속삭인다.

38 "아빠께 내일 안경을 가져가시라고 상기시켜 드려."

● 우리말을 참고하여 본문을 영작하시오.

1 미래를 상상하다

➡ _____

2 오전 7시이다.

➡ _____

3 침대가 흔들리고 김민지가 "5분만 더!"라고 소리를 지른다.

➡ _____

4 침대가 흔들기를 멈춘다.

➡ _____

5 갑자기, 민지의 엄마가 벽 스크린에 나타나 말한다. "학교에 늦겠구나!"

➡ _____

_____

6 민지는 눈을 비비며 "창문을 투명하게 해 줘."라고 말한다.

➡ _____

7 어두운 창문이 투명해지며 창문으로 햇살이 밝게 비춘다.

➡ _____

8 욕실에서 빨간 빛이 민지의 몸을 정밀 검사한다.

➡ _____

9 목소리가 "54킬로그램. 건강 상태가 매우 좋습니다."라고 말한다.

➡ _____

10 그녀가 샤워실 안에 발을 디디자, 물이 위와 양측에서 나온다.

➡ _____

11 샤워 후에, 따뜻한 공기가 나와 그녀를 말린다.

➡ _____

12 그녀가 나가자, 서랍이 열리며 오늘의 옷이 나타난다.

➡ _____

13 부엌에서 민지의 아빠가 "좋은 아침이구나, 얘야. 아침으로 무엇을 먹고 싶니?"라고 말한다.

➡ _____

14 민지는 "늘 먹던 걸로 주세요."라고 말한다.

➡ _____

15 아빠가 요리 기계의 버튼 몇 개를 누른다.

➡ _____

16 기계는 베이컨, 달걀, 빵을 만들어 낸다.

➡ _____

17 아빠는 작별 인사를 하고 문 밖으로 급히 나간다.

➡ _____

18 몇 분 후에, 민지의 아빠가 스크린에 나타나 소리친다. "안경을 깜빡했어요!"
➡ _____

19 민지의 엄마가 미소 지으며 답한다. "괜찮아요. 드론을 당신의 사무실로 보낼게요."
➡ _____

20 민지의 아빠가 "정말 고마워요!"라고 말한다.
➡ _____

21 민지의 엄마와 민지는 운전자가 필요 없는 비행 자동차에 탄다.
➡ _____

22 두 사람은 탁자 주변의 편안한 의자에 앉는다.
➡ _____

23 민지의 엄마가 이번 주 식료품을 선택하기 위해 자동차 창문을 터치한다.
➡ _____

24 그녀는 센서에 손가락을 대서 식료품 값을 지불한다.
➡ _____

25 식료품은 집으로 배달될 것이다.
➡ _____

26 자동차는 150층 빌딩의 꼭대기에 있는 민지의 학교에 내린다.
➡ _____

27 오늘 민지는 미국에 있는 학생 Dona와 함께 발표를 할 것이다.
➡ _____

28 하지만 민지가 미국에 갈 필요는 없다.
➡ _____

29 VR(가상 현실) 교실 덕분에, 그들은 같은 교실에 있는 것처럼 느낄 것이다.
➡ _____

30 민지의 가족이 집에 돌아오자 저녁이 준비된다.
➡ _____

31 그들은 식사를 하며 그 날에 관해 이야기한다.
➡ _____

32 맛있는 저녁 식사 후에, 청소 로봇이 식탁을 치우고 설거지를 한다.
➡ _____

33 민지가 "오늘 체스라고 불리는 놀이를 배웠어요. 해 보실래요?"라고 말한다.
➡ _____

34 모두가 동의한다.
➡ _____

35 탁자 위에 삼차원 체스판이 나타난다.
➡ _____

36 그들은 아주 즐거운 시간을 보낸다.
➡ _____

37 민지는 자러 가기 직전에, 자신의 손목시계에 속삭인다.
➡ _____

38 "아빠께 내일 안경을 가져가시라고 상기시켜 드려."
➡ _____

[01~02] 다음 빈칸에 공통으로 들어갈 말을 쓰시오.

01
- She made all the u_____ excuses.
- I'll have the u_____, please.

02
- We were tired _____ waiting for him to call.
- The house is located on top _____ a hill.

03 다음 빈칸에 알맞은 단어를 〈보기〉에서 골라 쓰시오.

> ┤ 보기 ├
> clear   comfortable   story

(1) His office is on the top floor of a thirty-_____ building.

(2) I was so _____ and warm in bed that I didn't want to get up.

(3) Will you please help me _____ the table?

04 우리말에 맞게 주어진 단어를 알맞게 배열하시오.

(1) 그의 좋지 않은 건강 때문에 그는 대학을 마치지 못했다. (finish, condition, of, he, bad, his, couldn't, college, because, health)

➡ _____

(2) 한 남자가 나무 뒤에서 갑자기 나타났다. (a, a, tree, suddenly, from, man, behind, appeared)

➡ _____

(3) 달이 하늘에서 밝게 빛났다. (shone, in, the, sky, moon, the, brightly)

➡ _____
_____.

05 주어진 영영풀이를 보고 빈칸에 알맞은 단어를 주어진 철자로 시작하여 쓰시오.

> to make someone remember something that they must do

> R_____ me to buy some milk tonight.

06 다음 밑줄 친 부분 중 그 쓰임이 어색한 것을 모두 찾아 고치시오.

> ⓐ I stopped to read and turned out the light.
> ⓑ The drought is over, thanks to the recent heavy rains.
> ⓒ By use the Internet you can do your shopping from home.

➡ _____

07 다음 우리말에 맞게 괄호 안의 단어를 알맞게 바꿔 빈칸에 쓰시오.

> Google says the _____(driver) cars are safer than those with human drivers.
> (구글은 운전자가 없는 자동차가 사람이 운전하는 자동차보다 안전하다고 말하고 있다.)

08 다음 문장을 수동태로 고쳤을 때 알맞은 것은?

> We cannot see the island from here.

① The island cannot see from here.
② The island is not seen from here.
③ The island not be seen from here.
④ The island cannot see from here.
⑤ The island cannot be seen from here.

09 다음 문장의 밑줄 친 부분을 강조하여 쓰시오.

(1) <u>Right before Minji goes to bed</u>, she whispers to her watch.

➡ _____

_____

(2) <u>Water</u> comes out from the top and sides.

➡ _____

(3) Mr. Kim presses <u>a few buttons</u> on the cooking machine.

➡ _____

_____

(4) The car lands <u>on top of a 150-story building</u>.

➡ _____

_____

10 다음 우리말을 괄호 안에 주어진 어휘를 이용하여 영작하시오.

> 당신에게 Peters라는 이름을 가진 고객이 있습니까? (a client, name, 7 단어)

➡ _____

[11~13] 다음 글을 읽고 물음에 답하시오.

A few minutes later, Minji's father appears on a screen and shouts, "I forgot my glasses!" Ms. Kim smiles and answers, "No problem. I'll send a drone to your office." Mr. Kim says, "Thanks a million!"

Ms. Kim and Minji get into a driverless flying car. They sit in comfortable chairs around a table. Ms. Kim touches the car window to select the groceries for this week. (A)그녀는 센서에 손가락을 대서 식료품 값을 지불한다. They will ⓐ to her house.

11 위 글의 빈칸 ⓐ에 deliver를 알맞은 형태로 쓰시오.

➡ _____

12 How will Mr. Kim get his glasses that he left at home? Fill in the blanks (A) and (B) with suitable words.

> Ms. Kim will send (A)_____ _____ to (B)_____ _____ with his glasses.

13 위 글의 밑줄 친 (A)의 우리말에 맞게 주어진 어휘를 알맞게 배열하시오.

> on / them / pays / putting / she / a sensor / by / her finger / for

➡ _____

_____

[14~16] 다음 글을 읽고 물음에 답하시오.

ⓐThe car lands at Minji's school on top of a 150-stories building. Today Minji will give a presentation with Dona, a student in America. ⓑBut Minji doesn't have to go to America. Thanks to a VR classroom, they will feel like they are in the same classroom.

14 위 글의 밑줄 친 ⓐ에서 어법상 <u>틀린</u> 부분을 찾아 고치시오.

_____ ➡ _____

15 위 글의 밑줄 친 ⓑ를 다음과 같이 바꿔 쓸 때 빈칸에 들어갈 알맞은 말을 두 단어로 쓰시오.

But Minji _____ _____ go to America.

16 How will it be possible for Minji and Dona, a student in America, to feel like they are in the same classroom? Fill in the blanks with suitable words.

Thanks to _____ _____ _____, it will be possible for them to feel like they are in the same classroom.

[17~18] 다음 글을 읽고 물음에 답하시오.

It's 7 a.m. The bed shakes and Minji Kim yells, "Five more minutes!" ⓐThe bed stops to shake. Suddenly, Minji's mom appears on a screen on the wall and says, "You're going to be late for school!" Minji rubs her eyes and says, "Clear the windows." The dark windows become clear and the sun shines brightly through ⓑthem.

17 위 글의 밑줄 친 ⓐ에서 어법상 <u>틀린</u> 부분을 찾아 고치시오.

_____ ➡ _____

18 위 글의 밑줄 친 ⓑthem이 가리키는 것을 본문에서 찾아 쓰시오.

➡ _____

[19~21] 다음 글을 읽고 물음에 답하시오.

In the bathroom, a red light (A)[scans / skips] Minji's body. A voice says, "54 kilograms. Your health condition is excellent." When she steps in the shower, water comes out from the top and sides. After her shower, warm air comes out and dries her. When she gets out, a drawer opens with today's (B)[cloths / clothes].

In the kitchen, her father says, "Good morning, Honey. What do you want for breakfast?" Minji says, "The usual, please." Mr. Kim presses (C)[a few / a little] buttons on the cooking machine. The machine prints out some bacon, eggs and bread. Mr. Kim says goodbye and rushes out the door.

19 위 글의 괄호 (A)~(C)에서 문맥이나 어법상 알맞은 낱말을 골라 쓰시오.

(A) _____ (B) _____ (C) _____

20 What happens when Minji finishes her shower? Answer in English in a full sentence.

➡ _____

21 주어진 영영풀이에 해당하는 단어를 본문에서 찾아 쓰시오.

part of a desk, chest, or other piece of furniture that is shaped like a box and is designed for putting things in

➡ _____

01
✎ 출제율 95%

다음 빈칸에 알맞은 단어를 〈보기〉에서 골라 쓰시오

보기
for   on   out   to

(1) The tower is located _____ top of a hill.

(2) The reality is that there is not enough money to pay _____ this project.

(3) Could you please print _____ this document?

(4) He sent a dozen red roses _____ his girlfriend on her birthday.

02
✎ 출제율 90%

다음 주어진 단어의 영영풀이가 잘못된 것을 고르시오.

① select: to choose something or someone by thinking carefully about which is the best, most suitable etc

② whisper: to shout or say something very loudly, especially because you are frightened, angry, or excited

③ press: to push a button, switch etc to make a machine start, a bell ring etc

④ shine: to produce bright light

⑤ appear: to start to be seen, to arrive, or to exist in a place, especially suddenly

03
✎ 출제율 95%

다음 밑줄 친 부분과 바꿔 쓸 수 있는 말을 고르시오.

It's important that parents select the right school for a child with learning difficulties.

① collect   ② create

③ require   ④ include

⑤ choose

04
✎ 출제율 90%

빈칸에 들어갈 접미사가 나머지와 다른 하나를 고르시오.

① It only takes one care_____ driver to cause an accident.

② The company is currently testing a driver_____ car.

③ Smoking has a harm_____ effect on people's health.

④ It's use_____ worrying about it.

⑤ Music is a source of end_____ pleasure to many people.

05
✎ 출제율 100%

다음 우리말에 맞도록 빈칸에 알맞은 말을 쓰시오. (철자가 주어진 것도 있음.)

(1) 나는 그것을 설명하는 것에 싫증이 난다.

➡ I'm t_____ _____ explaining it.

(2) Jenny가 올 때 그녀의 노트북을 가져오라고 상기시켜라.

➡ _____ Jenny _____ bring her laptop when she comes.

(3) 갑자기 모두가 말하는 것을 멈췄다.

➡ Suddenly everyone _____ t_____ .

06 출제율 95%

다음 빈칸 (A)와 (B)에 들어갈 말로 알맞은 것끼리 짝지어진 것을 고르시오.

> • I always ask how much time I have to (A)_____ my presentation.
> • The front door opens automatically when you (B)_____ in front of it.

	(A)	(B)		(A)	(B)
①	give	– attach	②	give	– avoid
③	give	– step	④	take	– avoid
⑤	take	– step			

07 출제율 100%

다음 중 어법상 어색한 것은?

① A few minutes later, Minji's father appears on a screen and shouts, "I forgot my glasses!"
② I tried to offer a few word of comfort.
③ Very few of his books are worth reading.
④ He has very little sight in his right eye.
⑤ I have a little money in the bank to fall back on.

08 출제율 90%

그림을 보고 주어진 어휘를 이용하여 빈칸을 알맞게 채우시오.

_____ _____ _____, the cleaning starts. (press, the button)

09 출제율 90%

그림을 보고, 주어진 어휘를 이용하여 빈칸을 알맞게 채우시오.

The table _____ _____ _____ with flowers by my mom. (will, decorate)

10 출제율 95%

다음 문장에서 어법상 어색한 것을 바르게 고치시오.

> Tiring after a long walk, Minji went to bed early.

➡ _____

_____

11 출제율 95%

다음의 부사절은 분사구문으로, 분사구문은 부사절로 바꿔 쓰시오.

(1) Minji's mom appears on a screen on the wall and says, "You're going to be late for school!"

➡ _____

_____

(2) Being late, she hurried to work.

➡ _____

_____

(3) Being an architect, what will you choose from nature?

➡ _____

_____

12 다음 문장을 수동태로 바꿔 쓰시오.

(1) Many teens will love this movie.

➡ _____

(2) We should not destroy the environment.

➡ _____

(3) They can make the fruit into delicious jam.

➡ _____

(4) You have to deliver what you promised.

➡ _____

---

13 다음 ⓐ~ⓕ 중 어법상 옳은 것을 <u>모두</u> 고르시오.

ⓐ Personal calls must be taken outside of the office area.

ⓑ After today heavy snow, many roads are still blocked.

ⓒ Minji's father is appeared on a screen and shouts, "I forgot my glasses!"

ⓓ Being delicate, the egg is strong enough to protect its contents.

ⓔ It is from oil drums that Nicholas made violins.

ⓕ As he climbed the hill, the old man had to stop catching his breath every few minutes.

➡ _____

[14~15] 다음 글을 읽고 물음에 답하시오.

(①) Ms. Kim and Minji get into a driverless flying car. (②) They sit in comfortable chairs around a table. (③) She pays for them by putting her finger on a sensor. (④) ⓐ<u>They</u> will be delivered to her house. (⑤)

---

14 위 글의 흐름으로 보아, 주어진 문장이 들어가기에 가장 적절한 곳은?

Ms. Kim touches the car window to select the groceries for this week.

①　　②　　③　　④　　⑤

---

15 위 글의 밑줄 친 ⓐThey가 가리키는 것을 본문에서 찾아 쓰시오.

➡ _____

[16~17] 다음 글을 읽고 물음에 답하시오.

When Minji's family comes back home, dinner is ready. They eat and talk about their day. After a delicious dinner, the cleaning robot clears the table and washes the dishes. Minji says, "ⓐ<u>I learned a game called chess today.</u> Do you want to play?" Everyone agrees. A 3-D chess board appears on the table. They have lots of fun.

Right before Minji goes to bed, she whispers to her watch. "Remind Daddy to take his glasses tomorrow."

---

16 위 글의 밑줄 친 문장 ⓐ에서 생략된 부분을 넣어 문장을 다시 쓰시오.

➡ _____

---

17 위 글의 주제로 알맞은 것을 고르시오.

① the difficulties people will experience in the future

② a scene of the life in the future

③ the development of the cleaning robot

④ how to play chess on a 3-D chess board

⑤ how to use the watch to remind something

[18~20] 다음 글을 읽고 물음에 답하시오.

In the bathroom, a red light scans Minji's body. A voice says, "54 kilograms. Your health condition is excellent." When she steps in the shower, water comes out from the top and sides. After her shower, warm air comes out and dries her. When she gets out, a drawer opens with today's clothes.

In the kitchen, her father says, "Good morning, Honey. What do you want ⓐ breakfast?" Minji says, "(A)늘 먹던 걸로 주세요." Mr. Kim presses a few buttons ⓑ the cooking machine. The machine prints out some bacon, eggs and bread. Mr. Kim says goodbye and rushes out the door.

18 위 글의 빈칸 ⓐ와 ⓑ에 들어갈 전치사가 바르게 짝지어진 것은?

	ⓐ	ⓑ			ⓐ	ⓑ
①	for	on		②	in	by
③	in	on		④	for	to
⑤	on	to				

19 위 글의 밑줄 친 (A)의 우리말에 맞게 3 단어로 영작하시오.

➡ _____

20 According to the passage, which is NOT true?

① Minji's health condition is excellent.
② When Minji steps in the shower, water comes out from the top and sides.
③ Minji opens a drawer to choose today's clothes.
④ The cooking machine prints out some bacon, eggs and bread.
⑤ Minji's father says goodbye and rushes out the door.

[21~23] 다음 글을 읽고 물음에 답하시오.

It's 7 a.m. The bed shakes and Minji Kim yells, "Five more minutes!" The bed stops ⓐshaking. ⓑSuddenly, Minji's mom is appeared on a screen on the wall and says, "You're going to be late for school!" Minji rubs her eyes and says, "Clear the windows." The dark windows become clear and the sun shines brightly through them.

21 위 글의 밑줄 친 ⓐshaking과 문법적 쓰임이 같은 것을 모두 고르시오.

① I heard him singing a song.
② Who is the girl playing the piano?
③ Taking a walk every day is very good for the health.
④ She is learning English now.
⑤ Why did you go there without saying anything?

22 위 글의 밑줄 친 ⓑ에서 어법상 틀린 부분을 찾아 고치시오.

_____ ➡ _____

23 Which question CANNOT be answered after reading the passage?

① How does the bed wake Minji up?
② Does Minji get up instantly in the morning?
③ How does Minji's mom wake Minji up?
④ What does Minji say to her mom?
⑤ What does Minji do to make the dark windows become clear?

MEMO

MEMO

INSIGHT
on the textbook
교과서 파헤치기

※ 다음 영어를 우리말로 쓰시오.

01 solar

02 average

03 blood

04 spot

05 probably

06 smash

07 complete

08 scenery

09 article

10 completely

11 abroad

12 serve

13 distance

14 enemy

15 species

16 surface

17 fool

18 forecast

19 octopus

20 wonder

21 million

22 surround

23 communicate

24 temperature

25 monster

26 clam

27 mop

28 nearby

29 breathe

30 calculate

31 discover

32 tightly

33 tool

34 vacuum

35 give up

36 go without

37 in a line

38 be full of

39 melt away

40 in the end

41 be covered with

42 this time of year

43 be different from

※ 다음 우리말을 영어로 쓰시오.

01 적 _____

02 지방 _____

03 해외에, 해외로 _____

04 피 _____

05 둘러싸다 _____

06 평균의, 보통의 _____

07 완전히 _____

08 경치, 풍경 _____

09 발견하다 _____

10 거리 _____

11 완성하다 _____

12 기사 _____

13 마침내 _____

14 예측, 예보 _____

15 수면, 표면 _____

16 조개 _____

17 추측하다 _____

18 때려 부수다, 깨뜨리다 _____

19 100만; 수많은 _____

20 대걸레로 닦다 _____

21 경이, 경탄; 궁금하다 _____

22 인근의, 가까운 곳의 _____

23 (입으로) 불다 _____

24 속이다; 바보 _____

25 진공청소기로 청소하다 _____

26 도구 _____

27 계산하다 _____

28 괴물 _____

29 문어 _____

30 아마 _____

31 태양의 _____

32 온도, 기온 _____

33 단단히, 꽉 _____

34 숨을 쉬다 _____

35 ～로 덮여 있다 _____

36 포기하다 _____

37 마침내, 결국 _____

38 차츰 사라지다 _____

39 한 줄로 _____

40 잠들다 _____

41 ～ 없이 지내다 _____

42 ～로 가득 차다 _____

43 ～와 다르다 _____

※ 다음 영영풀이에 알맞은 단어를 <보기>에서 골라 쓴 후, 우리말 뜻을 쓰시오.

1 _____ : the number 1,000,000: _____

2 _____ : the area around the North Pole: _____

3 _____ : to send out air from the mouth: _____

4 _____ : to finish making or doing something: _____

5 _____ : to move air into and out of your lungs: _____

6 _____ : to break something into many pieces: _____

7 _____ : a very large mammal that lives in the sea: _____

8 _____ : the amount of space between two places or things: _____

9 _____ : the upper layer of an area of land or water: _____

10 _____ : to trick someone into believing something that is not true: _____

11 _____ : to find a number, answer, etc. by using mathematical processes: _____

12 _____ : a piece of equipment you use with your hands for a particular task:
   _____

13 _____ : a statement about what you think is going to happen in the future:
   _____

14 _____ : a sea creature with a soft round body and eight long arms: _____

15 _____ : a set of animals or plants that have similar characteristics to each other:
   _____

16 _____ : to jump into water, especially with your arms and head going in first:
   _____

보기

species	whale	octopus	calculate
smash	Arctic	tool	million
dive	distance	fool	surface
forecast	blow	breathe	complete

※ 다음 우리말과 일치하도록 빈칸에 알맞은 말을 쓰시오.

Listen and Speak 1 A

B: We're _____ _____ _____ _____ the mountain.

G: I _____ _____ _____ this mountain is.

B: _____ _____ 2,000m _____.

G: Wow! This is a really _____ _____.

B: Yes, it is. Let's _____ _____.

B: 우리는 산 정상에 거의 다 왔어.
G: 나는 이 산이 얼마나 높은지 궁금해.
B: 이 산은 높이가 약 2,000미터야.
G: 우와! 정말 높은 산이구나.
B: 응, 맞아. 계속 올라가자.

Listen and Speak 1 B

B: Look _____ the baby penguins _____ TV. They're so cute.

G: Yes, but they _____ very _____ out there.

B: Yeah, the South Pole _____ _____ _____ Earth.

G: I wonder _____ _____ _____ _____ there.

B: The _____ temperature _____ about -58℃ _____ July and -26℃ _____ December.

G: Oh, _____, July is _____ _____ December there. Interesting!

B: Yes. _____ _____ very cold there, it _____ snow much.

G: That's _____, _____!

B: TV에 나온 아기 펭귄들을 봐. 아주 귀여워.
G: 응, 하지만 그들은 저곳에서 매우 추워 보여.
B: 응, 남극은 지구에서 가장 추운 곳이야.
G: 그곳이 얼마나 추운지 궁금해.
B: 평균 기온이 7월에는 약 섭씨 영하 58도이고, 12월에는 약 섭씨 영하 26도야.
G: 오, 그러면 그곳은 12월보다 7월이 더 춥구나. 흥미롭다!
B: 응. 비록 그곳은 매우 춥지만 눈은 많이 내리지 않아.
G: 그것도 흥미롭다!

Listen and Speak 1 C

1. **A:** We're _____ here.

   B: Yes, I'm so _____. Let's _____ _____.

   A: I _____ _____ the bus stop is.

   B: It's _____ _____ _____ the _____ _____.

   A: You're right. _____ go.

2. **A:** We're _____ _____.

   B: Yes, I'm so excited. Let's _____ _____.

   A: I _____ _____ _____ _____ is.

   B: It's _____ the library.

   A: You're _____. Let's go.

3. **A:** We're finally here.

   B: Yes, I'm so excited. _____ look around.

   A: _____ _____ _____ Green Park _____.

   B: It's _____ _____ the school.

   A: You're right. _____ _____.

1. A: 마침내 다 왔어.
   B: 맞아, 매우 신나. 둘러보자.
   A: 나는 버스 정류장이 어디에 있는지 궁금해.
   B: 경찰서 앞에 있어.
   A: 맞아. 가자.

2. A: 마침내 다 왔어.
   B: 맞아, 매우 신나. 둘러보자.
   A: 나는 안내 센터가 어디에 있는지 궁금해.
   B: 도서관 뒤에 있어.
   A: 맞아. 가자.

3. A: 마침내 다 왔어.
   B: 맞아, 매우 신나. 둘러보자.
   A: 나는 Green Park가 어디에 있는지 궁금해.
   B: 학교 옆에 있어.
   A: 맞아. 가자.

Listen and Speak 2 A

B: The weather is _____ nice _____.

G: Yeah. How _____ _____ _____ _____ this afternoon?

B: Good idea. Can you _____ the _____?

G: Oh, no! The weather _____ _____ _____ _____ in the afternoon.

B: Let's go _____ _____, then.

B: 바깥 날씨가 아주 좋아.
G: 응. 오늘 오후에 소풍 갈래?
B: 좋은 생각이야. 날씨를 확인해 주겠니?
G: 오, 안 돼! 일기 예보에 따르면 오후에 비가 올 거래.
B: 그러면 다음에 가자.

Listen and Speak 2 B

B: Sumin, what are you going _____ _____ on Sunday?

G: I'm going to _____ _____. Do you want to _____ _____?

B: I'd love to. _____ _____ _____ _____ _____ go?

G: I'm _____ _____ _____ to Namsan.

B: Oh, the _____ there is so beautiful _____ _____ _____ year.

G: Right. _____ _____ _____ _____ _____ _____ red _____ _____ now.

B: Great. _____ _____ does the shortest hiking course _____?

G: _____ _____ _____ _____ _____ about two hours.

B: Okay, see you _____ Sunday!

B: 수민아, 일요일에 무엇을 할 거니?
G: 나는 등산을 갈 거야. 나와 함께 가겠니?
B: 그러고 싶어. 어디로 가고 싶니?
G: 나는 남산에 가려고 생각 중이야.
B: 오, 매년 이맘때 그곳 경치는 아주 아름다워.
G: 맞아. 지금 빨간 단풍잎으로 덮여 있다고 들었어.
B: 좋아. 가장 짧은 등산 코스는 얼마나 걸리니?
G: 인터넷 정보에 따르면 약 두 시간 정도 걸린대.
B: 알겠어, 일요일에 봐!

Listen and Speak 2 C

1. A: _____ are you _____?

   B: I'm _____ the newspaper.

   A: Is there _____ _____?

   B: _____ _____ _____ _____ _____ _____ _____ _____ a new planet.

2. A: What are you doing?

   B: I'm reading _____ _____.

   A: Is there _____ _____?

   B: _____ _____ _____ _____ a whale family _____ _____ _____ _____ _____ _____ _____.

1. A: 뭐 하고 있니?
   B: 신문을 읽는 중이야.
   A: 흥미로운 것이 있니?
   B: 이 기사에 따르면 과학자들이 새로운 행성을 발견했대.

2. A: 뭐 하고 있니?
   B: 신문을 읽는 중이야.
   A: 흥미로운 것이 있니?
   B: 이 기사에 따르면 고래 가족이 동해에서 발견됐대.

Real Life Talk Watch a Video

Suji: _____ _____ this picture!

Tony: Wow! The _____ are walking _____ _____ _____ _____ the desert.

Suji: Yeah. The desert looks very _____ and _____.

Tony: I _____ _____ _____ _____ _____ _____ _____ water in the desert.

Suji: Let's find _____ on the Internet.

Tony: Okay. _____ _____ _____ _____ they can go about two weeks _____ _____.

Suji: Wow, that's amazing! _____ _____ really _____ animals.

Tony: I want to _____ _____ _____ in the desert someday.

수지: 이 사진을 봐!

Tony: 우와! 낙타들이 사막에서 한 줄로 걸어가고 있네.

수지: 응. 사막은 매우 덥고 건조해 보여.

Tony: 낙타들이 사막에서 물 없이 얼마나 오래 갈 수 있는지 궁금해.

수지: 인터넷에서 찾아보자.

Tony: 그래. 인터넷 정보에 따르면 낙타는 물 없이 2주 정도 갈 수 있대.

수지: 우와, 굉장하다! 낙타는 정말 흥미로운 동물이구나.

Tony: 나는 언젠가 사막에서 그들과 함께 여행하고 싶어.

Real Life Talk Step 2

1. A: _____ is the _____ _____ on Earth?

   B: I thinks it's the _____ _____.

   A: _____ _____ _____ _____ it is.

   B: The book _____ the _____ _____ of the South Pole is _____ -49℃.

   A: That's _____!

2. A: Which planet is the _____ in the _____ _____?

   B: I thinks it's _____.

   A: _____ _____ _____ _____ it is.

   B: _____ _____ _____ Jupiter is over 11 _____ _____ Earth.

   A: That's amazing!

3. A: Where is the _____ _____ _____ Earth?

   B: I thinks it's the Sahara Desert.

   A: I wonder _____ _____ _____.

   B: The newspaper _____ the temperature of the Sahara Desert can _____ _____ 50℃.

   A: That's _____!

1. A: 지구에서 가장 추운 곳이 어디니?
   B: 남극이라고 생각해.
   A: 나는 그곳이 얼마나 추운지 궁금해.
   B: 책에 따르면 남극의 평균 온도가 섭씨 영하 49도래.
   A: 굉장하다!

2. A: 태양계에서 가장 큰 행성이 어느 것이니?
   B: 목성이라고 생각해.
   A: 나는 그것이 얼마나 큰지 궁금해.
   B: 인터넷에 따르면 목성은 지구보다 11배 이상 크다고 해.
   A: 굉장하다!

3. A: 지구에서 가장 더운 사막이 어디니?
   B: 사하라 사막이라고 생각해.
   A: 나는 그곳이 얼마나 더운지 궁금해.
   B: 신문에 따르면 사하라 사막 온도가 섭씨 50도까지 이룰 수 있다고 해.
   A: 굉장하다!

※ 다음 우리말에 맞도록 대화를 영어로 쓰시오.

 해석

Listen and Speak 1 A

B: _____

G: _____

B: _____

G: _____

B: _____

B: 우리는 산 정상에 거의 다 왔어.
G: 나는 이 산이 얼마나 높은지 궁금해.
B: 이 산은 높이가 약 2,000미터야.
G: 우와! 정말 높은 산이구나.
B: 응, 맞아. 계속 올라가자.

Listen and Speak 1 B

B: _____

G: _____

B: _____

G: _____

B: _____

G: _____

B: _____

G: _____

B: TV에 나온 아기 펭귄들을 봐. 아주 귀여워.
G: 응, 하지만 그들은 저곳에서 매우 추워 보여.
B: 응, 남극은 지구에서 가장 추운 곳이야.
G: 그곳이 얼마나 추운지 궁금해.
B: 평균 기온이 7월에는 약 섭씨 영하 58도이고, 12월에는 약 섭씨 영하 26도야.
G: 오, 그러면 그곳은 12월보다 7월이 더 춥구나. 흥미롭다!
B: 응. 비록 그곳은 매우 춥지만 눈은 많이 내리지 않아.
G: 그것도 흥미롭다!

Listen and Speak 1 C

1. A: _____
   B: _____
   A: _____
   B: _____
   A: _____

2. A: _____
   B: _____
   A: _____
   B: _____
   A: _____

3. A: _____
   B: _____
   A: _____
   B: _____
   A: _____

1. A: 마침내 다 왔어.
   B: 맞아, 매우 신나. 둘러보자.
   A: 나는 버스 정류장이 어디에 있는지 궁금해.
   B: 경찰서 앞에 있어.
   A: 맞아. 가자.

2. A: 마침내 다 왔어.
   B: 맞아, 매우 신나. 둘러보자.
   A: 나는 안내 센터가 어디에 있는지 궁금해.
   B: 도서관 뒤에 있어.
   A: 맞아. 가자.

3. A: 마침내 다 왔어.
   B: 맞아, 매우 신나. 둘러보자.
   A: 나는 Green Park가 어디에 있는지 궁금해.
   B: 학교 옆에 있어.
   A: 맞아. 가자.

Listen and Speak 2 A

B: _____

G: _____

B: _____

G: _____

B: _____

B: 바깥 날씨가 아주 좋아.

G: 응. 오늘 오후에 소풍 갈래?

B: 좋은 생각이야. 날씨를 확인해 주겠니?

G: 오, 안 돼! 일기 예보에 따르면 오후에 비가 올 거래.

B: 그러면 다음에 가자.

Listen and Speak 2 B

B: _____

G: _____

B: _____

G: _____

B: _____

G: _____

B: _____

G: _____

B: _____

B: 수민아, 일요일에 무엇을 할 거니?

G: 나는 등산을 갈 거야. 나와 함께 가겠니?

B: 그러고 싶어. 어디로 가고 싶니?

G: 나는 남산에 가려고 생각 중이야.

B: 오, 매년 이맘때 그곳 경치는 아주 아름다워.

G: 맞아. 지금 빨간 단풍잎으로 덮여 있다고 들었어.

B: 좋아. 가장 짧은 등산 코스는 얼마나 걸리니?

G: 인터넷 정보에 따르면 약 두 시간 정도 걸린대.

B: 알겠어, 일요일에 봐!

Listen and Speak 2 C

1. A: _____

   B: _____

   A: _____

   B: _____

2. A: _____

   B: _____

   A: _____

   B: _____

1. A: 뭐 하고 있니?
   B: 신문을 읽는 중이야.
   A: 흥미로운 것이 있니?
   B: 이 기사에 따르면 과학자들이 새로운 행성을 발견했대.

2. A: 뭐 하고 있니?
   B: 신문을 읽는 중이야.
   A: 흥미로운 것이 있니?
   B: 이 기사에 따르면 고래 가족이 동해에서 발견됐대.

Real Life Talk Watch a Video

Suji: _____

Tony: _____

Suji: _____

Tony: _____

Suji: _____

Tony: _____

Suji: _____

Tony: _____

수지: 이 사진을 봐!
Tony: 우와! 낙타들이 사막에서 한 줄로 걸어가고 있네.
수지: 응. 사막은 매우 덥고 건조해 보여.
Tony: 낙타들이 사막에서 물 없이 얼마나 오래 갈 수 있는지 궁금해.
수지: 인터넷에서 찾아보자.
Tony: 그래. 인터넷 정보에 따르면 낙타는 물 없이 2주 정도 갈 수 있대.
수지: 우와, 굉장하다! 낙타는 정말 흥미로운 동물이구나.
Tony: 나는 언젠가 사막에서 그들과 함께 여행하고 싶어.

Real Life Talk Step 2

1. A: _____

   B: _____

   A: _____

   B: _____

   A: _____

2. A: _____

   B: _____

   A: _____

   B: _____

   A: _____

3. A: _____

   B: _____

   A: _____

   B: _____

   A: _____

1. A: 지구에서 가장 추운 곳이 어디니?
   B: 남극이라고 생각해.
   A: 나는 그곳이 얼마나 추운지 궁금해.
   B: 책에 따르면 남극의 평균 온도가 섭씨 영하 49도래.
   A: 굉장하다!

2. A: 태양계에서 가장 큰 행성이 어느 것이니?
   B: 목성이라고 생각해.
   A: 나는 그것이 얼마나 큰지 궁금해.
   B: 인터넷에 따르면 목성은 지구보다 11배 이상 크다고 해.
   A: 굉장하다!

3. A: 지구에서 가장 더운 사막이 어디게?
   B: 사하라 사막이라고 생각해.
   A: 나는 그곳이 얼마나 더운지 궁금해.
   B: 신문에 따르면 사하라 사막 온도가 섭씨 50도까지 이를 수 있다고 해.
   A: 굉장하다!

※ 다음 우리말과 일치하도록 빈칸에 알맞은 것을 골라 쓰시오.

1 _____ the _____
A. Sea   B. Under

2 _____ of our _____ is _____ by _____ .
A. covered   B. two-thirds   C. oceans   D. planet

3 They are _____ of _____ and are home to _____ of _____ .
A. millions   B. wonder   C. species   D. full

4 _____ day, we are _____ _____ _____ about them.
A. things   B. every   C. new   D. learning

5 _____ _____ _____ about some interesting _____ animals.
A. find   B. sea   C. out   D. let's

6 _____ _____
A. Dreams   B. Sweet

7 Can you _____ _____ these _____ are _____ in the picture?
A. whales   B. what   C. guess   D. doing

8 It _____ _____ they are standing _____ in a _____ .
A. like   B. up   C. looks   D. group

9 But they are _____ _____ !
A. sleeping   B. actually

10 Humpback whales _____ _____ their _____ they sleep.
A. while   B. stand   C. tails   D. on

11 They _____ _____ the _____ .
A. near   B. surface   C. sleep

12 _____ they are not fish, they _____ to come _____ to _____ .
A. breathe   B. since   C. up   D. need

13 _____ , they don't _____ _____ completely.
A. asleep   B. also   C. fall

14 When they _____ up, they come out of the water for a _____ and dive back _____ the sea.
A. wake   B. breath   C. deep   D. into

15 _____ Your _____
A. Meal   B. Enjoy

16 If you think fish are not _____ , _____ a _____ _____ the tuskfish.
A. smart   B. look   C. take   D. at

1 바다 아래에

2 우리 행성의 3분의 2는 대양들로 덮여 있다.

3 대양들은 신기한 것으로 가득 차 있고 수많은 종의 서식지이다.

4 매일 우리는 그들에 관한 새로운 것들을 배우고 있다.

5 몇몇 흥미로운 바다 동물들을 알아보자.

6 좋은 꿈 꿔라

7 여러분은 그림 속 이 고래들이 무엇을 하고 있는지 추측할 수 있는가?

8 그들이 무리를 지어 서 있는 것처럼 보인다.

9 그러나 그들은 실제로는 잠을 자고 있다!

10 혹등고래들은 잠을 자는 동안 꼬리로 서 있다.

11 그들은 수면 근처에서 잠을 잔다.

12 그들은 물고기가 아니기 때문에 숨을 쉬기 위해 위로 나올 필요가 있다.

13 또한 그들은 완전히 잠들지 않는다.

14 그들은 잠에서 깨면 심호흡을 하러 물 밖으로 나왔다가 바다로 다시 뛰어든다.

15 맛있게 먹어라

16 만약 물고기가 똑똑하지 않다고 생각한다면 'tuskfish'를 보아라.

17 This small fish _____ favorite food is _____ uses a _____ to _____ them.

    A. tool   B. open   C. clams   D. whose

18 Clams usually _____ under the sand, so they _____ be _____ _____.

    A. easily   B. hide   C. discovered   D. cannot

19 The tuskfish _____ on the sand _____ a _____ _____.

    A. until   B. blows   C. appears   D. clam

20 The _____ is _____ _____, _____ the fish cannot eat it.

    A. so   B. closed   C. clam   D. tightly

21 But the tuskfish _____ _____ _____.

    A. up   B. give   C. doesn't

22 It _____ the clam _____ a _____.

    A. against   B. smashes   C. rock

23 _____ the _____, the clam _____ and dinner is _____.

    A. end   B. served   C. opens   D. in

24 One, Two, _____, _____!

    A. Jump   B. Three

25 You have _____ seen a bird _____ _____ to the sea to _____ a fish.

    A. catch   B. probably   C. down   D. fly

26 But have you ever _____ a fish _____ _____ _____ the water to catch a bird?

    A. out   B. seen   C. of   D. jump

27 Well, birds _____ to be _____ when a _____ trevally is _____.

    A. careful   B. have   C. around   D. giant

28 This fish can _____ _____ _____ 170cm and 80kg.

    A. up   B. grow   C. to

29 But don't _____ _____ _____ _____ you.

    A. fool   B. let   C. size   D. its

30 This _____ is _____ and _____.

    A. smart   B. fish   C. quick

31 It can _____ a _____ bird and _____ its speed and _____.

    A. distance   B. spot   C. calculate   D. flying

32 When the bird _____ _____, the giant trevally _____ out of the water and _____ it.

    A. jumps   B. flies   C. catches   D. nearby

---

17 가장 좋아하는 먹이가 조개인 이 작은 물고기는 조개를 열기 위해 도구를 사용한다.

18 조개는 대개 모래 아래에 숨어 있어서 쉽게 발견할 수 없다.

19 'tuskfish'는 조개가 나타날 때까지 모래에 입김을 분다.

20 조개가 단단히 닫혀 있어서 물고기는 이것을 먹을 수 없다.

21 그러나 'tuskfish'는 포기하지 않는다.

22 'tuskfish'는 돌에 조개를 내리친다.

23 마침내 조개가 열리고 밥상이 차려진다.

24 하나, 둘. 셋, 뛰어라!

25 여러분은 아마 새가 물고기를 잡기 위해 바다로 날아 내려가는 것을 본 적이 있을 것이다.

26 그러나 물고기가 새를 잡기 위해 물 밖으로 뛰어오르는 것을 본 적이 있는가?

27 자, 새들은 'giant trevally'가 주변에 있을 때 조심해야 한다.

28 이 물고기는 170센티미터에 80킬로그램까지 자랄 수 있다.

29 그러나 그 크기에 속지 마라.

30 이 물고기는 빠르고 똑똑하다.

31 이것은 날고 있는 새를 발견하고 그 새의 속도와 거리를 계산할 수 있다.

32 새가 근처에 날고 있을 때, 'giant trevally'는 물 밖으로 뛰어올라 새를 잡는다.

※ 다음 우리말과 일치하도록 빈칸에 알맞은 말을 쓰시오.

1 _____ the _____

2 _____ of our planet _____ _____ _____ oceans.

3 They _____ _____ _____ wonder and are home to _____ _____ _____.

4 Every day, we are learning _____ _____ about them.

5 _____ _____ _____ about some interesting _____ _____.

6 _____ Dreams

7 Can you guess _____ _____ _____ _____ _____ _____ _____ in the picture?

8 It _____ _____ they are standing up _____ _____ _____.

9 But they are _____ _____ !

10 Humpback whales _____ _____ _____ _____ _____ _____ _____.

11 They sleep _____ _____ _____.

12 _____ they are not fish, they _____ _____ _____ _____ _____ _____ _____.

13 Also, they don't _____ _____ _____.

14 When they wake up, they come out of the water _____ _____ _____ _____ and _____ _____ _____ the sea.

15 _____ Your _____

16 If you think fish are not smart, _____ _____ _____ _____ the tuskfish.

1 바다 아래에

2 우리 행성의 3분의 2는 대양들로 덮여 있다.

3 대양들은 신기한 것으로 가득 차 있고 수많은 종의 서식지이다.

4 매일 우리는 그들에 관한 새로운 것들을 배우고 있다.

5 몇몇 흥미로운 바다 동물들을 알아보자.

6 좋은 꿈 꿔라

7 여러분은 그림 속 이 고래들이 무엇을 하고 있는지 추측할 수 있는가?

8 그들이 무리를 지어 서 있는 것처럼 보인다.

9 그러나 그들은 실제로는 잠을 자고 있다!

10 혹등고래들은 잠을 자는 동안 꼬리로 서 있다.

11 그들은 수면 근처에서 잠을 잔다.

12 그들은 물고기가 아니기 때문에 숨을 쉬기 위해 위로 나올 필요가 있다.

13 또한 그들은 완전히 잠들지 않는다.

14 그들은 잠에서 깨면 심호흡을 하러 물 밖으로 나왔다가 바다로 다시 뛰어든다.

15 맛있게 먹어라

16 만약 물고기가 똑똑하지 않다고 생각한다면 'tuskfish'를 보아라.

17 This small fish _____ _____ _____ is clams uses a tool to _____ them.

18 Clams usually _____ under the sand, so they _____ _____ _____ _____.

19 The tuskfish _____ on the sand _____ a clam _____.

20 The clam _____ _____ _____, so the fish cannot eat it.

21 But the tuskfish doesn't _____ _____.

22 It _____ the clam _____ a rock.

23 _____ _____ _____, the clam opens and dinner _____ _____.

24 One, Two, Three, _____!

25 You _____ probably _____ a bird _____ _____ to the sea to catch a fish.

26 But _____ you _____ _____ a fish _____ _____ _____ _____ to catch a bird?

27 Well, birds _____ _____ be careful when a giant trevally _____ _____.

28 This fish can grow _____ _____ 170cm and 80kg.

29 But don't _____ its size _____ you.

30 This fish is _____ _____ _____.

31 It can _____ a flying bird and _____ its _____ and _____.

32 When the bird flies _____, the giant trevally _____ out of the water and _____ it.

17 가장 좋아하는 먹이가 조개인 이 작은 물고기는 조개를 열기 위해 도구를 사용한다.

18 조개는 대개 모래 아래에 숨어 있어서 쉽게 발견할 수 없다.

19 'tuskfish'는 조개가 나타날 때까지 모래에 입김을 분다.

20 조개가 단단히 닫혀 있어서 물고기는 이것을 먹을 수 없다.

21 그러나 'tuskfish'는 포기하지 않는다.

22 'tuskfish'는 돌에 조개를 내리친다.

23 마침내 조개가 열리고 밥상이 차려진다.

24 하나, 둘, 셋, 뛰어라!

25 여러분은 아마 새가 물고기를 잡기 위해 바다로 날아 내려가는 것을 본 적이 있을 것이다.

26 그러나 물고기가 새를 잡기 위해 물 밖으로 뛰어오르는 것을 본 적이 있는가?

27 자, 새들은 'giant trevally'가 주변에 있을 때 조심해야 한다.

28 이 물고기는 170센티미터에 80킬로그램까지 자랄 수 있다.

29 그러나 그 크기에 속지 마라.

30 이 물고기는 빠르고 똑똑하다.

31 이것은 날고 있는 새를 발견하고 그 새의 속도와 거리를 계산할 수 있다.

32 새가 근처에 날고 있을 때, 'giant trevally'는 물 밖으로 뛰어올라 새를 잡는다.

※ 다음 문장을 우리말로 쓰시오.

1 Under the Sea

➡ _____

2 Two-thirds of our planet is covered by oceans.

➡ _____

3 They are full of wonder and are home to millions of species.

➡ _____

4 Every day, we are learning new things about them.

➡ _____

5 Let's find out about some interesting sea animals.

➡ _____

6 Sweet Dreams

➡ _____

7 Can you guess what these whales are doing in the picture?

➡ _____

8 It looks like they are standing up in a group.

➡ _____

9 But they are actually sleeping!

➡ _____

10 Humpback whales stand on their tails while they sleep.

➡ _____

11 They sleep near the surface.

➡ _____

12 Since they are not fish, they need to come up to breathe.

➡ _____

13 Also, they don't fall asleep completely.

➡ _____

14 When they wake up, they come out of the water for a deep breath and dive back into the sea.

➡ _____

15 Enjoy Your Meal

➡ _____

16 If you think fish are not smart, take a look at the tuskfish.

➡ _____

17 This small fish whose favorite food is clams uses a tool to open them.

➡ _____

18 Clams usually hide under the sand, so they cannot be easily discovered.

➡ _____

19 The tuskfish blows on the sand until a clam appears.

➡ _____

20 The clam is closed tightly, so the fish cannot eat it.

➡ _____

21 But the tuskfish doesn't give up.

➡ _____

22 It smashes the clam against a rock.

➡ _____

23 In the end, the clam opens and dinner is served.

➡ _____

24 One, Two, Three, Jump!

➡ _____

25 You have probably seen a bird fly down to the sea to catch a fish.

➡ _____

26 But have you ever seen a fish jump out of the water to catch a bird?

➡ _____

27 Well, birds have to be careful when a giant trevally is around.

➡ _____

28 This fish can grow up to 170cm and 80kg.

➡ _____

29 But don't let its size fool you.

➡ _____

30 This fish is quick and smart.

➡ _____

31 It can spot a flying bird and calculate its speed and distance.

➡ _____

32 When the bird flies nearby, the giant trevally jumps out of the water and catches it.

➡ _____

※ 다음 괄호 안의 단어들을 우리말에 맞도록 바르게 배열하시오.

1 (the / Under / Sea)
➡ _____

2 (of / two-thirds / our / is / planet / by / covered / oceans.)
➡ _____

3 (are / they / of / full / and / wonder / home / are / millions / to / species. / of)
➡ _____

4 (day, / every / are / we / new / learning / about / them. / things)
➡ _____

5 (find / let's / about / out / interesting / some / animals. / sea)
➡ _____

6 (Dreams / Sweet)
➡ _____

7 (you / can / what / guess / whales / these / doing / are / the / in / picture?)
➡ _____

8 (looks / it / they / like / standing / are / in / up / group. / a)
➡ _____

9 (they / but / actually / are / sleeping!)
➡ _____

10 (whales / humpback / on / stand / tails / their / they / while / sleep.)
➡ _____

11 (sleep / they / the / near / surface.)
➡ _____

12 (they / since / not / are / fish, / need / they / come / to / to / up / breathe.)
➡ _____

13 (they / also, / fall / don't / completely. / asleep)
➡ _____

14 (they / when / up, / wake / come / they / of / out / water / the / a / for / breath / deep / and / back / dive / the / into / sea.)
➡ _____
➡ _____

15 (Your / Meal / Enjoy)
➡ _____

16 (you / if / fish / think / not / are / smart, / a / take / at / look / tuskfish. / the)
➡ _____

1 바다 아래에

2 우리 행성의 3분의 2는 대양들로 덮여 있다.

3 대양들은 신기한 것으로 가득 차 있고 수많은 종의 서식지이다.

4 매일 우리는 그들에 관한 새로운 것들을 배우고 있다.

5 몇몇 흥미로운 바다 동물들을 알아보자.

6 좋은 꿈 꿔라

7 여러분은 그림 속 이 고래들이 무엇을 하고 있는지 추측할 수 있는가?

8 그들이 무리를 지어 서 있는 것처럼 보인다.

9 그러나 그들은 실제로는 잠을 자고 있다!

10 혹등고래들은 잠을 자는 동안 꼬리로 서 있다.

11 그들은 수면 근처에서 잠을 잔다.

12 그들은 물고기가 아니기 때문에 숨을 쉬기 위해 위로 나올 필요가 있다.

13 또한 그들은 완전히 잠들지 않는다.

14 그들은 잠에서 깨면 심호흡을 하러 물 밖으로 나왔다가 바다로 다시 뛰어든다.

15 맛있게 먹어라

16 만약 물고기가 똑똑하지 않다고 생각한다면 'tuskfish'를 보아라.

17 (small / this / whose / fish / food / favorite / clams / is / a / uses / to / tool / them. / open)

➡ _____

18 (usally / clams / under / hide / sand, / the / they / so / be / cannot / discovered. / easily)

➡ _____

19 (tuskfish / the / on / blows / sand / the / a / until / appears. / clam)

➡ _____

20 (clam / the / closed / is / tightly, / the / so / cannot / fish / it. / eat)

➡ _____

21 (the / but / doesn't / is / tuskfish / up. / give)

➡ _____

22 (smashes / it / clam / the / a / against / rock.)

➡ _____

23 (the / end, / in / clam / the / and / opens / is / dinner / served.)

➡ _____

24 (Two, / One, / Jump! / Three,)

➡ _____

25 (have / you / seen / probably / bird / a / down / fly / the / to / to / sea / a / catch / fish.)

➡ _____

26 (have / but / ever / you / a / seen / jump / fish / of / out / water / the / to / a / catch / bird?)

➡ _____

27 (birds / well, / to / have / careful / be / a / when / trevally / giant / around. / is)

➡ _____

28 (fish / this / grow / can / to / up / 80kg. / and 170cm)

➡ _____

29 (don't / but / its / let / fool / size / you.)

➡ _____

30 (fish / this / quick / is / smart. / and)

➡ _____

31 (can / it / a / spot / bird / flying / and / its / calculate / speed / distance. / and)

➡ _____

32 (the / when / flies / bird / nearby, / giant / the / jumps / trevally / of / out / water / the / catches / and / it.)

➡ _____

17 가장 좋아하는 먹이가 조개인 이 작은 물고기는 조개를 열기 위해 도구를 사용한다.

18 조개는 대개 모래 아래에 숨어 있어서 쉽게 발견할 수 없다.

19 'tuskfish'는 조개가 나타날 때까지 모래에 입김을 분다.

20 조개가 단단히 닫혀 있어서 물고기는 이것을 먹을 수 없다.

21 그러나 'tuskfish'는 포기하지 않는다.

22 'tuskfish'는 돌에 조개를 내리친다.

23 마침내 조개가 열리고 밥상이 차려진다.

24 하나, 둘, 셋, 뛰어라!

25 여러분은 아마 새가 물고기를 잡기 위해 바다로 날아 내려가는 것을 본 적이 있을 것이다.

26 그러나 물고기가 새를 잡기 위해 물 밖으로 뛰어오르는 것을 본 적이 있는가?

27 자, 새들은 'giant trevally'가 주변에 있을 때 조심해야 한다.

28 이 물고기는 170센티미터에 80킬로그램까지 자랄 수 있다.

29 그러나 그 크기에 속지 마라.

30 이 물고기는 빠르고 똑똑하다.

31 이것은 날고 있는 새를 발견하고 그 새의 속도와 거리를 계산할 수 있다.

32 새가 근처에 날고 있을 때, 'giant trevally'는 물 밖으로 뛰어올라 새를 잡는다.

※ 다음 우리말을 영어로 쓰시오.

1 바다 아래에

➡ _____

2 우리 행성의 3분의 2는 대양들로 덮여 있다.

➡ _____

3 대양들은 신기한 것으로 가득 차 있고 수많은 종의 서식지이다.

➡ _____

4 매일 우리는 그들에 관한 새로운 것들을 배우고 있다.

➡ _____

5 몇몇 흥미로운 바다 동물들을 알아보자.

➡ _____

6 좋은 꿈 꿔라

➡ _____

7 여러분은 그림 속 이 고래들이 무엇을 하고 있는지 추측할 수 있는가?

➡ _____

8 그들이 무리를 지어 서 있는 것처럼 보인다.

➡ _____

9 그러나 그들은 실제로는 잠을 자고 있다!

➡ _____

10 혹등고래들은 잠을 자는 동안 꼬리로 서 있다.

➡ _____

11 그들은 수면 근처에서 잠을 잔다.

➡ _____

12 그들은 물고기가 아니기 때문에 숨을 쉬기 위해 위로 나올 필요가 있다.

➡ _____

13 또한 그들은 완전히 잠들지 않는다.

➡ _____

14 그들은 잠에서 깨면 심호흡을 하러 물 밖으로 나왔다가 바다로 다시 뛰어든다.

➡ _____

15 맛있게 먹어라

➡ _____

16 만약 물고기가 똑똑하지 않다고 생각한다면 'tuskfish'를 보아라.
➡ _____

17 가장 좋아하는 먹이가 조개인 이 작은 물고기는 조개를 열기 위해 도구를 사용한다.
➡ _____

18 조개는 대개 모래 아래에 숨어 있어서 쉽게 발견할 수 없다.
➡ _____

19 'tuskfish'는 조개가 나타날 때까지 모래에 입김을 분다.
➡ _____

20 조개가 단단히 닫혀 있어서 물고기는 이것을 먹을 수 없다.
➡ _____

21 그러나 'tuskfish'는 포기하지 않는다.
➡ _____

22 'tuskfish'는 돌에 조개를 내리친다.
➡ _____

23 마침내 조개가 열리고 밥상이 차려진다.
➡ _____

24 하나, 둘, 셋, 뛰어라!
➡ _____

25 여러분은 아마 새가 물고기를 잡기 위해 바다로 날아 내려가는 것을 본 적이 있을 것이다.
➡ _____

26 그러나 물고기가 새를 잡기 위해 물 밖으로 뛰어오르는 것을 본 적이 있는가?
➡ _____

27 자, 새들은 'giant trevally'가 주변에 있을 때 조심해야 한다.
➡ _____

28 이 물고기는 170센티미터에 80킬로그램까지 자랄 수 있다.
➡ _____

29 그러나 그 크기에 속지 마라.
➡ _____

30 이 물고기는 빠르고 똑똑하다.
➡ _____

31 이것은 날고 있는 새를 발견하고 그 새의 속도와 거리를 계산할 수 있다.
➡ _____

32 새가 근처에 날고 있을 때, 'giant trevally'는 물 밖으로 뛰어올라 새를 잡는다.
➡ _____

※ 다음 우리말과 일치하도록 빈칸에 알맞은 말을 쓰시오.

After You Read A. Read and Correct

1. I _____ _____ _____ today.

2. _____ of our planet _____ _____ _____ oceans.

3. They are home to _____ _____ _____ .

4. _____ _____ _____ _____ _____ about sea animals.

5. _____ _____ , humpback whales _____ _____ _____ _____ they sleep, and they sleep _____ _____ _____ .

Word Power

1. He found a _____ _____ _____ _____ the car.

2. I can _____ you _____ _____ _____ _____ .

3. _____ _____ _____ _____ his cute looks.

4. Experience _____ even _____ _____ .

Think and Write Step 3

1. My _____ _____ : Beluga whale

2. I _____ _____ the beluga _____ .

3. It lives in _____ _____ _____ . It has _____ _____ _____ .

4. It _____ _____ fish and _____ .

5. _____ _____ _____ about the beluga whale is _____ it is _____ _____ _____ .

6. _____ _____ people _____ _____ the _____ _____ .

7. _____ it _____ _____ , it is _____ .

8. But when it _____ _____ , its body _____ _____ _____ !

9. I want to see this animal _____ _____ _____ _____ !

1. 나는 오늘 바다에 대해 배웠다.
2. 우리 행성의 3분의 2는 대양들로 덮여 있다.
3. 그것들은 수많은 종의 서식지이다.
4. 바다 동물들에 관한 많은 흥미로운 사실들이 있다.
5. 예를 들어, 혹등고래들은 잠을 자는 동안 꼬리로 서 있고, 그들은 수면 근처에서 잠을 잔다.

1. 그는 차를 주차하기 좋은 장소를 발견했다.
2. 나는 관중 속에서 너를 발견할 수 있다.
3. 그의 귀여운 외모에 속지 마라.
4. 경험은 바보조차도 현명하게 만든다.

1. 나의 재미있는 동물: 벨루가 고래
2. 저는 벨루가 고래를 소개할게요.
3. 벨루가 고래는 북극해에 살아요. 둥근 머리를 가졌어요.
4. 벨루가 고래는 주로 물고기와 조개를 먹어요.
5. 벨루가 고래에 관한 흥미로운 사실은 온몸이 하얗다는 거예요.
6. 그것이 사람들이 벨루가 고래를 흰고래라고 부르는 이유예요.
7. 벨루가 고래는 태어날 때, 회색이에요.
8. 그러나 다 자라면, 몸은 하얀색이 돼요!
9. 저는 제 눈으로 이 동물을 보고 싶어요!

※ 다음 우리말을 영어로 쓰시오.

After You Read A. Read and Correct

1. 나는 오늘 바다에 대해 배웠다.

   ➡ _____

2. 우리 행성의 3분의 2는 대양들로 덮여 있다.

   ➡ _____

3. 그것들은 수많은 종의 서식지이다.

   ➡ _____

4. 바다 동물들에 관한 많은 흥미로운 사실들이 있다.

   ➡ _____

5. 예를 들어, 혹등고래들은 잠을 자는 동안 꼬리로 서 있고, 그들은 수면 근처에서 잠을 잔다.

   ➡ _____

Word Power

1. 그는 차를 주차하기 좋은 장소를 발견했다.

   ➡ _____

2. 나는 관중 속에서 너를 발견할 수 있다.

   ➡ _____

3. 그의 귀여운 외모에 속지 마라.

   ➡ _____

4. 경험은 바보조차도 현명하게 만든다.

   ➡ _____

Think and Write Step 3

1. 나의 재미있는 동물: 벨루가 고래

   ➡ _____

2. 저는 벨루가 고래를 소개할게요.

   ➡ _____

3. 벨루가 고래는 북극해에 살아요. 둥근 머리를 가졌어요.

   ➡ _____

4. 벨루가 고래는 주로 물고기와 조개를 먹어요.

   ➡ _____

5. 벨루가 고래에 관한 흥미로운 사실은 온몸이 하얗다는 거예요.

   ➡ _____

6. 그것이 사람들이 벨루가 고래를 흰고래라고 부르는 이유예요.

   ➡ _____

7. 벨루가 고래는 태어날 때, 회색이에요.

   ➡ _____

8. 그러나 다 자라면, 몸은 하얀색이 돼요!

   ➡ _____

9. 저는 제 눈으로 이 동물을 보고 싶어요!

   ➡ _____

※ 다음 영어를 우리말로 쓰시오.

01 protect _____

02 active _____

03 contribute _____

04 merchant _____

05 due _____

06 unbelievable _____

07 mistake _____

08 dynamite _____

09 fault _____

10 graduate _____

11 headline _____

12 appreciate _____

13 describe _____

14 article _____

15 heart attack _____

16 including _____

17 regret _____

18 graduation _____

19 habit _____

20 invention _____

21 actually _____

22 inventor _____

23 shocked _____

24 opinion _____

25 disappointed _____

26 originally _____

27 participate _____

28 audience _____

29 normal _____

30 award _____

31 perfect _____

32 spill _____

33 mistakenly _____

34 stomachache _____

35 give up _____

36 put off _____

37 think of A as B _____

38 take eyes off _____

39 catch one's breath _____

40 rather than _____

41 keep in touch _____

42 take part in _____

43 describe A as B _____

※ 다음 우리말을 영어로 쓰시오.

01 보통의, 정상적인 _____

02 의견 _____

03 사실 _____

04 기술하다, 묘사하다 _____

05 잘못 _____

06 졸업하다 _____

07 고맙게 생각하다 _____

08 ~을 포함해서 _____

09 완벽한 _____

10 충격을 받은 _____

11 보호하다, 지키다 _____

12 감동시키다 _____

13 관객 _____

14 상인 _____

15 후회; 후회하다 _____

16 실망한, 낙담한 _____

17 실수, 잘못 _____

18 습관 _____

19 상, 시상 _____

20 실수로 _____

21 쏟아지다, 쏟다 _____

22 ~하기로 되어 있는, 예정된 _____

23 원래는, 처음에는 _____

24 기여하다, 공헌하다 _____

25 몹시, 깊이, 매우 _____

26 발명품 _____

27 기사 _____

28 (신문 기사 등의) 표제 _____

29 복통 _____

30 심장 마비 _____

31 믿을 수 없는, 믿기 어려운 _____

32 다이너마이트 _____

33 졸업(식) _____

34 신뢰하다, 믿다 _____

35 지각하다 _____

36 놀라서 _____

37 미루다, 연기하다 _____

38 ~에 참가하다 _____

39 ~보다는 _____

40 포기하다 _____

41 안 자다, 깨어 있다 _____

42 연락하고 지내다 _____

43 A를 B라고 생각하다 _____

※ 다음 영영풀이에 알맞은 단어를 <보기>에서 골라 쓴 후, 우리말 뜻을 쓰시오.

1 _____: a powerful explosive: _____

2 _____: to flow over the edge of a container: _____

3 _____: to be grateful for something: _____

4 _____: to explain about something: _____

5 _____: to feel sorry or unhappy about something: _____

6 _____: to gain a goal or point in a sport or game: _____

7 _____: a thing or an idea that has been invented: _____

8 _____: to help to cause something to happen: _____

9 _____: a person who sells products in large amounts: _____

10 _____: expected at or planned for a certain time: _____

11 _____: a ceremony at which degrees or diplomas are given out: _____

12 _____: difficult or impossible to believe: _____

13 _____: the group of people who have gathered to watch or listen to something:

_____

14 _____: the title written in large letters over a story in a newspaper:

_____

15 _____: to cause someone to feel an emotion and especially sadness or sympathy:

_____

16 _____: to give information about something via newspaper, TV or radio:

_____

보기			
report	describe	move	score
due	regret	unbelievable	dynamite
audience	appreciate	headline	invention
merchant	contribute	graduation	spill

※ 다음 우리말과 일치하도록 빈칸에 알맞은 말을 쓰시오.

해석

Listen and Speak 1 A

G: Mike, why _____ _____ _____ _____ class?

B: I had a bad _____.

G: Oh, no! _____ you _____ now?

B: Yeah. I _____ _____ _____ _____ last night.

G: Mike, 왜 수업에 늦었니?
B: 배가 많이 아팠어.
G: 오, 저런! 지금은 괜찮니?
B: 응. 어젯밤 덜 먹었어야 했어.

Listen and Speak 1 B

G: Jiho, what's _____? You look _____.

B: Yeah. I _____ _____ _____ last night.

G: Did you _____ computer games _____?

B: No, _____ this time. I _____ _____ _____ my history project.

G: Is it _____ today?

B: Yeah. I _____ _____ _____ _____ _____ the _____ _____.

G: Hmm, I understand. I often have _____ _____ problem.

B: Really? Well, let's _____ _____ _____ our bad _____.

G: 지호야, 무슨 일이니? 너 피곤해 보여.
B: 응. 어젯밤에 늦게까지 깨어 있었어.
G: 너 또 컴퓨터 게임을 했니?
B: 아니, 이번엔 아니야. 나는 역사 과제를 끝내야 했어.
G: 그 과제가 오늘까지니?
B: 응. 나는 마지막 순간까지 미루지 말았어야 했어.
G: 음, 이해해. 나도 종종 같은 문제를 겪어.
B: 정말? 음, 우리의 나쁜 습관을 바꾸도록 노력하자.

Listen and Speak 1 C

1. A: What's _____?
   B: I _____ _____ _____ the rain.
   A: Oh, I'm _____ _____ _____ that.
   B: I should _____ _____ an umbrella.

2. A: _____ wrong?
   B: I _____ the test.
   A: Oh, I'm sorry to _____ _____.
   B: I _____ _____ _____ _____.

3. A: What's _____?
   B: I _____ my bike.
   A: Oh, I'm sorry _____ _____ that.
   B: _____ _____ _____ _____ it.

4. A: What's wrong?
   B: I _____ _____ _____ school.
   A: Oh, I'm _____ _____ _____ _____.
   B: I _____ _____ _____ _____ _____.

1. A: 무슨 일 있니?
   B: 오, 비를 맞았어.
   A: 안됐구나.
   B: 나는 우산을 가져왔어야 했어.

2. A: 무슨 일 있니?
   B: 시험에 떨어졌어.
   A: 오, 안됐구나.
   B: 나는 공부를 열심히 했어야 했어.

3. A: 무슨 일 있니?
   B: 자전거를 잃어버렸어.
   A: 오, 안됐구나.
   B: 나는 사슬로 묶어놨어야 했어.

4. A: 무슨 일 있니?
   B: 학교에 늦었어.
   A: 오, 안됐구나.
   B: 나는 일찍 일어났어야 했어.

Listen and Speak 2 A

G: Jinsu, what are you _____ _____ _____ _____ the vacation?

B: I'm going to read _____ books. _____ _____ you?

G: I'm _____ _____ _____ my grandparents in Busan.

B: Sounds great. I _____ _____ _____ a wonderful vacation.

G: 진수야, 방학 동안 무엇을 할 거니?
B: 나는 책을 많이 읽을 거야. 너는 어떠니?
G: 나는 부산에 계신 조부모님을 방문할 계획이야.
B: 좋구나. 멋진 방학을 보내길 바라.

Listen and Speak 2 B

G: Jaemin, are you _____ _____ the singing contest?

B: Well, _____ _____ _____ _____ _____ _____ _____, Tina.

G: Why? I _____ you really _____ _____ _____ _____ _____ the contest.

B: I don't think I'm a _____ _____.

G: Come on. You're _____ _____ _____ _____ _____ _____.

B: Do you really _____ _____?

G: Of _____. You have a really nice _____.

B: Thank _____ _____ _____ so, I'll _____ _____ _____ _____.

B: _____ _____ _____ _____ the contest.

G: 재민아, 노래 경연 대회에 나갈 준비는 됐니?
B: 음, 포기할까 생각 중이야, Tina.
G: 왜? 나는 네가 그 대회에 정말로 참가하고 싶어 한다고 생각했어.
B: 나는 내가 노래를 잘하는 것 같지 않아.
G: 그러지 말고, 너는 내가 아는 노래를 가장 잘하는 사람이야.
B: 정말로 그렇게 생각하니?
G: 물론이지. 너는 정말 멋진 목소리를 가졌어.
B: 그렇게 말해 줘서 고마워. 최선을 다해 볼게.
G: 네가 대회에서 우승하기를 바라.

Listen and Speak 2 C

1. A: What _____ you _____ _____ do tomorrow?
   B: I'm _____ _____ _____ _____ in the school festival.
   A: Great! I _____ _____ _____ _____ the _____.
   B: Thanks. I _____ _____, too.

2. A: What are you going to do tomorrow?
   B: I'm _____ _____ _____ soccer.
   A: Great! I _____ _____ _____ _____ _____ _____ _____.
   B: Thanks. I hope so, _____.

3. A: What are you going to do tomorrow?
   B: I'm going to _____ _____ the _____.
   A: Great! _____ _____ _____ _____ _____ the contest.
   B: Thanks. _____ _____ _____ _____, too.

1. A: 너는 내일 무엇을 할 계획이니?
   B: 학교 축제에서 노래 부를 거야.
   A: 멋지네! 나는 네가 청중을 감동시키기를 바라.
   B: 고마워. 나도 그러길 바라.

2. A: 너는 내일 무엇을 할 계획이니?
   B: 축구를 할 거야.
   A: 멋지네! 나는 네가 득점하기를 바라.
   B: 고마워. 나도 그러길 바라.

3. A: 너는 내일 무엇을 할 계획이니?
   B: 연설 대회에 참가할 거야.
   A: 멋지네! 나는 네가 대회에서 우승하기를 바라.
   B: 고마워. 나도 그러길 바라.

Real Life Talk Watch a Video

Minho: Linda, what are you _____?

Linda: I'm reading _____ _____ from my classmates.

Minho: Oh, it _____ _____ they had _____ _____ _____ to you.

Linda: Many of them _____ _____ they like my _____.

Minho: That's nice. What _____?

Linda: _____ _____ _____ said I didn't _____ _____ _____ _____ them.

Minho: That's not your _____. You were always _____.

Linda: Yeah, but I _____ _____ _____ _____ my classmates.

Minho: You still have time _____ _____.

Linda: You're _____.

Minho: I _____ _____ _____ _____ _____ _____ your classmates _____ _____.

Linda: Thanks. _____ _____ _____, too.

Minho: Linda, 무엇을 읽고 있니?

Linda: 나는 학급 친구들에게 받은 졸업 메시지를 읽고 있어.

Minho: 오, 친구들이 너에게 할 말이 많은 것 같구나.

Linda: 그들 중 많은 친구들이 나의 미소를 좋아한다고 적었어.

Minho: 멋지네. 그 외에는?

Linda: 그들 중 몇몇은 내가 그들과 충분히 어울리지 않았다고 말했어.

Minho: 그건 네 잘못이 아니야. 너는 항상 바빴잖아.

Linda: 응, 하지만 나는 학급 친구들과 더 많은 시간을 보냈어야 했어.

Minho: 졸업 후에도 여전히 시간이 있어.

Linda: 네 말이 맞아.

Minho: 네가 졸업 후에도 학급 친구들과 계속 연락하기를 바라.

Linda: 고마워. 나도 그러길 바라.

Real Life Talk Step 2

1. A: I _____ _____ we're _____ soon.

   B: Yeah. Is _____ _____ you _____ about your middle school life?

   A: Yes. I _____ _____ _____ _____ _____ _____ _____.

   B: Well, you _____ _____ _____ _____ _____ in high school.

   A: I _____ you're right.

   B: I _____ _____ _____ _____ in classes in high school.

2. A: I can't _____ _____ _____ _____ soon.

   B: Yeah. Is there _____ _____ _____ _____ your middle school life?

   A: Yes. I _____ _____ _____ _____ _____ _____ many school events.

   B: Well, you have a _____ _____ in high school.

   A: I _____ you're _____.

   B: I _____ _____ _____ _____ _____ many school events in high school.

1. A: 우리가 곧 졸업하는 것을 믿을 수 없어.
   B: 응. 중학교 생활에서 네가 후회하는 것이 있니?
   A: 응. 나는 수업에서 적극적이었어야 했어.
   B: 음, 너는 고등학교에서 다시 한 번 기회가 있어.
   A: 네 말이 맞는 것 같아.
   B: 고등학교에서는 네가 수업에서 적극적이기를 바라.

2. A: 우리가 곧 졸업하는 것을 믿을 수 없어.
   B: 응. 중학교 생활에서 네가 후회하는 것이 있니?
   A: 응. 나는 학교 행사에 많이 참여했어야 했어.
   B: 음, 너는 고등학교에서 다시 한 번 기회가 있어.
   A: 네 말이 맞는 것 같아.
   B: 고등학교에서는 네가 많은 학교 행사에 참여하기를 바라.

※ 다음 우리말에 맞도록 대화를 영어로 쓰시오.

 해석

Listen and Speak 1 A

G: _____

B: _____

G: _____

B: _____

G: Mike, 왜 수업에 늦었니?
B: 배가 많이 아팠어.
G: 오, 저런! 지금은 괜찮니?
B: 응. 어젯밤 덜 먹었어야 했어.

Listen and Speak 1 B

G: _____

B: _____

G: _____

B: _____

G: _____

B: _____

G: _____

B: _____

G: 지호야, 무슨 일이니? 너 피곤해 보여.
B: 응. 어젯밤에 늦게까지 깨어 있었어.
G: 너 또 컴퓨터 게임을 했니?
B: 아니, 이번엔 아니야. 나는 역사 과제를 끝내야 했어.
G: 그 과제가 오늘까지니?
B: 응. 나는 마지막 순간까지 미루지 말았어야 했어.
G: 음, 이해해. 나도 종종 같은 문제를 겪어.
B: 정말? 음, 우리의 나쁜 습관을 바꾸도록 노력하자.

Listen and Speak 1 C

1. A: _____

   B: _____

   A: _____

   B: _____

2. A: _____

   B: _____

   A: _____

   B: _____

3. A: _____

   B: _____

   A: _____

   B: _____

4. A: _____

   B: _____

   A: _____

   B: _____

1. A: 무슨 일 있니?
   B: 오, 비를 맞았어.
   A: 안됐구나.
   B: 나는 우산을 가져왔어야 했어.

2. A: 무슨 일 있니?
   B: 시험에 떨어졌어.
   A: 오, 안됐구나.
   B: 나는 공부를 열심히 했어야 했어.

3. A: 무슨 일 있니?
   B: 자전거를 잃어버렸어.
   A: 오, 안됐구나.
   B: 나는 사슬로 묶어놨어야 했어.

4. A: 무슨 일 있니?
   B: 학교에 늦었어.
   A: 오, 안됐구나.
   B: 나는 일찍 일어났어야 했어.

Listen and Speak 2 A

G: _____
B: _____
G: _____
B: _____

G: 진수야, 방학 동안 무엇을 할 거니?
B: 나는 책을 많이 읽을 거야. 너는 어떠니?
G: 나는 부산에 계신 조부모님을 방문할 계획이야.
B: 좋구나. 멋진 방학을 보내길 바라.

Listen and Speak 2 B

G: _____
B: _____
G: _____
B: _____
G: _____
B: _____
G: _____
B: _____
B: _____

G: 재민아, 노래 경연 대회에 나갈 준비는 됐니?
B: 음, 포기할까 생각 중이야, Tina.
G: 왜? 나는 네가 그 대회에 정말로 참가하고 싶어 한다고 생각했어.
B: 나는 내가 노래를 잘하는 것 같지 않아.
G: 그러지 말고. 너는 내가 아는 노래를 가장 잘하는 사람이야.
B: 정말로 그렇게 생각하니?
G: 물론이지. 너는 정말 멋진 목소리를 가졌어.
B: 그렇게 말해 줘서 고마워. 최선을 다해 볼게.
G: 네가 대회에서 우승하기를 바라.

Listen and Speak 2 C

1. A: _____
   B: _____
   A: _____
   B: _____

2. A: _____
   B: _____
   A: _____
   B: _____

3. A: _____
   B: _____
   A: _____
   B: _____

1. A: 너는 내일 무엇을 할 계획이니?
   B: 학교 축제에서 노래 부를 거야.
   A: 멋지네! 나는 네가 청중을 감동시키기를 바라.
   B: 고마워. 나도 그러길 바라.

2. A: 너는 내일 무엇을 할 계획이니?
   B: 축구를 할 거야.
   A: 멋지네! 나는 네가 득점하기를 바라.
   B: 고마워. 나도 그러길 바라.

3. A: 너는 내일 무엇을 할 계획이니?
   B: 연설 대회에 참가할 거야.
   A: 멋지네! 나는 네가 대회에서 우승하기를 바라.
   B: 고마워. 나도 그러길 바라.

Real Life Talk Watch a Video

Minho: _____

Linda: _____

Minho: _____

Linda: _____

Minho: _____

Linda: _____

Minho: _____

Linda: _____

Minho: _____

Linda: _____

Minho: _____

Linda: _____

Minho: Linda, 무엇을 읽고 있니?

Linda: 나는 학급 친구들에게 받은 졸업 메시지를 읽고 있어.

Minho: 오, 친구들이 너에게 할 말이 많은 것 같구나.

Linda: 그들 중 많은 친구들이 나의 미소를 좋아한다고 적었어.

Minho: 멋지네. 그 외에는?

Linda: 그들 중 몇몇은 내가 그들과 충분히 어울리지 않았다고 말했어.

Minho: 그건 네 잘못이 아니야. 너는 항상 바빴잖아.

Linda: 응, 하지만 나는 학급 친구들과 더 많은 시간을 보냈어야 했어.

Minho: 졸업 후에도 여전히 시간이 있어.

Linda: 네 말이 맞아.

Minho: 네가 졸업 후에도 학급 친구들과 계속 연락하기를 바라.

Linda: 고마워. 나도 그러길 바라.

Real Life Talk Step 2

1. A: _____

   B: _____

   A: _____

   B: _____

   A: _____

   B: _____

2. A: _____

   B: _____

   A: _____

   B: _____

   A: _____

   B: _____

1. A: 우리가 곧 졸업하는 것을 믿을 수 없어.

   B: 응. 중학교 생활에서 네가 후회하는 것이 있니?

   A: 응. 나는 수업에서 적극적이었어야 했어.

   B: 음, 너는 고등학교에서 다시 한 번 기회가 있어.

   A: 네 말이 맞는 것 같아.

   B: 고등학교에서는 네가 수업에서 적극적이기를 바라.

2. A: 우리가 곧 졸업하는 것을 믿을 수 없어.

   B: 응. 중학교 생활에서 네가 후회하는 것이 있니?

   A: 응. 나는 학교 행사에 많이 참여했어야 했어.

   B: 음, 너는 고등학교에서 다시 한 번 기회가 있어.

   A: 네 말이 맞는 것 같아.

   B: 고등학교에서는 네가 많은 학교 행사에 참여하기를 바라.

※ 다음 우리말과 일치하도록 빈칸에 알맞은 것을 골라 쓰시오.

1 _____ Will You _____ _____ ?
A. Be   B. How   C. Remembered

2 It was _____ a _____ _____ .
A. normal   B. just   C. morning

3 Alfred Nobel _____ _____ his _____ _____ read the newspaper.
A. chair   B. in   C. to   D. sat

4 _____ he was drinking his coffee, a _____ _____ his _____ : *The Merchant of Death, Alfred Nobel, Is Dead.*
A. headline   B. eye   C. while   D. caught

5 " _____ ? What is _____ ?"
A. this   B. what

6 Reading the _____ , he _____ his cup _____ _____ .
A. surprise   B. article   C. dropped   D. in

7 His coffee _____ all _____ his clothes and desk, but he couldn't _____ his eyes _____ the newspaper.
A. take   B. spilled   C. off   D. over

8 The _____ was about _____ _____ _____ !
A. death   B. article   C. own   D. his

9 It said Nobel had _____ in France _____ a _____ _____ .
A. attack   B. died   C. heart   D. from

10 "Oh _____ _____ ! Am I _____ ?"
A. dead   B. goodness   C. my

11 _____ his _____ , Nobel _____ _____ .
A. kept   B. catching   C. reading   D. breath

12 Soon, he became _____ _____ _____ .
A. shocked   B. even   C. more

13 The article _____ him _____ the _____ of dynamite and _____ dangerous objects for war.
A. as   B. other   C. described   D. inventor

14 It said that he had _____ _____ from the _____ of _____ .
A. deaths   B. become   C. others   D. rich

15 He _____ _____ his _____ .
A. eyes   B. believe   C. couldn't

16 It was _____ that dynamite was _____ _____ his many _____ .
A. inventions B. true   C. one   D. of

---

1 당신은 어떻게 기억될까요?

2 그저 평범한 아침이었다.

3 Alfred Nobel은 신문을 읽기 위해 의자에 앉았다.

4 커피를 마시는 동안 한 기사 제목이 그의 눈길을 끌었다. "죽음의 상인, Alfred Nobel 사망하다"

5 "뭐라고? 이게 뭐지?"

6 기사를 읽으며 그는 놀라서 컵을 떨어뜨렸다.

7 커피가 그의 옷과 책상 온 곳에 쏟아졌지만 그는 신문에서 눈을 뗄 수 없었다.

8 기사는 그 자신의 죽음에 관한 것이었다!

9 기사에는 Nobel이 심장 마비로 프랑스에서 죽었다고 쓰여 있었다.

10 "오, 이럴 수가! 내가 죽었다고?"

11 숨을 고른 후, Nobel은 계속 읽었다.

12 곧, 그는 훨씬 더 충격을 받게 되었다.

13 기사는 그를 전쟁에 쓰이는 다이너마이트와 다른 위험한 물건의 발명가로 기술했다.

14 기사에는 그가 다른 사람들의 죽음으로 인해 부유해졌다고 쓰여 있었다.

15 그는 자신의 눈을 믿을 수 없었다.

16 다이너마이트가 그의 많은 발명품 중 하나인 것은 사실이었다.

17 But he never _____ that the world would _____ _____ him _____ "the merchant of death."

    A. as   B. imagined   C. of   D. think

18 Nobel _____ _____ _____.

    A. deeply   B. was   C. disappointed

19 " _____ _____ this _____ ?

    A. be   B. could   C. how

20 _____ is _____ !

    A. unbelievable   B. This

21 I'm not a _____ _____ _____.

    A. death   B. merchant   C. of

22 I want to be _____ _____ a _____.

    A. remembered   B. different   C. in   D. way

23 I want to _____ _____ as a person who made the _____ _____."

    A. world   B. be   C. better   D. remembered

24 He decided _____ _____ _____ _____ about him.

    A. people's   B. to   C. opinions   D. change

25 In 1888, a French _____ _____ _____ Alfred Nobel's _____.

    A. death   B. mistakenly   C. newspaper   D. reported

26 The person _____ _____ _____ was his brother, Ludvig.

    A. died   B. had   C. actually   D. who

27 _____ _____ the report, _____, Nobel decided to do something to _____ to the world.

    A. however   B. thanks   C. contribute   D. to

28 In 1895, he _____ to _____ his money _____ _____ the Nobel Prize.

    A. to   B. decided   C. create   D. use

29 _____, there were _____ _____ _____.

    A. awards   B. originally   C. five   D. only

30 A _____ _____ was _____ in 1968.

    A. added   B. sixth   C. award

31 Today, when we _____ of Alfred Nobel, we think of the Nobel Prize, _____ _____ _____.

    A. than   B. think   C. rather   D. dynamite

---

17 하지만 그는 세상이 그를 '죽음의 상인'으로 생각할 거라고는 결코 상상하지 못했다.

18 Nobel은 몹시 실망했다.

19 "어떻게 이럴 수가 있지?

20 이건 믿을 수 없어!

21 나는 죽음의 상인이 아니야.

22 나는 다르게 기억되고 싶어.

23 나는 세상을 더 좋게 만든 사람으로 기억되고 싶어."

24 그는 자신에 대한 사람들의 견해를 바꾸기로 결심했다.

25 1888년에, 한 프랑스 신문에서 실수로 Alfred Nobel의 죽음을 보도했다.

26 실제로 죽은 사람은 Alfred Nobel의 형인 Ludvig였다.

27 하지만 그 보도 덕분에, Nobel은 세상에 공헌하기 위해 무언가를 하기로 결심했다.

28 1895년에, 그는 자신의 돈을 노벨상을 만드는 데 사용하기로 결정했다.

29 원래 다섯 종류의 상만 있었다.

30 여섯 번째 상은 1968년에 추가되었다.

31 오늘날 우리가 Alfred Nobel을 생각할 때, 우리는 다이너마이트보다는 노벨상을 떠올린다.

※ 다음 우리말과 일치하도록 빈칸에 알맞은 것을 골라 쓰시오.

1 _____ Will You _____ _____?

2 It was _____ a _____ _____.

3 Alfred Nobel _____ _____ _____ _____ _____ _____ the newspaper.

4 _____ he was drinking his coffee, a _____ _____ _____ _____: *The Merchant of Death, Alfred Nobel, Is Dead.*

5 "_____? What is this?"

6 _____ the article, he dropped his cup _____ _____.

7 His coffee _____ all over his clothes and desk, but he couldn't _____ _____ _____ _____ the newspaper.

8 The article was _____ _____ _____ _____!

9 It said Nobel _____ _____ in France _____ _____ _____ _____.

10 "Oh _____ _____! Am I dead?"

11 _____ _____ _____ _____, Nobel _____ _____.

12 Soon, he became _____ _____ _____.

13 The article _____ him _____ the inventor of dynamite and _____ _____ _____ for war.

14 It said that he _____ _____ _____ from the _____ _____ _____.

15 He _____ _____ his eyes.

16 _____ was true _____ dynamite was _____ _____ _____ _____.

---

1 당신은 어떻게 기억될까요?

2 그저 평범한 아침이었다.

3 Alfred Nobel은 신문을 읽기 위해 의자에 앉았다.

4 커피를 마시는 동안 한 기사 제목이 그의 눈길을 끌었다. "죽음의 상인, Alfred Nobel 사망하다"

5 "뭐라고? 이게 뭐지?"

6 기사를 읽으며 그는 놀라서 컵을 떨어뜨렸다.

7 커피가 그의 옷과 책상 온 곳에 쏟아졌지만 그는 신문에서 눈을 뗄 수 없었다.

8 기사는 그 자신의 죽음에 관한 것이었다!

9 기사에는 Nobel이 심장 마비로 프랑스에서 죽었다고 쓰여 있었다.

10 "오, 이럴 수가! 내가 죽었다고?"

11 숨을 고른 후, Nobel은 계속 읽었다.

12 곧, 그는 훨씬 더 충격을 받게 되었다.

13 기사는 그를 전쟁에 쓰이는 다이너마이트와 다른 위험한 물건의 발명가로 기술했다.

14 기사에는 그가 다른 사람들의 죽음으로 인해 부유해졌다고 쓰여 있었다.

15 그는 자신의 눈을 믿을 수 없었다.

16 다이너마이트가 그의 많은 발명품 중 하나인 것은 사실이었다.

17 But he never imagined that the world would _____ _____ him _____ "the _____ _____ _____."

18 Nobel was _____ _____.

19 "_____ could this _____?

20 This is _____!

21 I'm not a _____ _____ _____.

22 I want to be remembered _____ _____ _____ _____ _____.

23 I want to _____ _____ _____ _____ a person who made _____ _____ _____."

24 He decided _____ _____ _____ _____ _____ about him.

25 In 1888, a French newspaper _____ _____ Alfred Nobel's death.

26 The person _____ _____ _____ _____ _____ was his brother, Ludvig.

27 _____ _____ the report, however, Nobel _____ do something to _____ _____ the world.

28 In 1895, he decided to use his money _____ _____ the Nobel Prize.

29 _____, there were _____ _____ _____.

30 A _____ _____ was _____ in 1968.

31 Today, when we _____ _____ Alfred Nobel, we think of the Nobel Prize, _____ _____ dynamite.

17 하지만 그는 세상이 그를 '죽음의 상인'으로 생각할 거라고는 결코 상상하지 못했다.

18 Nobel은 몹시 실망했다.

19 "어떻게 이럴 수가 있지?

20 이건 믿을 수 없어!

21 나는 죽음의 상인이 아니야.

22 나는 다르게 기억되고 싶어.

23 나는 세상을 더 좋게 만든 사람으로 기억되고 싶어."

24 그는 자신에 대한 사람들의 견해를 바꾸기로 결심했다.

25 1888년에, 한 프랑스 신문에서 실수로 Alfred Nobel의 죽음을 보도했다.

26 실제로 죽은 사람은 Alfred Nobel의 형인 Ludvig였다.

27 하지만 그 보도 덕분에, Nobel은 세상에 공헌하기 위해 무언가를 하기로 결심했다.

28 1895년에, 그는 자신의 돈을 노벨상을 만드는 데 사용하기로 결정했다.

29 원래 다섯 종류의 상만 있었다.

30 여섯 번째 상은 1968년에 추가되었다.

31 오늘날 우리가 Alfred Nobel을 생각할 때, 우리는 다이너마이트보다는 노벨상을 떠올린다.

※ 다음 문장을 우리말로 쓰시오.

1 How Will You Be Remembered?

➡ _____

2 It was just a normal morning.

➡ _____

3 Alfred Nobel sat in his chair to read the newspaper.

➡ _____

4 While he was drinking his coffee, a headline caught his eye: *The Merchant of Death, Alfred Nobel, Is Dead.*

➡ _____

5 "What? What is this?"

➡ _____

6 Reading the article, he dropped his cup in surprise.

➡ _____

7 His coffee spilled all over his clothes and desk, but he couldn't take his eyes off the newspaper.

➡ _____

8 The article was about his own death!

➡ _____

9 It said Nobel had died in France from a heart attack.

➡ _____

10 "Oh my goodness! Am I dead?"

➡ _____

11 Catching his breath, Nobel kept reading.

➡ _____

12 Soon, he became even more shocked.

➡ _____

13 The article described him as the inventor of dynamite and other dangerous objects for war.

➡ _____

14 It said that he had become rich from the deaths of others.

➡ _____

15 He couldn't believe his eyes.

➡ _____

16 It was true that dynamite was one of his many inventions.

➡ _____

17 But he never imagined that the world would think of him as "the merchant of death."

➡ _____

18 Nobel was deeply disappointed.

➡ _____

19 "How could this be?

➡ _____

20 This is unbelievable!

➡ _____

21 I'm not a merchant of death.

➡ _____

22 I want to be remembered in a different way.

➡ _____

23 I want to be remembered as a person who made the world better."

➡ _____

24 He decided to change people's opinions about him.

➡ _____

25 In 1888, a French newspaper mistakenly reported Alfred Nobel's death.

➡ _____

26 The person who had actually died was his brother, Ludvig.

➡ _____

27 Thanks to the report, however, Nobel decided to do something to contribute to the world.

➡ _____

28 In 1895, he decided to use his money to create the Nobel Prize.

➡ _____

29 Originally, there were only five awards.

➡ _____

30 A sixth award was added in 1968.

➡ _____

31 Today, when we think of Alfred Nobel, we think of the Nobel Prize, rather than dynamite.

➡ _____

※ 다음 괄호 안의 단어들을 우리말에 맞도록 바르게 배열하시오.

1 (Will / How / Be / You / Remembered?)
➡ _____

2 (was / it / a / just / morning. / normal)
➡ _____

3 (Nobel / Alfred / in / sat / chair / his / read / to / newspaper. / the)
➡ _____

4 (he / while / drinking / was / coffee, / his / headline / a / his / caught / eye: / *Merchant* / *The* / *Death,* / *of* / *Nobel,* / *Alfred* / *Dead.* / *Is*)
➡ _____
_____

5 ("what? // this?" / is / what)
➡ _____

6 (the / reading / article, / dropped / he / cup / his / surprise. / in)
➡ _____

7 (coffee / his / all / spilled / his / over / clothes / desk, / and / he / but / take / couldn't / his / eyes / the / off / newspaper.)
➡ _____
_____

8 (article / the / about / was / own / his / death!)
➡ _____

9 (said / it / had / Nobel / in / died / from / France / heart / a / attack.)
➡ _____

10 (my / "oh / goodness! // I / am / dead?")
➡ _____

11 (his / catching / breath, / kept / Nobel / reading.)
➡ _____

12 (he / soon, / even / became / shocked. / more)
➡ _____

13 (article / the / him / described / the / as / of / inventor / dynamite / other / and / objects / dangerous / war. / for)
➡ _____
_____

14 (said / it / he / that / become / had / from / rich / deaths / the / others. / of)
➡ _____

15 (couldn't / he / believe / eyes. / his)
➡ _____

16 (was / it / that / true / was / dynamite / of / one / his / inventions. / many)
➡ _____

---

1 당신은 어떻게 기억될까요?

2 그저 평범한 아침이었다.

3 Alfred Nobel은 신문을 읽기 위해 의자에 앉았다.

4 커피를 마시는 동안 한 기사 제목이 그의 눈길을 끌었다. "죽음의 상인, Alfred Nobel 사망하다"

5 "뭐라고? 이게 뭐지?"

6 기사를 읽으며 그는 놀라서 컵을 떨어뜨렸다.

7 커피가 그의 옷과 책상 온 곳에 쏟아졌지만 그는 신문에서 눈을 뗄 수 없었다.

8 기사는 그 자신의 죽음에 관한 것이었다!

9 기사에는 Nobel이 심장 마비로 프랑스에서 죽었다고 쓰여 있었다.

10 "오, 이럴 수가! 내가 죽었다고?"

11 숨을 고른 후, Nobel은 계속 읽었다.

12 곧, 그는 훨씬 더 충격을 받게 되었다.

13 기사는 그를 전쟁에 쓰이는 다이너마이트와 다른 위험한 물건의 발명가로 기술했다.

14 기사에는 그가 다른 사람들의 죽음으로 인해 부유해졌다고 쓰여 있었다.

15 그는 자신의 눈을 믿을 수 없었다.

16 다이너마이트가 그의 많은 발명품 중 하나인 것은 사실이었다.

17 (he / but / imagined / never / the / that / would / world / of / think / as / him / merchant / "the / death." / of)

➡ _____

_____

18 (was / Nobel / disappointed. / deeply)

➡ _____

19 (could / "how / be? / this)

➡ _____

20 (is / this / unbelievable!)

➡ _____

21 (not / I'm / merchant / a / death. / of)

➡ _____

22 (want / I / be / to / remembered / a / in / way. / different)

➡ _____

23 (want / I / be / to / as / remembered / person / a / made / who / world / the / better.")

➡ _____

24 (decided / he / change / to / opinions / people's / him. / about)

➡ _____

25 (1888, / in / newspaper French / a / reported / mistakenly / Nobel's / Alfred / death.)

➡ _____

26 (person / the / had / who / died / actually / his / was / Ludvig. / brother,)

➡ _____

27 (to / thanks / report, / the / Nobel / however, / to / decided / something / do / contribute / to / the / to / world.)

➡ _____

28 (1895, / in / decided / he / use / to / money / his / create / to / Nobel / the / Prize.)

➡ _____

29 (there / originally, / only / were / awards. / five)

➡ _____

30 (sixth / a / was / award / in / added / 1968.)

➡ _____

31 (when / today, / think / we / Alfred / of / we / Nobel, / of / think / the / Prize, / Nobel / than / rather / dynamite.)

➡ _____

_____

17 하지만 그는 세상이 그를 '죽음의 상인'으로 생각할 거라고는 결코 상상하지 못했다.

18 Nobel은 몹시 실망했다.

19 "어떻게 이럴 수가 있지?

20 이건 믿을 수 없어!

21 나는 죽음의 상인이 아니야.

22 나는 다르게 기억되고 싶어.

23 나는 세상을 더 좋게 만든 사람으로 기억되고 싶어."

24 그는 자신에 대한 사람들의 견해를 바꾸기로 결심했다.

25 1888년에, 한 프랑스 신문에서 실수로 Alfred Nobel의 죽음을 보도했다.

26 실제로 죽은 사람은 Alfred Nobel의 형인 Ludvig였다.

27 하지만 그 보도 덕분에, Nobel은 세상에 공헌하기 위해 무언가를 하기로 결심했다.

28 1895년에, 그는 자신의 돈을 노벨상을 만드는 데 사용하기로 결정했다.

29 원래 다섯 종류의 상만 있었다.

30 여섯 번째 상은 1968년에 추가되었다.

31 오늘날 우리가 Alfred Nobel을 생각할 때, 우리는 다이너마이트보다는 노벨상을 떠올린다.

※ 다음 우리말을 영어로 쓰시오.

1 당신은 어떻게 기억될까요?

➡ _____

2 그저 평범한 아침이었다.

➡ _____

3 Alfred Nobel은 신문을 읽기 위해 의자에 앉았다.

➡ _____

4 커피를 마시는 동안 한 기사 제목이 그의 눈길을 끌었다. "죽음의 상인, Alfred Nobel 사망하다"

➡ _____

_____

5 "뭐라고? 이게 뭐지?"

➡ _____

6 기사를 읽으며 그는 놀라서 컵을 떨어뜨렸다.

➡ _____

7 커피가 그의 옷과 책상 온 곳에 쏟아졌지만 그는 신문에서 눈을 뗄 수 없었다.

➡ _____

8 기사는 그 자신의 죽음에 관한 것이었다!

➡ _____

9 기사에는 Nobel이 심장 마비로 프랑스에서 죽었다고 쓰여 있었다.

➡ _____

10 "오, 이럴 수가! 내가 죽었다고?"

➡ _____

11 숨을 고른 후, Nobel은 계속 읽었다.

➡ _____

12 곧, 그는 훨씬 더 충격을 받게 되었다.

➡ _____

13 기사는 그를 전쟁에 쓰이는 다이너마이트와 다른 위험한 물건의 발명가로 기술했다.

➡ _____

14 기사에는 그가 다른 사람들의 죽음으로 인해 부유해졌다고 쓰여 있었다.

➡ _____

15 그는 자신의 눈을 믿을 수 없었다.

➡ _____

16 다이너마이트가 그의 많은 발명품 중 하나인 것은 사실이었다.

➡ _____

17 하지만 그는 세상이 그를 '죽음의 상인'으로 생각할 거라고는 결코 상상하지 못했다.

➡ _____

18 Nobel은 몹시 실망했다.

➡ _____

19 "어떻게 이럴 수가 있지?

➡ _____

20 이건 믿을 수 없어!

➡ _____

21 나는 죽음의 상인이 아니야.

➡ _____

22 나는 다르게 기억되고 싶어.

➡ _____

23 나는 세상을 더 좋게 만든 사람으로 기억되고 싶어."

➡ _____

24 그는 자신에 대한 사람들의 견해를 바꾸기로 결심했다.

➡ _____

25 1888년에, 한 프랑스 신문에서 실수로 Alfred Nobel의 죽음을 보도했다.

➡ _____

26 실제로 죽은 사람은 Alfred Nobel의 형인 Ludvig였다.

➡ _____

27 하지만 그 보도 덕분에, Nobel은 세상에 공헌하기 위해 무언가를 하기로 결심했다.

➡ _____

28 1895년에, 그는 자신의 돈을 노벨상을 만드는 데 사용하기로 결정했다.

➡ _____

29 원래 다섯 종류의 상만 있었다.

➡ _____

30 여섯 번째 상은 1968년에 추가되었다.

➡ _____

31 오늘날 우리가 Alfred Nobel을 생각할 때, 우리는 다이너마이트보다는 노벨상을 떠올린다.

➡ _____

구석구석 지문 Test

※ 다음 우리말과 일치하도록 빈칸에 알맞은 말을 쓰시오.

After You Read A. Read and Correct

1. WORLD NEWS / _____ 13, 1888

2. _____ _____ _____, Alfred Nobel, Is _____

3. Alfred Nobel _____ yesterday _____ France _____ _____ _____ _____.

4. He _____ _____ and _____ _____ _____ for war.

5. He _____ _____ from _____ _____ _____ _____ _____.

6. He _____ _____ _____ the deaths of _____ _____ _____.

7. The world will _____ him _____ "_____ _____ _____ _____."

1. 세계 뉴스 / 1888년 4월 13일
2. 죽음의 상인, Alfred Nobel 사망하다
3. Alfred Nobel이 어제 프랑스에서 심장마비로 사망했다.
4. 그는 전쟁에 쓰이는 다이너마이트와 다른 위험한 물건들을 발명했다.
5. 그는 다른 사람들의 죽음으로 인해 부유해졌다.
6. 그는 수천 명의 사람들의 죽음에 대해 책임이 있다.
7. 세상은 그를 "죽음의 상인"으로 기억할 것이다.

Word Power

1. Tim _____ _____ _____ _____ the beach.

2. Thomas Edison made _____ 1,000 _____ in _____ _____.

3. Who is _____ _____ of _____ _____?

1. Tim은 특별한 해변용 신발을 발명했다.
2. Thomas Edison은 일생 동안 천 개 이상의 발명품을 만들었다.
3. 비행기의 발명가는 누구인가?

Think and Write Step 2

1. _____ _____ this year, I'm glad _____ I _____ money _____ _____ in Africa.

2. I did this _____ I wanted _____ _____ _____ for children _____ _____.

3. _____ _____ money, I didn't buy snacks _____ _____ _____.

4. I _____ _____ _____ _____ UNICEF.

5. Before I donated, I sometimes _____ _____ _____ _____ _____.

6. Now I _____ _____ _____ _____ _____.

7. I'm _____ _____ _____.

1. 올해를 뒤돌아보니, 나는 아프리카의 아이들에게 돈을 기부해서 기쁘다.
2. 나는 어려움에 처한 아이들의 상황을 변화시키고 싶었기 때문에 기부를 했다.
3. 돈을 모으기 위해, 나는 한 달 동안 간식을 사지 않았다.
4. 나는 그 돈을 유니세프에 기부했다.
5. 나는 기부하기 전에는 가끔 접시에 음식을 남겼다.
6. 이제 나는 내 음식을 정말 고맙게 여긴다.
7. 나는 내 자신이 자랑스럽다.

※ 다음 우리말을 영어로 쓰시오.

After You Read A. Read and Correct

1. 세계 뉴스 / 1888년 4월 13일
   ➡ _____

2. 죽음의 상인, Alfred Nobel 사망하다
   ➡ _____

3. Alfred Nobel이 어제 프랑스에서 심장마비로 사망했다.
   ➡ _____

4. 그는 전쟁에 쓰이는 다이너마이트와 다른 위험한 물건들을 발명했다.
   ➡ _____

5. 그는 다른 사람들의 죽음으로 인해 부유해졌다.
   ➡ _____

6. 그는 수천 명의 사람들의 죽음에 대해 책임이 있다.
   ➡ _____

7. 세상은 그를 "죽음의 상인"으로 기억할 것이다.
   ➡ _____

Word Power

1. Tim은 특별한 해변용 신발을 발명했다.
   ➡ _____

2. Thomas Edison은 일생 동안 천 개 이상의 발명품을 만들었다.
   ➡ _____

3. 비행기의 발명가는 누구인가?
   ➡ _____

Think and Write Step 2

1. 올해를 뒤돌아보니, 나는 아프리카의 아이들에게 돈을 기부해서 기쁘다.
   ➡ _____

2. 나는 어려움에 처한 아이들의 상황을 변화시키고 싶었기 때문에 기부를 했다.
   ➡ _____

3. 돈을 모으기 위해, 나는 한 달 동안 간식을 사지 않았다.
   ➡ _____

4. 나는 그 돈을 유니세프에 기부했다.
   ➡ _____

5. 나는 기부하기 전에는 가끔 접시에 음식을 남겼다.
   ➡ _____

6. 이제 나는 내 음식을 정말 고맙게 여긴다.
   ➡ _____

7. 나는 내 자신이 자랑스럽다.
   ➡ _____

※ 다음 영어를 우리말로 쓰시오.

01	solution	
02	after	
03	clear	
04	health condition	
05	land	
06	appear	
07	select	
08	bathroom	
09	press	
10	special	
11	brightly	
12	rub	
13	scan	
14	usual	
15	shower	
16	whisper	
17	sensor	
18	shine	
19	future	
20	grocery	

21	comfortable	
22	shake	
23	drawer	
24	story	
25	yell	
26	driverless	
27	by -ing	
28	step in	
29	feel like	
30	be tired of	
31	come back	
32	stop -ing	
33	remind A to 동사원형	
34	give a presentation	
35	on top of	
36	pay for	
37	print out	
38	send A to B	
39	thanks to ~	
40	don't have to 동사원형	

※ 다음 우리말을 영어로 쓰시오.

01	빛나다, 비추다	
02	나타나다	
03	(건물의) 층	
04	일상의, 늘 먹던 것	
05	욕실	
06	맑게[투명하게] 하다; 투명한, 맑은	
07	특별한	
08	미래	
09	식료품 및 잡화	
10	건강 상태	
11	센서, 감지기	
12	내려앉다, 착륙하다	
13	누르다	
14	~ 후에	
15	문지르다, 비비다	
16	흔들리다, 흔들다	
17	운전자가 필요 없는	
18	정밀 검사[촬영]하다	
19	밝게	
20	선택하다	

21	서랍	
22	샤워실, 샤워	
23	속삭이다	
24	소리치다, 외치다	
25	편안한, 안락한	
26	해결책	
27	~에 발을 디디다	
28	~인 것처럼 느끼다	
29	돌아오다	
30	~에 싫증이 나다	
31	~의 값을 지불하다	
32	~함으로써	
33	~의 꼭대기에	
34	~할 필요가 없다	
35	~을 멈추다	
36	발표를 하다	
37	(프린트로) 출력하다	
38	~ 덕분에	
39	A에게 ~할 것을 상기시키다	
40	A를 B에게 보내다	

※ 다음 영영풀이에 알맞은 단어를 <보기>에서 골라 쓴 후, 우리말 뜻을 쓰시오.

1 _____ : a level of a building; a floor: _____

2 _____ : to produce bright light: _____

3 _____ : to return to the ground or another surface after a flight: _____

4 _____ : to choose someone or something from a group: _____

5 _____ : a room with a sink and toilet and usually a bathtub or shower: _____

6 _____ : feeling physically relaxed, without pain or other unpleasant feelings: _____

7 _____ : food and other goods sold in a grocery store or at a supermarket: _____

8 _____ : to start to be seen, to arrive, or to exist in a place, especially suddenly: _____

9 _____ : to push a button, switch, etc. to make a machine start, a bell ring, etc.: _____

10 _____ : to speak or say something very quietly, using your breath rather than your voice: _____

11 _____ : to choose something or someone by thinking carefully about which is the best, most suitable, etc.: _____

12 _____ : a device that can react to light, heat, pressure, etc. in order to make a machine, etc. do something or show something: _____

13 _____ : to shout or say something very loudly, especially because you are frightened, angry, or excited: _____

14 _____ : a box that slides into and out of a piece of furniture such as a desk and that is used to store things: _____

15 _____ : to move your hand, or something such as a cloth, backwards and forwards over a surface while pressing firmly: _____

16 _____ : to move suddenly from side to side or up and down, usually with a lot of force, or to make something or someone do this: _____

보기			
yell	select	drawer	bathroom
whisper	shine	press	sensor
rub	comfortable	shake	grocery
appear	story	select	land

※ 다음 우리말과 일치하도록 빈칸에 알맞은 것을 골라 쓰시오.

1 _____ the _____
A. Future   B. Picture

2 _____ 7 _____
A. a.m.   B. it's

3 The bed _____ and Minji Kim _____, "Five more _____!"
A. yells   B. minutes   C. shakes

4 The bed _____ _____.
A. shaking   B. stops

5 _____, Minji's mom _____ on a screen on the wall and says, "You're _____ to be _____ for school!"
A. late   B. appears   C. suddenly   D. going

6 Minji _____ her _____ and _____, "_____ the windows."
A. eyes   B. clear   C. rubs   D. says

7 The dark windows _____ clear and the sun _____ _____ them.
A. through   B. brightly   C. become   D. shines

8 In the bathroom, a red _____ _____ Minji's _____.
A. scans   B. body   C. light

9 A _____ says, "54 kilograms. Your _____ _____ is _____."
A. excellent   B. voice   C. condition   D. health

10 When she _____ in the shower, water comes _____ from the _____ and _____.
A. sides   B. steps   C. out   D. top

11 After her shower, _____ air _____ _____ and _____ her.
A. dries   B. warm   C. out   D. comes

12 When she _____ _____, a drawer opens _____ today's _____.
A. out   B. with   C. gets   D. clothes

13 In the _____, her father _____, "Good morning, Honey. What do you want _____ _____?"
A. kitchen   B. for   C. says   D. breakfast

14 Minji _____, "The _____, please."
A. usual   B. says

15 Mr. Kim _____ a _____ buttons on the _____ _____.
A. presses   B. machine   C. few   D. cooking

16 The _____ _____ _____ some bacon, eggs and bread.
A. prints   B. machine   C. out

17 Mr. Kim _____ goodbye and _____ _____ the door.
A. rushes   B. says   C. out

18 A few minutes _____, Minji's father _____ on a screen and _____, "I _____ my glasses!"
A. shouts   B. forgot   C. later   D. appears

19 Ms. Kim _____ and _____, "No _____. I'll _____ a drone to your office."
A. send   B. smiles   C. problem   D. answers

1 미래를 상상하다

2 오전 7시이다.

3 침대가 흔들리고 김민지가 "5분만 더!"라고 소리를 지른다.

4 침대가 흔들기를 멈춘다.

5 갑자기, 민지의 엄마가 벽 스크린에 나타나 말한다. "학교에 늦겠구나!"

6 민지는 눈을 비비며 "창문을 투명하게 해 줘."라고 말한다.

7 어두운 창문이 투명해지며 창문으로 햇살이 밝게 비춘다.

8 욕실에서 빨간 빛이 민지의 몸을 정밀 검사한다.

9 목소리가 "54킬로그램. 건강 상태가 매우 좋습니다."라고 말한다.

10 그녀가 샤워실 안에 발을 디디자, 물이 위와 양측에서 나온다.

11 샤워 후에, 따뜻한 공기가 나와 그녀를 말린다.

12 그녀가 나가자, 서랍이 열리며 오늘의 옷이 나타난다.

13 부엌에서 민지의 아빠가 "좋은 아침이구나, 얘야. 아침으로 무엇을 먹고 싶니?"라고 말한다.

14 민지는 "늘 먹던 걸로 주세요." 라고 말한다.

15 아빠가 요리 기계의 버튼 몇 개를 누른다.

16 기계는 베이컨, 달걀, 빵을 만들어 낸다.

17 아빠는 작별 인사를 하고 문 밖으로 급히 나간다.

18 몇 분 후에, 민지의 아빠가 스크린에 나타나 소리친다. "안경을 깜빡했어요!"

19 민지의 엄마가 미소 지으며 답한다. "괜찮아요. 드론을 당신의 사무실로 보낼게요."

20 Mr. Kim _____, "_____ a _____!"
    A. million   B. says   C. thanks

21 Ms. Kim and Minji _____ _____ a _____ car.
    A. flying   B. get   C. driverless   D. into

22 They _____ _____ _____ chairs _____ a table.
    A. around   B. comfortable   C. in   D. sit

23 Ms. Kim _____ the car window to _____ the _____ _____ this week.
    A. select   B. touches   C. groceries   D. for

24 She _____ for them _____ _____ her finger on a _____.
    A. putting   B. pays   C. sensor   D. by

25 They _____ _____ _____ _____ her house.
    A. be   B. will   C. to   D. delivered

26 The car _____ at Minji's school _____ _____ of a 150-_____ building.
    A. top   B. lands   C. story   D. on

27 Today Minji will _____ a _____ _____ Dona, a student _____ America.
    A. with   B. give   C. in   D. presentation

28 But Minji _____ _____ _____ _____ to America.
    A. to   B. doesn't   C. have   D. go

29 _____ _____ a VR classroom, they will feel _____ they are in the _____ classroom.
    A. to   B. like   C. same   D. thanks

30 _____ Minji's family _____ _____ home, dinner is _____.
    A. ready   B. back   C. when   D. comes

31 They eat and _____ _____ their _____.
    A. talk   B. day   C. about

32 After a _____ dinner, the cleaning robot _____ the table and _____ the _____.
    A. washes   B. delicious   C. clears   D. dishes

33 Minji says, "I _____ a game _____ _____ today. Do you want to _____?"
    A. called   B. play   C. learned   D. chess

34 _____ _____.
    A. agrees   B. everyone

35 A _____ chess _____ _____ the table.
    A. on   B. board   C. 3-D   D. appears

36 They have _____ _____ _____.
    A. fun   B. of   C. lots

37 _____ _____ Minji goes to bed, she _____ to her _____.
    A. before   B. whispers   C. right   D. watch

38 "_____ Daddy _____ his _____ tomorrow."
    A. take   B. remind   C. glasses   D. to

20 민지의 아빠가 "정말 고마워요!" 라고 말한다.

21 민지의 엄마와 민지는 운전자가 필요 없는 비행 자동차에 탄다.

22 두 사람은 탁자 주변의 편안한 의자에 앉는다.

23 민지의 엄마가 이번 주 식료품을 선택하기 위해 자동차 창문을 터치한다.

24 그녀는 센서에 손가락을 대서 식료품 값을 지불한다.

25 식료품은 집으로 배달될 것이다.

26 자동차는 150층 빌딩의 꼭대기에 있는 민지의 학교에 내린다.

27 오늘 민지는 미국에 있는 학생 Dona와 함께 발표를 할 것이다.

28 하지만 민지가 미국에 갈 필요는 없다.

29 VR(가상 현실) 교실 덕분에, 그들은 같은 교실에 있는 것처럼 느낄 것이다.

30 민지의 가족이 집에 돌아오자 저녁이 준비된다.

31 그들은 식사를 하며 그 날에 관해 이야기한다.

32 맛있는 저녁 식사 후에, 청소 로봇이 식탁을 치우고 설거지를 한다.

33 민지가 "오늘 체스라고 불리는 놀이를 배웠어요. 해 보실래요?"라고 말한다.

34 모두가 동의한다.

35 탁자 위에 삼차원 체스판이 나타난다.

36 그들은 아주 즐거운 시간을 보낸다.

37 민지는 자러 가기 직전에, 자신의 손목시계에 속삭인다.

38 "아빠께 내일 안경을 가져가시라고 상기시켜 드려."

※ 다음 우리말과 일치하도록 빈칸에 알맞은 말을 쓰시오.

1 _____ the _____

2 _____ 7 a.m.

3 The bed _____ and Minji Kim _____, "_____ _____ _____!"

4 The bed _____ _____.

5 Suddenly, Minji's mom _____ on a screen on the wall and says, "You're going to _____ _____ _____ school!"

6 Minji _____ _____ _____ and says, "_____ the windows."

7 The dark windows _____ _____ and the sun _____ _____ through them.

8 In the bathroom, a red light _____ _____ _____ _____.

9 A _____ says, "54 kilograms. Your _____ _____ is excellent."

10 When she _____ _____ the shower, water _____ _____ _____ the _____ and _____.

11 After her shower, warm air _____ _____ and _____ her.

12 When she _____ _____, a drawer opens _____ _____ _____.

13 In the kitchen, her father says, "Good morning, Honey. What do you want _____ _____?"

14 Minji says, "_____ _____, please."

15 Mr. Kim _____ _____ _____ buttons _____ the cooking machine.

16 The machine _____ _____ some bacon, eggs and bread.

17 Mr. Kim says goodbye and _____ _____ the door.

---

1 미래를 상상하다

2 오전 7시이다.

3 침대가 흔들리고 김민지가 "5분만 더!"라고 소리를 지른다.

4 침대가 흔들기를 멈춘다.

5 갑자기, 민지의 엄마가 벽 스크린에 나타나 말한다. "학교에 늦겠구나!"

6 민지는 눈을 비비며 "창문을 투명하게 해 줘."라고 말한다.

7 어두운 창문이 투명해지며 창문으로 햇살이 밝게 비춘다.

8 욕실에서 빨간 빛이 민지의 몸을 정밀 검사한다.

9 목소리가 "54킬로그램. 건강 상태가 매우 좋습니다."라고 말한다.

10 그녀가 샤워실 안에 발을 디디자, 물이 위와 양측에서 나온다.

11 샤워 후에, 따뜻한 공기가 나와 그녀를 말린다.

12 그녀가 나가자, 서랍이 열리며 오늘의 옷이 나타난다.

13 부엌에서 민지의 아빠가 "좋은 아침이구나. 얘야. 아침으로 무엇을 먹고 싶니?"라고 말한다.

14 민지는 "늘 먹던 걸로 주세요."라고 말한다.

15 아빠가 요리 기계의 버튼 몇 개를 누른다.

16 기계는 베이컨, 달걀, 빵을 만들어 낸다.

17 아빠는 작별 인사를 하고 문 밖으로 급히 나간다.

18 _____ _____ _____ _____, Minji's father appears on a screen and shouts, "I _____ my glasses!"

19 Ms. Kim smiles and answers, "No problem. I'll _____ _____ _____ _____ your office."

20 Mr. Kim says, "Thanks _____ _____!"

21 Ms. Kim and Minji get into a _____ _____ _____.

22 They sit _____ _____ _____ _____ a table.

23 Ms. Kim touches the car window _____ _____ the _____ for this week.

24 She _____ _____ them _____ _____ her finger _____ _____ _____.

25 They _____ _____ _____ to her house.

26 The car _____ at Minji's school on top of a _____ building.

27 Today Minji will _____ _____ _____ _____ Dona, a student in America.

28 But Minji _____ _____ _____ go to America.

29 _____ _____ a VR classroom, they will _____ _____ they are in the _____ _____.

30 When Minji's family _____ _____ home, dinner _____ _____.

31 They eat and _____ _____ their day.

32 After a _____ _____, the cleaning robot clears the table and _____ _____ _____.

33 Minji says, "I learned a game _____ _____ today. Do you want _____ _____?"

34 Everyone _____.

35 A _____ _____ _____ _____ on the table.

36 They have _____ _____ _____ _____.

37 Right before Minji goes to bed, she _____ _____ her watch.

38 "_____ Daddy _____ _____ his glasses tomorrow."

---

18 몇 분 후에, 민지의 아빠가 스크린에 나타나 소리친다. "안경을 깜빡했어요!"

19 민지의 엄마가 미소 지으며 답한다. "괜찮아요. 드론을 당신의 사무실로 보낼게요."

20 민지의 아빠가 "정말 고마워요!"라고 말한다.

21 민지의 엄마와 민지는 운전자가 필요 없는 비행 자동차에 탄다.

22 두 사람은 탁자 주변의 편안한 의자에 앉는다.

23 민지의 엄마가 이번 주 식료품을 선택하기 위해 자동차 창문을 터치한다.

24 그녀는 센서에 손가락을 대서 식료품 값을 지불한다.

25 식료품은 집으로 배달될 것이다.

26 자동차는 150층 빌딩의 꼭대기에 있는 민지의 학교에 내린다.

27 오늘 민지는 미국에 있는 학생 Dona와 함께 발표를 할 것이다.

28 하지만 민지가 미국에 갈 필요는 없다.

29 VR(가상 현실) 교실 덕분에, 그들은 같은 교실에 있는 것처럼 느낄 것이다.

30 민지의 가족이 집에 돌아오자 저녁이 준비된다.

31 그들은 식사를 하며 그 날에 관해 이야기한다.

32 맛있는 저녁 식사 후에, 청소 로봇이 식탁을 치우고 설거지를 한다.

33 민지가 "오늘 체스라고 불리는 놀이를 배웠어요. 해 보실래요?"라고 말한다.

34 모두가 동의한다.

35 탁자 위에 삼차원 체스판이 나타난다.

36 그들은 아주 즐거운 시간을 보낸다.

37 민지는 자러 가기 직전에, 자신의 손목시계에 속삭인다.

38 "아빠께 내일 안경을 가져가시라고 상기시켜 드려."

※ 다음 문장을 우리말로 쓰시오.

1 Picture the Future

➡ _____

2 It's 7 a.m.

➡ _____

3 The bed shakes and Minji Kim yells, "Five more minutes!"

➡ _____

4 The bed stops shaking.

➡ _____

5 Suddenly, Minji's mom appears on a screen on the wall and says, "You're going to be late for school!"

➡ _____

6 Minji rubs her eyes and says, "Clear the windows."

➡ _____

7 The dark windows become clear and the sun shines brightly through them.

➡ _____

8 In the bathroom, a red light scans Minji's body.

➡ _____

9 A voice says, "54 kilograms. Your health condition is excellent."

➡ _____

10 When she steps in the shower, water comes out from the top and sides.

➡ _____

11 After her shower, warm air comes out and dries her.

➡ _____

12 When she gets out, a drawer opens with today's clothes.

➡ _____

13 In the kitchen, her father says, "Good morning, Honey. What do you want for breakfast?"

➡ _____

14 Minji says, "The usual, please."

➡ _____

15 Mr. Kim presses a few buttons on the cooking machine.

➡ _____

16 The machine prints out some bacon, eggs and bread.

➡ _____

17 Mr. Kim says goodbye and rushes out the door.

➡ _____

18 ➤ A few minutes later, Minji's father appears on a screen and shouts, "I forgot my glasses!"
➡ _____

19 ➤ Ms. Kim smiles and answers, "No problem. I'll send a drone to your office."
➡ _____

20 ➤ Mr. Kim says, "Thanks a million!"
➡ _____

21 ➤ Ms. Kim and Minji get into a driverless flying car.
➡ _____

22 ➤ They sit in comfortable chairs around a table.
➡ _____

23 ➤ Ms. Kim touches the car window to select the groceries for this week.
➡ _____

24 ➤ She pays for them by putting her finger on a sensor.
➡ _____

25 ➤ They will be delivered to her house.
➡ _____

26 ➤ The car lands at Minji's school on top of a 150-story building.
➡ _____

27 ➤ Today Minji will give a presentation with Dona, a student in America.
➡ _____

28 ➤ But Minji doesn't have to go to America.
➡ _____

29 ➤ Thanks to a VR classroom, they will feel like they are in the same classroom.
➡ _____

30 ➤ When Minji's family comes back home, dinner is ready.
➡ _____

31 ➤ They eat and talk about their day.
➡ _____

32 ➤ After a delicious dinner, the cleaning robot clears the table and washes the dishes.
➡ _____

33 ➤ Minji says, "I learned a game called chess today. Do you want to play?"
➡ _____

34 ➤ Everyone agrees.
➡ _____

35 ➤ A 3-D chess board appears on the table.
➡ _____

36 ➤ They have lots of fun.
➡ _____

37 ➤ Right before Minji goes to bed, she whispers to her watch.
➡ _____

38 ➤ "Remind Daddy to take his glasses tomorrow."
➡ _____

※ 다음 괄호 안의 단어들을 우리말에 맞도록 바르게 배열하시오.

1 (the / Future / Picture)
➡ _____

2 (7 / it's / a.m.)
➡ _____

3 (bed / the / and / shakes / Kim / Minji / yells, / more / "five / minutes!")
➡ _____

4 (bed / the / shaking. / stops)
➡ _____

5 (Minji's / suddenly, / appears / mom / a / on / screen / the / on / wall / says, / and / "you're / to / going / be / for / late / school!")
➡ _____

6 (rubs / Minji / eyes / her / says, / and / the / "clear / windows.")
➡ _____

7 (dark / the / become / windows / and / clear / sun / the / brightly / shines / them. / through)
➡ _____

8 (the / in / bathroom, / red / a / scans / light / body. / Minji's)
➡ _____

9 (voice / a / says, / kilograms. / "54 // health / your / is / condition / excellent.")
➡ _____

10 (she / when / in / steps / shower, / the / comes / water / from / out / top / the / sides. / and)
➡ _____

11 (her / after / shower, / air / warm / out / comes / her. / and / dries)
➡ _____

12 (she / when / out, / gets / drawer / a / with / opens / clothes. / today's)
➡ _____

13 (the / in / kitchen, / father / her / says, / morning, / "good / Honey. // do / what / you / for / want / breakfast?")
➡ _____

14 (says, / Minji / usual, / "the / please.")
➡ _____

15 (Kim / Mr. / a / presses / buttons / few / the / on / machine. / cooking)
➡ _____

16 (machine / the / out / prints / bacon, / some / and / bread. / eggs)
➡ _____

17 (Kim / Mr. / goodbye / says / and / out / rushes / door. / the)
➡ _____

18 (few / a / later, / minutes / father / Minji's / appears / a / on / and / screen / shouts, / forgot / "I / glasses!" / my)
➡ _____

19 (Kim / Ms. / answers, / and / smiles / probelm. / "no // send / I'll / drone / a / your / to / office.")
➡ _____

1 미래를 상상하다

2 오전 7시이다.

3 침대가 흔들리고 김민지가 "5분만 더!"라고 소리를 지른다.

4 침대가 흔들기를 멈춘다.

5 갑자기, 민지의 엄마가 벽 스크린에 나타나 말한다. "학교에 늦겠구나!"

6 민지는 눈을 비비며 "창문을 투명하게 해 줘."라고 말한다.

7 어두운 창문이 투명해지며 창문으로 햇살이 밝게 비춘다.

8 욕실에서 빨간 빛이 민지의 몸을 정밀 검사한다.

9 목소리가 "54킬로그램. 건강 상태가 매우 좋습니다."라고 말한다.

10 그녀가 샤워실 안에 발을 디디자, 물이 위와 양측에서 나온다.

11 샤워 후에, 따뜻한 공기가 나와 그녀를 말린다.

12 그녀가 나가자, 서랍이 열리며 오늘의 옷이 나타난다.

13 부엌에서 민지의 아빠가 "좋은 아침이구나, 얘야. 아침으로 무엇을 먹고 싶니?"라고 말한다.

14 민지는 "늘 먹던 걸로 주세요." 라고 말한다.

15 아빠가 요리 기계의 버튼 몇 개를 누른다.

16 기계는 베이컨, 달걀, 빵을 만들어 낸다.

17 아빠는 작별 인사를 하고 문 밖으로 급히 나간다.

18 몇 분 후에, 민지의 아빠가 스크린에 나타나 소리친다. "안경을 깜빡했어요!"

19 민지의 엄마가 미소 지으며 답한다. "괜찮아요. 드론을 당신의 사무실로 보낼게요."

20 (Kim / Mr. / says, / a / million!" / "thanks)
➡ _____

21 (Kim / Ms. / and / get / Minji / a / into / flying / driverless / car.)
➡ _____

22 (sit / they / comfortable / in / around / chairs / table. / a)
➡ _____

23 (Kim / Ms. / the / touches / car / to / window / select / groceries / the / this / for / week.)
➡ _____

24 (pays / she / them / for / putting / by / finger / her / on / sensor. / a)
➡ _____

25 (will / they / delivered / be / her / to / house.)
➡ _____

26 (car / the / at / lands / school / Minji's / top / on / a / of / building. / 150-story)
➡ _____

27 (Minji / today / give / will / with / presentation / a / Dona, / student / a / America. / in)
➡ _____

28 (Minji / but / have / doesn't / go / to / America. / to)
➡ _____

29 (to / thanks / VR / a / classroom, / will / they / like / feel / they / in / are / same / the / classroom.)
➡ _____

30 (Minji's / when / comes / family / home, / back / is / dinner / ready.)
➡ _____

31 (eat / they / talk / and / their / about / day.)
➡ _____

32 (a / after / dinner, / delicious / cleaning / the / clears / robot / table / the / washes / and / dishes. / the)
➡ _____

33 (says, / Minji / learned / "I / game / a / chess / called / today. // you / do / to / want / play?")
➡ _____

34 (agrees. / everyone)
➡ _____

35 (3-D / a / board / chess / on / appears / table. / the)
➡ _____

36 (have / they / fun. / of / lots)
➡ _____

37 (before / right / goes / Minji / bed, / to / whispers / she / her / to / watch.)
➡ _____

38 (Daddy / "remind / take / to / glasses / his / tomorrow.")
➡ _____

20 민지의 아빠가 "정말 고마워요!"라고 말한다.

21 민지의 엄마와 민지는 운전자가 필요 없는 비행 자동차에 탄다.

22 두 사람은 탁자 주변의 편안한 의자에 앉는다.

23 민지의 엄마가 이번 주 식료품을 선택하기 위해 자동차 창문을 터치한다.

24 그녀는 센서에 손가락을 대서 식료품 값을 지불한다.

25 식료품은 집으로 배달될 것이다.

26 자동차는 150층 빌딩의 꼭대기에 있는 민지의 학교에 내린다.

27 오늘 민지는 미국에 있는 학생 Dona와 함께 발표를 할 것이다.

28 하지만 민지가 미국에 갈 필요는 없다.

29 VR(가상 현실) 교실 덕분에, 그들은 같은 교실에 있는 것처럼 느낄 것이다.

30 민지의 가족이 집에 돌아오자 저녁이 준비된다.

31 그들은 식사를 하며 그 날에 관해 이야기한다.

32 맛있는 저녁 식사 후에, 청소 로봇이 식탁을 치우고 설거지를 한다.

33 민지가 "오늘 체스라고 불리는 놀이를 배웠어요. 해 보실래요?"라고 말한다.

34 모두가 동의한다.

35 탁자 위에 삼차원 체스판이 나타난다.

36 그들은 아주 즐거운 시간을 보낸다.

37 민지는 자러 가기 직전에, 자신의 손목시계에 속삭인다.

38 "아빠께 내일 안경을 가져가시라고 상기시켜 드려."

※ 다음 우리말을 영어로 쓰시오.

1 미래를 상상하다
➡ _____

2 오전 7시이다.
➡ _____

3 침대가 흔들리고 김민지가 "5분만 더!"라고 소리를 지른다.
➡ _____

4 침대가 흔들기를 멈춘다.
➡ _____

5 갑자기, 민지의 엄마가 벽 스크린에 나타나 말한다. "학교에 늦겠구나!"
➡ _____
_____

6 민지는 눈을 비비며 "창문을 투명하게 해 줘."라고 말한다.
➡ _____

7 어두운 창문이 투명해지며 창문으로 햇살이 밝게 비춘다.
➡ _____

8 욕실에서 빨간 빛이 민지의 몸을 정밀 검사한다.
➡ _____

9 목소리가 "54킬로그램. 건강 상태가 매우 좋습니다."라고 말한다.
➡ _____

10 그녀가 샤워실 안에 발을 디디자, 물이 위와 양측에서 나온다.
➡ _____

11 샤워 후에, 따뜻한 공기가 나와 그녀를 말린다.
➡ _____

12 그녀가 나가자, 서랍이 열리며 오늘의 옷이 나타난다.
➡ _____

13 부엌에서 민지의 아빠가 "좋은 아침이구나, 얘야. 아침으로 무엇을 먹고 싶니?"라고 말한다.
➡ _____

14 민지는 "늘 먹던 걸로 주세요."라고 말한다.
➡ _____

15 아빠가 요리 기계의 버튼 몇 개를 누른다.
➡ _____

16 기계는 베이컨, 달걀, 빵을 만들어 낸다.
➡ _____

17 아빠는 작별 인사를 하고 문 밖으로 급히 나간다.
➡ _____

18 몇 분 후에, 민지의 아빠가 스크린에 나타나 소리친다. "안경을 깜빡했어요!"
➡ _____

19 민지의 엄마가 미소 지으며 답한다. "괜찮아요. 드론을 당신의 사무실로 보낼게요."
➡ _____

20 민지의 아빠가 "정말 고마워요!"라고 말한다.
➡ _____

21 민지의 엄마와 민지는 운전자가 필요 없는 비행 자동차에 탄다.
➡ _____

22 두 사람은 탁자 주변의 편안한 의자에 앉는다.
➡ _____

23 민지의 엄마가 이번 주 식료품을 선택하기 위해 자동차 창문을 터치한다.
➡ _____

24 그녀는 센서에 손가락을 대서 식료품 값을 지불한다.
➡ _____

25 식료품은 집으로 배달될 것이다.
➡ _____

26 자동차는 150층 빌딩의 꼭대기에 있는 민지의 학교에 내린다.
➡ _____

27 오늘 민지는 미국에 있는 학생 Dona와 함께 발표를 할 것이다.
➡ _____

28 하지만 민지가 미국에 갈 필요는 없다.
➡ _____

29 VR(가상 현실) 교실 덕분에, 그들은 같은 교실에 있는 것처럼 느낄 것이다.
➡ _____

30 민지의 가족이 집에 돌아오자 저녁이 준비된다.
➡ _____

31 그들은 식사를 하며 그 날에 관해 이야기한다.
➡ _____

32 맛있는 저녁 식사 후에, 청소 로봇이 식탁을 치우고 설거지를 한다.
➡ _____

33 민지가 "오늘 체스라고 불리는 놀이를 배웠어요. 해 보실래요?"라고 말한다.
➡ _____

34 모두가 동의한다.
➡ _____

35 탁자 위에 삼차원 체스판이 나타난다.
➡ _____

36 그들은 아주 즐거운 시간을 보낸다.
➡ _____

37 민지는 자러 가기 직전에, 자신의 손목시계에 속삭인다.
➡ _____

38 "아빠께 내일 안경을 가져가시라고 상기시켜 드려."
➡ _____

영어 기출 문제집

적중100

2학기

정답 및 해설

동아 | 이병민

중 3

적중100

영어 기출 문제집

적중'100

2학기

정답 및 해설

동아 | 이병민

중 3

Feel the Wonder

시험대비 실력평가
p.08

01 ④　　02 ②　　03 ⑤　　04 ④
05 ①

01 하나의 단어가 품사에 따라 완전히 다른 의미를 갖는 경우가 있다. land는 동사로는 '착륙하다'를, 명사로는 '땅'을 뜻한다. ④번은 명사로, 나머지 보기들은 동사로 사용되고 있다. ① 비행기가 공항에 착륙했다. ② 새가 물 위에 착륙했다. ③ 조종사가 가까스로 비행기를 안전하게 착륙시켰다. ④ 이 마을의 땅은 농사 짓기에 좋다. ⑤ 지금 착륙을 위해 들어오는 비행기 한 대가 있다.

02 ① camel: 낙타 / 사람들이 동물원에서 낙타를 구경하고 있다. ② complete: 완성하다 / 학생들은 그 과정을 마쳐야만 한다. ③ abroad: 해외에, 해외로 / Katya는 다음 달에 해외로 처음 여행을 갈 것이다. ④ 나의 부모님은 가끔 내가 적인 것처럼 대한다. ⑤ article: 기사 / 이 기사는 내가 신문에서 오려낸 거야.

03 ① from, be different from: ~와 다르다 / 런던은 대부분의 유럽의 도시들과는 다르다. ② up, give up: 포기하다 / 우리는 30분 동안 열쇠를 찾느라 시간을 보냈고, 결국 포기하고 집에 갔다. ③ away, melt away: 차츰 사라지다 / 아이스 호텔은 완전히 녹아서 강으로 흘러 들어갈 것입니다. ④ with, be covered with: ~로 덮여 있다. / 그의 책상은 책과 서류로 뒤덮여 있었다. ⑤ in, in a line: 한 줄로 / 그들은 한 줄로 늘어선 차들 속에 갇혀 있었다.

04 landscape: 풍경 scenery: 경치, 풍경 • 언덕에서 그는 평화로운 풍경을 내려다보았다.

05 Arctic: 북극 (지방) the area around the North Pole 북극의 주변 지역

서술형 시험대비
p.09

01 smash　　02 (1) (n)earby　(2) (f)orecast　(3) finally
(4) tightly　　03 record　　04 (f)ool
05 (1) spotted　(2) blow[blowing]　(3) Diving　(4) served
06 (1) The weather is very changeable at this time of year.
(2) There will be a chance for parents to look around the school.

01 smash: 때려 부수다, 깨뜨리다 / 무언가를 많은 조각으로 깨뜨리다 smash A against B: A를 B에 내리치다 / 그들은 바위에 조개가 깨져서 열릴 때까지 조개류를 세게 반복적으로 부딪친다.

02 (1) nearby: 인근에, 가까운 곳에 (2) forecast: 예측, 예보 (3) finally: 마침내 (4) tightly: 단단히, 꽉

03 하나의 단어가 품사에 따라 완전히 다른 의미를 갖는 경우가 있다. record: (동) 녹음하다 (명) 기록 • 그녀는 스튜디오에서 신곡을 녹음하고 있다. • 그녀는 올림픽 기록을 세웠다.

04 fool: (동) 속이다 (명) 바보 / • TV 뉴스가 충분한 정보를 제공할 거라고 생각하는 사람은 바보다. • 너는 나를 속일 수 없어. 나는 그가 이미 너에게 돈을 주었다는 것을 알아.

05 (1) spot: 발견하다, 찾아내다 / 나는 방금 전에 우리 뒤에 있는 경찰차를 발견했다. (2) blow: (입으로) 불다 / 나는 그녀가 커피를 식히기 위해서 커피를 부는 것을 보았다. (3) dive: 뛰어들다, 다이빙하다 / 절벽에서 다이빙하는 것은 위험하다. (4) serve: (음식을) 제공하다, 차려 주다 / 티케이크는 버터와 같이 뜨겁게 제공되어야 한다.

06 (1) at this time of year: 이맘때는, 이맘때쯤이면 (2) look around: 둘러보다

교과서 Conversation

핵심 Check
p.10~11

1 (1) I wonder where the museum is.
　(2) I wonder how long the Amazon River is.
2 (1) The Internet says　(2) The book says
3 ③

교과서 대화문 익히기

Check(√) True or False
p.12~13

1 F　2 T　3 T　4 F　5 F　6 T　7 T　8 F

교과서 확인학습
p.15~17

Listen and Speak 1 A
almost at / wonder how high / It's about / keep going

Listen and Speak 1 B
at, on / look / is the coldest place on / how cold it is

/ average, is, in, in / then, colder than / Although it's, doesn't / interesting

Listen and Speak 1 C

1. finally / excited, look around / wonder where / in front of
2. finally here / wonder where the information center / behind
3. I wonder where, is / next to

Listen and Speak 2 A

so / about going on a picnic / check / forecast says it'll be rainy / another time

Listen and Speak 2 B

to do / join me / Where do you want to / thinking of going / scenery, this time of / I heard that it's covered with / How long, take / The Internet says it takes / on

Listen and Speak 2 C

1. What, doing / anything interesting / This article says scientists have discovered
2. the newspaper / anything interesting / This article says, was seen in the East Sea

Real Life Talk Watch a Video

Check out / camels, in a line in / wonder how long camels can go / out / The Internet says / Camels are, interesting / travel with them

Real Life Talk Step 2

1. Where / I wonder how cold / says, average temperature, about / amazing
2. solar system / I wonder how big / The Internet says, times bigger than
3. on / how hot it is / says / reach up to

시험대비 기본평가   p.18

01 ②   02 ④   03 ①

01 'I wonder ~.'는 '나는 ~이 궁금하다.'라는 뜻으로 어떤 것에 대해 궁금할 때 사용하는 표현이다. wonder 다음에는 의문사절이나 if/whether절이 온다. 형용사 'curious(궁금한, 호기심이 많은)'를 사용해서 'I'm curious ~.'로 궁금한 점을 나타내는 표현을 할 수 있다.

02 '~ says (that) ...'(~에 따르면 …이다)는 어딘가에서 보거나 들은 내용을 상대방에게 보고하거나 전달할 때 사용하는 표현이다. 동사 'say'는 '~라고 말하다'는 뜻으로 흔히 사용되지만, 여기서는 '~라고 되어[쓰여] 있다, ~라고 나와 있다, (글, 표지판 등이) 나타내다, ~에 따르면 …이다' 등의 의미로 사용되었다.

03 궁금증을 표현할 때 '~를 궁금해하다'라는 의미를 가진 동

사 wonder를 이용하여 'I wonder ~.'라고 말한다. 궁금증을 나타내는 다른 표현으로 'I'm curious about ~.', 'I don't know why ~.' 'Can you tell me more about ~?', 'I'm interested to know ~.', 'I'd like to know ~.', 'I wish I knew ~.' 등으로 바꿔 사용할 수 있다.

시험대비 실력평가   p.19~20

01 ①   02 going   03 ⑤   04 ②
05 ③   06 (A) says (B) away   07 ⑤
08 ④   09 (a) on (b) than   10 ③
11 ⑤

01 'I wonder ~.'는 '나는 ~이 궁금하다.'라는 뜻으로 어떤 것에 대해 궁금할 때 사용하는 표현이다.

02 keep -ing: 계속 ~하다

03 ① 산 정상에 도착하기 위해서, 그들은 2시간 정도 올라가야 한다.(산 정상까지 얼마의 시간이 남았는지 정보가 나와 있지 않다.) ② 소년은 산이 얼마나 높은지 모른다.(산 높이를 물어보는 질문에 소년이 2,000미터라고 대답했다.) ③ 그들은 그들이 올라가고 있는 산이 높지 않다고 생각한다.(높다고 생각했다.) ④ 그들은 막 정상에 도착했다.(도착하지 못 했다.) ⑤ 소녀는 산이 얼마나 높은지 알기를 원한다.

04 세상에서 가장 높은 산에 대해 궁금증을 나타내는 말에는 높이를 말하는 ②번의 '인터넷에 따르면 그것은 약 8,850m라고 해.'가 적절하다.

05 누가 노래를 불렀는지 궁금해하는 말에 인터넷에 따르면 Jack이 노래를 썼다고 말하는 것은 어색하다.

06 (A) '~ says (that) ...'(~에 따르면 …이다)는 어딘가에서 보거나 들은 내용을 상대방에게 보고하거나 전달할 때 사용하는 표현이다. (B) melt away: 차츰 사라지다

07 마지막에 G가 말하고 있는 'That's interesting, too!'의 That이 가리키는 것이 주어진 문장이므로 주어진 문장(비록 그곳은 매우 춥지만 눈은 많이 내리지 않아.)은 ⑤번에 들어가는 것이 적절하다.

08 'I wonder ~.'는 '나는 ~이 궁금하다.'라는 뜻으로 어떤 것에 대해 궁금할 때 사용하는 표현이다. wonder 다음에는 의문사절이나 if/whether절이 온다. 궁금증을 나타내는 다른 표현으로 'I'm curious about ~.', 'I don't know why ~.', 'Can you tell me more about ~?', 'I'd like to know ~.', 등으로 바꿔 사용할 수 있다.

09 (a) on Earth: 지구상에서, (b) 비교급+than

10 ① 남극은 얼마나 추운가?(7월에 약 섭씨 영하 58도이고, 12월에는 약 섭씨 영하 26도이다.) ② 그들은 TV에서 무엇을 보고 있는가?(아기 펭귄들) ③ 남극의 연평균 기온은 몇 도인가? (대화에서 7월과 12월의 온도가 나와 있고, 연평균 기온은 나와 있

지 않았다.) ④ 어디가 지구에서 가장 추운 곳인가? (남극) ⑤ 남극에서 눈이 많이 내리는가?(많이 내리지 않는다.)

11 일요일에 무엇을 할 것인지 질문을 하자 (C) 등산을 갈 거라 말하며, 같이 가자고 제안하자 (D) 그러고 싶다고 대답하며 어디로 가는지 질문한다. (B) 남산에 가려고 생각 중이라고 대답하자 (A) 이맘때 그 곳 경치가 아름답다고 말하니, 맞다고 하며 단풍잎으로 덮여 있다고 말한다.

 서술형 시험대비 p:21

01 out 02 how long
03 camels 04 (A) says (B) takes
05 I heard that it is covered with red autumn leaves now.
06 I wonder where Green Park is.

---

01 check out: (흥미로운 것을) 살펴보다, 확인하다 find out: 찾아내다, (조사하여) 발견하다

02 'The Internet says they can go about two weeks without water.(인터넷 정보에 따르면 낙타는 물 없이 2주 정도 갈 수 있대.)'를 볼 때 얼마나 오래 가는지 질문하는 것이 적절하므로 의문사 'how long'이 어울린다.

03 수지가 낙타가 흥미로운 동물이라고 말하는 것에 이어서 Tony가 언젠가 사막에서 그들과 함께 여행하고 싶다고 말하고 있으므로 them이 가리키는 것은 낙타이다.

04 (A) 'The Internet says ~.'는 '인터넷에 따르면.'라는 뜻으로 어딘가에서 보거나 들은 내용을 상대방에게 보고하거나 전달할 때 사용하는 표현이다. (B) take: (얼마의 시간이) 걸리다

05 어떤 내용을 들어서 알고 있음을 표현할 때 'I heard that+주어+동사 ~.'의 형태로 말할 수 있다. heard 대신에 현재완료 형태인 'have heard'를 사용할 수도 있다. be covered with: ~로 덮여 있다 autumn leaves: 단풍

06 궁금증을 표현할 때 '~를 궁금해 하다'라는 의미를 가진 동사 wonder를 이용하여 'I wonder ~.'라고 말한다. I wonder 뒤에는 간접의문문의 어순인 '의문사(where)+주어(Green Park)+동사(is)'의 순서로 문장을 쓴다.

교과서
Grammar

핵심 Check p.22~23

1 (1) whose (2) of which
2 (1) I think we should wait until tempers have cooled.
  (2) Give me your hand while we cross the road.

시험대비 기본평가 p.24

01 ④ 02 ① 03 ②
04 (1) when (2) after (3) until

---

01 뒤에 명사가 이어지는 소유격 관계대명사가 필요한 자리이다. 선행사가 'This small fish'이므로 of which나 whose를 쓴다. of which를 쓸 경우에는 이어지는 명사에 the가 붙어야 한다는 것에 주의한다.

02 첫 문장과 두 번째 문장이 '인과' 관계나 '역접'의 관계 등이 보이지 않으므로 '~하는 동안'을 의미하는 while이 가장 적절하다.

03 두 문장에서 공통되는 것이 'the woman'과 'Her'이므로 소유격 부분을 소유격 관계대명사로 전환하여 쓴다. 선행사가 사람으로 'of which'는 쓸 수 없으므로 'whose'가 적절하다.

04 (1) 문맥상 when이 적절하다. (2) 문맥상 after가 적절하다. (3) 문맥상 until이 적절하다.

시험대비 실력평가 p.25~27

01 ③ 02 ⑤ 03 I met a girl whose name is the same as mine. 04 Be quiet while I'm speaking. 05 ① 06 ③ 07 of which price → of which the price 08 ②
09 ④ 10 ⑤ 11 ③ 12 ②
13 ⑤ 14 ① 15 (1) whose (2) whose (3) of which (4) while (5) are (6) until 16 ④, ⑤

---

01 '그 다큐멘터리는 그것에서 자신들의 생활이 묘사된 노동자들 사이에서 많은 불쾌감을 자아냈다.'는 문장이다. 사람이 선행사인 경우 소유격 관계대명사는 whose만 가능하다.

02 '암컷은 알이 부화할 때까지 알을 품는다.' 문맥상 after를 until로 바꾸는 것이 적절하다.

03 관계대명사의 소유격이 있으므로 선행사 a girl 뒤에 whose name을 배열하는 것이 적절하다.

04 '~하는 동안'이라는 뜻을 가진 시간을 나타내는 부사절을 이끄는 접속사 while이 있으므로 'Be quiet'으로 명령문을 쓰고, 접속사 while을 쓴 후, 'I'm speaking.'을 쓴다.

05 뒤에 명사가 이어지는 소유격 관계대명사가 필요하며, 사람이 선행사인 경우에는 whose만 가능하다.

06 '~한 후에'를 의미하는 시간의 접속사 after를 쓰는 것이 적절하다.

07 of which의 경우 이어지는 명사에 the를 붙여야 한다. 또는 of which 대신 whose를 써도 된다.

08 ⓐ, ⓒ, ⓔ는 whose, ⓑ, ⓓ는 of which를 써야 한다. 사람이 선행사일 경우에는 소유격 관계대명사는 whose만 쓰며, 사물이 선행사일 경우에는 whose와 of which 둘 다 가능하며, of which를 쓸 경우에는 명사에 정관사가 붙는다.

09 ④번에서 until은 '~까지'의 뜻이므로 '~할 때'를 의미하는

---

when으로 바꾸는 것이 적절하다.

10 ⑤는 의문대명사의 소유격으로 쓰였다. 앞에 선행사가 없으며 정관사가 없는 것이 특징이다. 그 외에는 모두 선행사의 소유격 관계대명사 whose이다.

11 ③ I usually go to the gym during my lunch hour. while은 접속사로 다음에 '주어+동사'가 이어지지만 during은 전치사로 명사(구)가 이어진다. 각각 ① 시간(~ 전에), ② 조건(~한다면), ④ 이유(~ 때문에), ⑤ 양보(~일지라도)의 접속사이다.

12 ②번은 선행사 the beluga whale 뒤에 소유격 관계대명사가 알맞게 쓰였다. ① of which roof → whose roof 또는 of which the roof, ③ of which the hobby → whose hobby, ④ the → 삭제, ⑤ roof of which → the roof of which 또는 whose roof

13 '그녀는 이름이 Mark인 남자를 만났다.'라는 문장이다. His name을 대신하는 소유격 관계대명사 whose를 사용해서 하나의 문장으로 만드는 것이 적절하며, of which는 선행사가 사람인 경우에는 쓰지 않는다. whose 뒤에 정관사 the를 함께 쓰지 않는다.

14 War must be a word whose meaning has to disappear from our understanding. 또는 War must be a word the meaning of which[of which the meaning] has to disappear from our understanding.이 알맞다.

15 (1) 선행사가 사물이므로 'whose'나 'of which'를 쓸 수 있지만 'of which'를 쓸 경우 the가 명사 앞에 붙는다. (2) 뒤에 명사가 이어지고 완전한 절이 나오므로 소유격 관계대명사 whose가 적절하다. (3) 뒤에 the tail이 나오므로 of which가 적절하다. whose 다음에는 정관사가 있는 명사가 이어질 수 없다. (4) while은 접속사로 다음에 '주어+동사'가 이어지지만 during은 전치사로 명사(구)가 이어진다. (5) 시간의 접속사가 이끄는 부사절에서는 미래의 의미일지라도 현재시제를 쓴다. (6) 내용상 부사절을 이끄는 until이 적절하다.

16 선행사가 사물이므로 'whose+명사'나 'of which+the+명사' 또는 'the+명사+of which'의 형태로 쓸 수 있지만 'of which'를 쓸 경우 보통 the가 명사 앞에 붙으며, whose를 쓸 경우 the를 명사 앞에 쓸 수 없다.

🦉 서술형 시험대비
p.28~29

01 (1) Tony has seen the girl whose hair is red.
(2) They are private businesses whose main focus is making money.
(3) Humpback whales stand on their tails while they sleep.
(4) As soon as we arrived on the island, we were eager to explore.

02 (1) I met my friend while I was on my way to school.
(2) You will be instructed where to go as soon as the plane is ready.
(3) He grew and grew until he was taller than his father.
(4) You must be careful when you are handling chemicals.

03 (1) I have a cup the color of which[of which the color] is blue.
(2) I could not solve the science problem the solution of which[of which the solution] was very difficult.
(3) I want to enter an international school the students of which[of which the students] come from many countries.
(4) Years ago I happened to get a very old-looking jar the owner of which[of which the owner] is not known up to now.

04 (1) the → 삭제 (2) owner → the owner
(3) which → of which (4) who → whose
(5) whose → who (6) who → whose

05 of which the top[the top of which] is covered with

06 While Jinsu was talking with Mark

07 (1) The tuskfish blows on the sand until a clam appears.
(2) You can select the album the cover of which you'd like to change.
(3) Humanity can be quite cold to those whose eyes see the world differently.

01 소유격 관계대명사 whose와 시간을 나타내는 접속사 등에 유의하여, 주어진 단어들을 적절히 배열한다.

02 while(~하는 동안에), as soon as(~하자마자), until(~까지), when(~할 때) 등의 접속사가 시간을 나타내는 부사절을 이끌도록 쓴다.

03 소유격 관계대명사가 필요한데, which를 이용하라고 했고 선행사가 사물이므로 'the+명사+of which' 또는 'of which+the+명사'의 어순으로 연결한다.

04 어색한 단어를 하나만 찾아야 하므로, 관계대명사의 쓰임에 주의해서 찾아 적절하게 고치도록 한다. (5)번은 소유격이 아니라 주격 관계대명사를 써야 하는 것에 유의한다.

05 선행사는 the mountain이고, the top이 있으므로 관계대명사 소유격 whose를 쓸 수 없다. of which를 써서 'the top of which'나 'of which the top'을 써야 한다. 산이 눈으로 덮인 것이므로 cover를 'be covered with'로 변형시켜야 함에도 유의한다.

06 '~하는 동안'은 접속사 While로 나타내고 6 단어이므로 진행형을 이용하여, 'was talking with'로 표현하는 것에 유의한다.

5

07 (1) '~까지'를 의미하는 until을 추가한다. (2) 주어진 어휘에 cover of가 있으므로, 'the cover of which'로 표현해야 하므로 the와 which를 추가한다. (3)은 선행사가 those로 사람이므로 관계대명사 whose를 써야 하므로 whose를 추가한다.

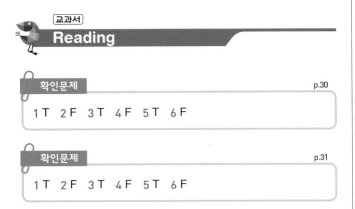

Reading

확인문제   p.30

1 T 2 F 3 T 4 F 5 T 6 F

확인문제   p.31

1 T 2 F 3 T 4 F 5 T 6 F

교과서 확인학습 A   p.32~33

01 Under	02 Two-thirds
03 millions of species	04 new things
05 Let's find out	06 Sweet
07 what these whales are doing	
08 in a group	09 actually
10 stand on their tails	11 near the surface
12 need to come up	13 fall asleep
14 for a deep breath	15 Enjoy
16 take a look at	17 whose favorite food
18 cannot be easily discovered	
19 until, appears	20 is closed tightly
21 give up	22 smashes, against
23 is served	24 Jump
25 fly down	26 jump out of the water
27 is around	28 up to
29 let, fool	30 quick and smart
31 spot, calculate	32 nearby, jumps, catches

교과서 확인학습 B   p.34~35

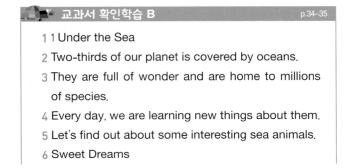

1 1 Under the Sea
2 Two-thirds of our planet is covered by oceans.
3 They are full of wonder and are home to millions of species.
4 Every day, we are learning new things about them.
5 Let's find out about some interesting sea animals.
6 Sweet Dreams

7 Can you guess what these whales are doing in the picture?
8 It looks like they are standing up in a group.
9 But they are actually sleeping!
10 Humpback whales stand on their tails while they sleep.
11 They sleep near the surface.
12 Since they are not fish, they need to come up to breathe.
13 Also, they don't fall asleep completely.
14 When they wake up, they come out of the water for a deep breath and dive back into the sea.
15 Enjoy Your Meal
16 If you think fish are not smart, take a look at the tuskfish.
17 This small fish whose favorite food is clams uses a tool to open them.
18 Clams usually hide under the sand, so they cannot be easily discovered.
19 The tuskfish blows on the sand until a clam appears.
20 The clam is closed tightly, so the fish cannot eat it.
21 But the tuskfish doesn't give up.
22 It smashes the clam against a rock.
23 In the end, the clam opens and dinner is served.
24 One, Two, Three, Jump!
25 You have probably seen a bird fly down to the sea to catch a fish.
26 But have you ever seen a fish jump out of the water to catch a bird?
27 Well, birds have to be careful when a giant trevally is around.
28 This fish can grow up to 170cm and 80kg.
29 But don't let its size fool you.
30 This fish is quick and smart.
31 It can spot a flying bird and calculate its speed and distance.
32 When the bird flies nearby, the giant trevally jumps out of the water and catches it.

시험대비 실력평가   p.36~39

01 are → is   02 oceans   03 ④   04 is closed   05 clams   06 gives up eating it → doesn't give up (eating it)   07 ②   08 (A) are (B) uses (C) give up   09 a rock   10 As

[Because/Since]　　11 ①, ③, ④　　12 ②

13 (A) jumps　(B) catches　14 clams

15 It smashes the clam against a rock.

16 It blows on the sand until a clam appears.

17 ③　　　　18 ①, ③　　　19 sleepy → asleep

20 ③　　　　21 ⑤　　　　22 ⑤　　　　23 ②

24 ②　　　　25 ④

01 '부분이나 분수를 나타내는 말+단수명사'는 단수로 취급해야 하므로 are를 is로 고치는 것이 적절하다.

02 They는 앞 문장의 'oceans'를 가리킨다.

03 몇몇 흥미로운 바다 동물들을 알아보자고 했으므로, 뒤에 올 내용으로는 '몇몇 흥미로운 바다 동물들에 대한 이야기들'이 적절하다.

04 조개가 단단히 '닫혀 있다'고 해야 하므로 'is closed'로 쓰는 것이 적절하다.

05 '조개'를 가리킨다.

06 조개가 단단히 닫혀 있어서 tuskfish가 그것을 먹을 수 없을 때, 그 물고기는 '(그것을 먹는 것을) 포기하지 않는다.'

07 appears는 자동사이므로 수동태로 쓸 수 없다.

08 (A) 명사 fish는 단수형과 복수형이 동일한 단어인데, a fish는 단수 취급, fish는 복수 취급하므로 are가 적절하다. (B) 주어인 fish 앞에 This small이 있으므로 단수 취급하여 uses가 적절하다. (C) 그러나 tuskfish는 '포기하지 않는다'고 해야 하므로 give up이 적절하다. give up: 포기하다, keep trying: 계속 노력하다

09 tuskfish는 조개가 단단히 닫혀 있어서 먹을 수 없을 때 포기하지 않고 돌에 조개를 내리친다고 했으므로, 조개를 열기 위해 사용한 도구는 '돌'이라고 하는 것이 적절하다.

10 so는 '그래서, 그 결과'라는 뜻의 접속사인데, so를 생략하는 경우에는 이유를 나타내는 접속사 As[Because/Since]로 문장을 시작하는 것이 적절하다.

11 ⓐ와 ①, ③, ④: 현재분사, ②, ⑤: 동명사

12 이 글은 'giant trevally가 물 밖으로 뛰어올라 새를 잡는' 것에 관한 글이므로, 주제로는 ②번 'giant trevally는 새를 잡기 위해 물 밖으로 뛰어오르는 물고기이다'가 적절하다.

13 새가 근처에 날고 있을 때, giant trevally가 물 밖으로 '뛰어올라' 새를 '잡기' 때문이다.

14 '조개'를 가리킨다.

15 smash A against B: A를 B에 내리치다

16 그것(tuskfish)은 조개가 나타날 때까지 모래에 입김을 분다.

17 ⓐ in a group: 한 무리를 이루어, ⓑ on their tails: 꼬리로, on: 무엇에 기대거나 받쳐져 있음을 나타냄(on one foot: 한 발로)

18 ⓒ와 ①, ③: 부사적 용법, ②, ⑤: 명사적 용법, ④: 형용사적 용법

19 '동작을 나타내는 자동사+형용사'는 become의 뜻이 된다. asleep: 잠이 든, 자고 있는, fall asleep: 잠들다

20 이 글은 'giant trevally가 물 밖으로 뛰어올라 새를 잡는' 것에 관한 글이므로, 제목으로는 ③번 '하나, 둘, 셋, 뛰어라!'가 적절하다.

21 ⓑ와 ⑤: (특정한 수·정도 등)까지 (less than), ① ~하고 있는 (doing), ② ~의 책임인, ~에게 달려 있는, ③ ~할 수 있는(육체적으로나 정신적으로), 너 이 일을 할 능력이 있니? ④ (특정한 위치·시점)까지 (until)

22 'giant trevally가 날고 있는 새의 속도와 거리를 어떻게 계산할 수 있는지'는 대답할 수 없다. ① Yes, there is. ② It can grow up to 170cm and 80kg. ③ Yes, it is. ④ It can spot a flying bird.

23 이 글은 'humpback whale들의 잠을 자는 모습과 그들의 심호흡'에 관한 내용의 글이므로, 제목으로는 ②번 '좋은 꿈 꿔라'가 적절하다.

24 주어진 문장의 But에 주목한다. ②번 앞 문장의 내용과 상반되는 내용이 뒤에 이어지므로 ②번이 적절하다.

25 'humpback whale'들은 '완전히 잠들지 않는다.'

🦉 서술형 시험대비　　　　p.40~41

01 Two-thirds of our planet

02 with　　　03 millions of species

04 Can you guess what these whales are doing in the picture?

05 (A) while　(B) near　(C) to breathe

06 (A) out of the water　(B) dive back

07 (1) in order that　(2) so that

08 to jump → jump[jumping]

09 (A) quick and smart　(B) size

10 the bird　　11 whose　　12 is served

13 the tuskfish[this small fish] cannot discover them easily.

14 (A) smashes　(B) against

01 Two-thirds는 '3분의 2'를 나타내는 분수 표현이며 분자는 기수로, 분모는 서수로 쓴다.

02 be full of = be filled with

03 '수많은 종'을 가리킨다.

04 'what these whales are doing in the picture'는 동사 guess의 목적어로, '의문사+주어+동사'의 어순으로 쓰인 간접 의문문이다.

05 (A) 뒤에 '주어+동사'가 이어지므로 while이 적절하다. while+주어+동사, during+기간을 나타내는 명사, (B) 수면 '근처에서'라고 해야 하므로 near가 적절하다. near: (거리상으

로) ~에서 가까이(전치사), nearby: 인근의, 가까운 곳의(형용사), the nearby surface처럼 주로 명사 앞에 씀), 인근에, 가까운 곳에(부사), (C) '숨을 쉬기 위해' 위로 나올 필요가 있다고 해야 하므로 to breathe가 적절하다.

06 혹등고래는 물고기가 아니기 때문에 잠에서 깨면 심호흡을 하러 '물 밖으로' 나왔다가 바다로 '다시 뛰어든다.'

07 부사적 용법의 목적을 나타내는 to부정사는 'in order that ~ can[may]'이나 'so that ~ can[may]'을 사용하여 복문으로 고치는 것이 적절하다.

08 지각동사 see+목적어+동사원형/현재분사: (목적어)가 ~하는 것을 보다

09 비록 giant trevally가 170센티미터에 80킬로그램까지 자랄 수 있지만 그것은 '빠르고 똑똑하다.' 그러므로, 그 '크기'에 속지 않는 것이 좋을 것이다. 왜냐하면 새가 근처에 날고 있을 때, 그것은 날고 있는 새를 발견하고 그 새의 속도와 거리를 계산하고 그 새를 잡기 위해 물 밖으로 뛰어오르기 때문이다.

10 '새'를 가리킨다.

11 소유격 관계대명사 whose로 쓰는 것이 적절하다.

12 밥상이 '차려진다'고 해야 하므로 'is served'로 쓰는 것이 적절하다.

13 생략된 'by the tuskfish[this small fish]'의 'the tuskfish[this small fish]'를 주어로 사용하여 능동태로 고치는 것이 적절하다.

14 조개가 모래로부터 나타날 때, 그것은 단단히 닫혀 있다. 그러면 tuskfish는 그것을 열기 위해 '돌에 조개를 내리친다.' smash A against B: A를 B에 내리치다

영역별 핵심문제   p.43~47

01 ②, ④, ⑤   02 wonder   03 ①   04 ③
05 I wonder how high this mountain is.   06 ①
07 ④   08 ③   09 forecast   10 ⑤
11 in   12 The Internet says they can go about two weeks without water.   13 ②
14 ①   15 ⑤   16 ④   17 whose night view is wonderful   18 ③   19 ②
20 ④   21 breath   22 ③, ④   23 to breathe   25 ④   25 This small fish whose favorite food is clams uses a tool to open them.
26 ②   27 ①, ⑤   28 ④
29 because → why   30 (A) gray[grey] (B) white

01 spot은 동사로 '발견하다, 찾아내다'의 뜻이며, 명사로는 '장소, 위치'이다. ⓑ, ⓒ는 '장소, 위치' ⓐ, ⓓ, ⓔ는 '발견하다, 찾아내다'의 의미로 사용되었다. ⓐ 만약에 엄마와 아빠가 오시는 것을 발견한다면, 나에게 경고해 줘. ⓑ 주차할 장소를 찾느라 약

20분이 걸렸다. ⓒ 이곳은 멈춰서 쉬기에 좋은 장소처럼 보인다. ⓓ 만약에 네가 운이 좋다면, 너는 사슴 한 마리 혹은 두 마리를 발견할 것이다. ⓔ 이 개미들은 비교적 찾기 쉽다.

02 wonder: (명) 경이, 경탄, 놀라움 (동) 궁금하다 • 가끔 그는 왜 그의 아버지가 그를 싫어하는지 궁금했다. • 타지마할의 경관은 우리를 경탄으로 가득 채웠다.

03 average: (명) 평균 (형) 평균의 / 3, 8, 10의 평균은 7이다.

04 (A) be full of: ~로 가득 차다 • 부엌은 연기로 가득 찼다. (B) this time of year: 이맘때는, 이맘때쯤이면 • 보스턴은 이맘때쯤이면 매우 아름답다.

05 궁금증을 표현할 때 '~를 궁금해하다'라는 의미를 가진 동사 wonder를 이용하여 'I wonder ~.'라고 말한다. I wonder 뒤에는 간접의문문의 어순인 '의문사(how high)+주어(this mountain)+동사(is)'의 순서로 문장을 쓴다.

06 숫자 앞의 about은 '대략, 약'의 의미이다.

07 주어진 문장은 '정말 높은 산이구나.'로, 상대방의 말에 맞다고 하는 'Yes, it is.'와 연결될 수 있으므로 ④가 적절하다.

08 주어진 문장은 상대방에게 날씨를 확인해 달라고 요청하는 말이며, 다음에 날씨를 확인하고 일기 예보에 따르면 오후에 비가 올 것이라는 말하는 내용이 나오는 것이 자연스러우므로 ③번이 적절하다.

09 forecast: 예측, 예보 / 당신이 생각하기에 미래에 무엇이 일어날지에 대한 언급

10 ⓐ 오늘 오후에 날씨는 어떤가?(비가 온다) ⓑ 누가 일기 예보를 확인했는가?(G) ⓒ 그들은 무슨 요일에 소풍을 갈 예정인가?(다음에 가자고 말했지 정확히 언제 가자고 말하지 않았다.) ⓓ 지금 바깥 날씨가 좋은가?(네) ⓔ 누가 소풍을 가자고 제안했는가?(G)

11 in a line: 한 줄로, in+장소: ~에서

12 '~가 …라고 말하다'라는 의미의 '주어+say(s)+that+주어+동사 ~.' 구문을 이용해 주어가 한 말인 that절의 내용을 상대방에게 보고하거나 전해줄 수 있다. 이때 접속사 that은 생략 가능하다. about: 대략, 약 without: ~ 없이

13 <보기>와 ②의 when은 시간의 접속사로 쓰였다. ① 관계부사 ③ 의문부사 ④ 대명사 ⑤ 명사

14 <보기>와 ①의 whose는 관계대명사의 소유격이다. 나머지는 모두 의문사로 '누구의'라는 의미로 사용되었다.

15 나에게는 '아빠가 유명한 배우인 친구가 있다.'는 문장이다. 선행사가 사람이므로 관계대명사의 소유격 whose를 사용해서 하나의 문장으로 만드는 것이 적절하다.

16 '꼬리가 매우 짧은 개를 봐라.'라는 문장이다. 선행사가 사람이므로 관계대명사의 소유격 'of which'나 'whose'를 사용해서 하나의 문장으로 만드는 것이 적절하며, 'of which'를 쓸 경우 정관사 the가 있어야 함에 주의한다.

17 5 단어이므로 소유격 관계대명사 whose를 활용하여, 'whose

night view'로 표현하는 것에 유의한다.

18 가장 어울리는 의미의 접속사를 찾는다. '비가 그칠 때까지 여기서 기다리자.'라는 의미가 가장 적절하다.

19 ② Linda lost her husband when she was 40. 보통 접속사 when은 '바로 그 때(at that time)'의 상황이나 동작을 나타낼 때 사용하고 접속사 while은 특정하게 길이가 있는 기간을 나타낼 때 쓰며 '동시에 일어나는(happening at the same time)' 상황이나 동작을 나타낼 때 사용한다. 남편과 사별하는 것은 한순간의 일이므로 while과는 어울리지 않는다.

20 문장의 의미에 맞게 적절한 접속사를 찾는다. (A) 그는 여행을 하는 동안 책을 썼다. (B) 그는 나를 보자마자 도망쳤다. (C) 그의 엄마는 청소를 끝낸 후에 꽃을 탁자 위에 놓았다.

21 '심호흡을 하러'라고 해야 하므로, breathe의 명사 breath를 쓰는 것이 적절하다. a deep breath: 심호흡

22 (A)와 ③, ④: [이유를 나타내어] ~이므로, ~이니까(접속사), ①, ⑤: [종종 계속을 나타내는 완료형의 동사를 가진 주절 뒤에서] ~한 이래 (죽), ~한 때부터 내내(접속사), ② 그 이래(부사)

23 그들은 잠에서 깨면 '숨을 쉬기 위해' 물 밖으로 나오려고 그렇게 한다.

24 이 글은 'tuskfish가 가장 좋아하는 먹이인 조개를 열기 위해 도구를 사용하는 것'에 관한 글이므로, 제목으로는 ⑤번 '맛있게 먹어라'가 적절하다.

25 선행사인 This small fish 다음에 소유격 관계대명사 whose를 쓰는 것이 적절하다.

26 ② '이 작은 물고기는' 조개를 열기 위해 도구를 사용한다고 했으므로, tuskfish는 '작은 물고기'라는 것을 알 수 있다.

27 ⓐ와 ①, ⑤: 경험 용법, ② 계속 용법, ③ 결과 용법, ④ 완료 용법

28 ④는 '날고 있는 새'를 가리키고, 나머지는 다 'giant trevally'를 가리킨다.

29 벨루가 고래는 온몸이 하얗기 때문에 사람들이 벨루가 고래를 흰고래라고 부른다고 해야 하므로, because를 why로 고치는 것이 적절하다. That's why+결과, That's because+이유

30 벨루가 고래는 태어날 때, '회색'이지만, 다 자라면, 몸은 '하얀색'이 된다. (A)에는 'The beluga whale is born'이라는 1형식 문장에 형용사 gray를 유사보어로 사용하여 답하는 것이 적절하다.

단원별 예상문제
p.48~51

01 ⓐ, ⓓ와 ⓑ, ⓒ, ⓔ   02 ⑤

03 (1) Arctic   (2) breathe   04 out   05 ②

06 I wonder how cold it is.   07 ③   08 ⓐ July

ⓑ December   09 I wonder how cold it is there.

10 ②   11 ①   12 The Internet says it

---

takes about two hours.   13 ③

14 (1) whose   (2) of which   (3) who   (4) whose
   (5) of which   (6) which

15 ③   16 ④   17 don't let its size fool

you   18 ①   19 ①   20 ④

21 ⑤   22 ③   23 ④

01 land는 동사로는 '착륙하다, 떨어지다'의 의미이며, 명사로는 '땅'의 의미로 사용된다. ⓐ와 ⓓ는 '착륙하다'로, ⓑ, ⓒ, ⓔ는 '땅'의 의미로 사용되었다. ⓐ 그것은 공이 어디에 떨어지는지 보여준다. ⓑ 그들의 여정은 그들을 많은 외국의 땅으로 이끌었다. ⓒ 그들은 시골로 이사 가서 약간의 땅을 샀다. ⓓ 그는 비행기가 착륙하는 소리를 듣지 못했다. ⓔ 비행기가 땅으로 내려갔는지 바다로 내려갔는지는 명확하지 않다.

02 tightly: 단단히, firmly: 단단히 • 대문이 잠겼고, 모든 창문이 단단히 닫혀 있다.

03 (1) Arctic: 북극 (지방) (2) breathe: 숨을 쉬다

04 check out: (흥미로운 것을) 살펴보다, 확인하다 • 저희 새 매장에서 가격들을 한번 살펴보세요! find out: 찾아내다, (조사하여) 발견하다 • 그 회의가 몇 시에 시작하는지 알아 볼 수 있어요? out of: ~ 밖으로 • 창 밖으로 기대지 마.

05 temperature: 온도, 기온

06 궁금증을 표현할 때 '~를 궁금해하다'라는 의미를 가진 동사 wonder를 이용하여 'I wonder ~.'라고 말한다. wonder 다음에는 의문사절이나 if/whether절이 온다. 여기서는 의문사절인 '의문사+주어+동사'를 사용하였다.

07 (A) 펭귄들이 귀엽다는 것과 그것들이 추워 보인다는 내용은 접속사 'but(하지만)'으로 연결될 수 있다. (B) '매우 춥지만, 눈은 많이 내리지 않아.'가 내용상 어울리므로 although가 적절하다.
although: 비록 ~일지라도, ~이긴 하지만

08 7월이 약 섭씨 영하 58도이고, 12월은 약 섭씨 영하 26도이므로, 7월이 12월보다 춥다.

09 궁금증을 표현할 때 '~를 궁금해하다'라는 의미를 가진 동사 wonder를 이용하여 'I wonder ~.'라고 말한다. I wonder 뒤에는 간접의문문의 어순인 '의문사(how cold)+주어(it)+동사(is)'의 순서로 문장을 쓴다.

10 주어진 문장은 '어디로 가고 싶니?'로 이 질문에 대한 대답으로 가고 싶은 장소가 나오는 것이 어울리므로, 장소를 말하고 있는 'I'm thinking of going to Namsan.(나는 남산에 가려고 생각 중이야.)'이 대답이 될 수 있다. 그러므로 주어진 문장은 ②에 들어가야 알맞다.

11 (A) 'I'm thinking of ~.'는 '나는 ~할까 생각 중이다'라는 뜻으로 of 뒤에 동명사를 취해 의도나 계획을 나타낼 때 쓰는 표현

이다. (B) 어떤 내용을 들어서 알고 있음을 표현할 때 'I heard that+주어+동사 ~.'의 형태로 말할 수 있다. heard 대신에 현재완료형의 형태인 have heard를 사용할 수도 있다. (C) be covered with: ~로 덮여 있다

12 'The Internet says ~.'는 '인터넷에 따르면 ~'이라는 뜻으로 어딘가에서 보거나 들은 내용을 상대방에게 보고하거나 전달할 때 사용하는 표현이다. take: (얼마의 시간이) 걸리다 about: 대략, 약

13 He won't rest until he finds her. 시간의 접속사가 이끄는 부사절에서는 미래의 의미일지라도 현재시제를 쓴다.

14 (1), (4)는 소유격 관계대명사 whose가 적절하다. (2), (5)는 내용상 소유격이 필요한데, 정관사 the가 있으므로 'of which'가 적절하다. (3)은 주격 관계대명사 who가 적절하다. (6)은 전치사 for의 목적어 자리에 쓰인 관계대명사로 which가 적절하다.

15 ⓐ와 ③: 접속사, ① 지시형용사, ② 지시부사, ④ 지시대명사, ⑤ 관계대명사

16 '문어가 어떻게 피부색을 바꿀 수 있는지'는 알 수 없다. ① It lives on the ocean floor. ② It usually eats small fish. ③ It can change the color of its skin to hide from its enemies. ⑤ It shoots out dark black ink and swims away.

17 사역동사(let)+목적어+동사원형: '(목적어)가 ~하도록 허락하다', fool: '속이다, 기만하다'

18 글의 첫 부분에서 '여러분은 아마 새가 물고기를 잡기 위해 바다로 날아 내려가는 것을 본 적이 있을 것'이라고 했다.

19 ⓐ out of: ~에서 밖으로, ~의 밖으로, ⓑ into: ~ 안으로

20 이 글은 'humpback whale들의 잠을 자는 모습과 그들의 심호흡'에 관한 내용의 글이므로, 주제로는 ④번 'humpback whale들은 어떻게 잠을 자고 호흡하는가?'가 적절하다.

21 주어진 문장의 But에 주목한다. ⑤번 앞 문장의 내용과 상반되는 내용이 뒤에 이어지므로 ⑤번이 적절하다.

22 ⓐ와 ①, ④: 부사적 용법, ②: 형용사적 용법, ③, ⑤: 명사적 용법

23 'tuskfish가 조개를 여는데 얼마나 오래 걸리는지'는 대답할 수 없다. ① Its favorite food is clams. ② They usually hide under the sand. ③ It blows on the sand until a clam appears. ⑤ To open the clam.

![owl icon] **서술형 실전문제**   p.52~53

01 (1) I wonder how long the shortest hiking course takes.

(2) I'm curious (about) how long the shortest hiking course takes.

02 (1) This article says scientists have discovered a new planet.

(2) According to this article, scientists have discovered a new planet.

03 I wonder how long can camels go without water in the desert. → I wonder how long camels can go without water in the desert.

04 (1) I interviewed a man whose dream is to climb Baekdusan.

(2) The cat whose name[the name of which, of which the name] is Molly is sitting on the table.

05 (1) You have to finish your homework before you go to bed.

(2) Tom waited in front of the door until someone came out.

06 they don't fall asleep completely

07 bottom of the sea → surface

08 (A) fish   (B) a deep breath

09 (A) fly   (B) nearby   (C) out of

10 to fool   11 spot

01 'I wonder ~.'는 '나는 ~이 궁금하다.'라는 뜻으로 어떤 것에 대해 궁금할 때 사용하는 표현이다. 궁금증을 나타내는 다른 표현으로 curious를 사용해 'be[become] curious about ~'으로 나타낼 수 있다.

02 '~ says (that) …'(~에 따르면 …이다)는 어딘가에서 보거나 들은 내용을 상대방에게 보고하거나 전달할 때 사용하는 표현이다. '~에 따르면'이라는 뜻으로 'according to'를 사용할 수 있다. *article: 기사

03 궁금증을 표현할 때 '~를 궁금해 하다'라는 의미를 가진 동사 wonder를 이용하여 'I wonder ~.'라고 말한다. wonder 다음에는 의문사절(의문사+주어+동사)이 나올 수 있다.

04 (1) a man이 선행사이므로, 사람을 선행사로 하는 소유격 관계대명사 whose를 이용하여 두 문장을 연결하는 것이 적절하다. (2) The cat이 선행사이므로, 소유격 관계대명사 whose나 'of which'를 활용한다.

05 (1) 잠자리에 들기 전에 숙제를 끝내라고 하는 것이 적절하다. (2) 누군가가 나올 때까지 기다렸다고 하는 것이 적절하다.

06 fall asleep: 잠들다

07 humpback whale들은 '수면' 근처에서 잠을 잔다.

08 그들은 '물고기'가 아니기 때문에, 잠에서 깨면 '심호흡'을 하러 물 밖으로 나올 필요가 있다.

09 (A) '지각동사 see+목적어+동사원형: (목적어)가 ~하는 것을 보다'라고 해야 하므로 fly가 적절하다. (B) 새가 '근처에' 날고

있을 때라고 해야 하므로 nearby가 적절하다. nearby: 인근에, 가까운 곳에(부사), 인근의, 가까운 곳의(형용사), the nearby surface처럼 주로 명사 앞에 씀, nearly: 거의, (C) giant trevally는 물 '밖으로' 뛰어올라 새를 잡는다고 해야 하므로 out of가 적절하다.

10 사역동사(let)+목적어+동사원형 = allow+목적어+to부정사: (목적어)가 ~하도록 허락하다

11 spot: 발견하다, 찾아내다, 어떤 것 또는 어떤 사람을 주목하다, 알아채다

창의사고력 서술형 문제   p.54

|모범답안|

01 I wonder what this is. / The Internet says it is / I'm curious where it is.

02 (A) in the Arctic Ocean (B) a round head (C) fish and clams (D) it is white all over (E) gray (F) white

01 I wonder ~: 나는 ~이 궁금하다. ~ says (that) ···: ~에 따르면 ···이다

단원별 모의고사   p.55~59

01 ⑤

02 (1) nearby (2) friendly (3) completely (4) finally

03 ④

04 (1) was full (2) go on a picnic (3) grow up to (4) millions of

05 (A) → (C) → (D) → (B)

06 I wonder where the bus stop is.

07 in front of   08 going

09 (1) The weather forecast says it'll be rainy in the afternoon.
(2) According to the weather forecast, it'll be rainy in the afternoon.

10 the scenery there is so beautiful this time of year

11 ③   12 ③   13 ①   14 ⑤

15 I have a friend whose hobby is to play basketball.

16 When he comes back home, he will call his father.

17 (1) Charlotte is a wise spider whose best friend is Wilbur. 또는 Charlotte is a wise spider of which the best friend is Wilbur.
(2) The girl whose dress is yellow is Bora.
(3) I'll take care of your dog while you are away.

18 ⑤   19 ③

---

20 (A) the surface (B) their tails (C) completely

21 breathe → breath   22 ⑤   23 ②

24 the clam

25 have you ever seen a fish jump out of the water to catch a bird?

26 ②

27 one hundred and seventy centimeters and eighty kilograms

01 (A) fall asleep: 잠들다 • 아까 커피를 많이 마셔서 지금은 잠들 수 없다. (B) keep -ing: 계속해서 ~하다 • 중요한 것은 계속 시도하는 것이다.

02 (1) nearby: 인근에, 가까운 곳에 / 나는 인근에 있는 작은 가게에 갔어. (2) friendly: 친절한 / 호텔 직원들이 매우 친절하고 도움이 많이 되었다. (3) completely: 완전히 / 나는 오늘이 그의 생일이라는 것을 완전히 잊었다. (4) 우리는 마침내 한밤중에 집에 도착했다.

03 ① take, take: (얼마의 시간이) 걸리다 / 이것은 얼마나 걸릴 거야? ② surrounded, surround: 둘러싸다 / 너는 포위되었다! 무기를 내려놓아라. ③ hide, hide: 숨다, 숨기다 / 그녀가 도착하지 않자 그는 실망감을 감추기가 어려웠다. ④ smashed, smash: 때려 부수다, 깨뜨리다 ⑤ calculate, calculate: 계산하다 / 아무리 계산해도 3천 원이 빈다.

04 (1) be full of: ~로 가득 차다 (2) go on a picnic: 소풍가다 (3) grow up to: 자라서 ~이 되다 (4) millions of: 수백만의

05 (A) 무엇을 하고 있는지 질문을 하자 (C) 신문을 읽고 있다고 대답한다. (D) 신문에서 흥미로운 것이 있는지 질문하자 (B) 고래 가족이 동해에서 발견되었다는 것을 얘기해준다.

06 'I wonder ~.'는 '나는 ~이 궁금하다.'라는 뜻으로 어떤 것에 대해 궁금할 때 사용하는 표현이다. wonder 다음에는 의문사절이나 if/whether절이 온다. 여기서는 '의문사(where)+주어(the bus stop)+동사(is)'인 의문사절을 wonder의 목적어로 사용한다.

07 버스 정류장은 경찰서 앞에 있다. in front of: ~ 앞에

08 How about -ing?: ~하는 것이 어떠니?

09 '~ says (that) ···'(~에 따르면 ···이다)는 어딘가에서 보거나 들은 내용을 상대방에게 보고하거나 전달할 때 사용하는 표현이다. 동사 'say'는 '~라고 말하다'는 뜻으로 흔히 사용되지만, 여기에서는 '~라고 되어[쓰여] 있다, ~라고 나와 있다, (글, 표지판 등이) 나타내다'라는 뜻으로 사용되었다. '~에 따르면'이라는 뜻으로 'according to'를 사용할 수 있다. weather forecast: 일기 예보

10 scenery: 경치, 풍경 this time of year: 이맘때는, 이맘때쯤

이면

11 be covered with: ~로 덮여 있다

12 ⓐ 수민이는 어디를 갈 예정인가?(남산) ⓑ 남산에는 얼마나 많은 하이킹 코스가 있는가?(모른다.) ⓒ 어디서 남자아이가 한강의 가장 짧은 코스를 찾는가?(한강이 아니라 남산이다.) ⓓ 무슨 요일에 그들은 만날 것인가?(일요일) ⓔ 수민이는 이번 일요일에 무엇을 할 예정인가?(등산을 갈 것이다.)

13 during은 다음에 명사(구)가 이어지고, while은 다음에 절(주어+동사)이 이어진다.

14 ① who → whose, ② of which → whose, ③ of whose → whose, ④ window → the window

15 소유격 관계대명사 whose를 활용한다.

16 시간의 접속사가 이끄는 부사절에서는 미래의 의미일지라도 현재 시제를 쓴다.

17 (1) 뒤에 명사가 이어지고 완전한 절이 나오므로 소유격 관계대명사로 whose 또는 'of which'를 쓴다. (2) 선행사가 The girl로 사람일 때, 소유격 관계대명사는 whose만 가능하다. (3) 시간의 접속사가 이끄는 부사절에서는 미래의 의미일지라도 현재시제를 쓴다.

18 ① the 생략 ② of which price → whose price 또는 of which the price ③ will be → is ④ as soon as → until

19 ③ exactly: 정확히, ⓐ와 ①, ②, ④, ⑤: 실제로는

20 혹등고래들은 '꼬리로' 선 채로 '수면' 근처에서 잠을 자며, 그들은 '완전히' 잠들지 않는다.

21 breathe는 동사이므로 명사형인 breath로 고쳐야 한다.

22 'humpback whale들이 심호흡을 하러 얼마나 자주 물 밖으로 나오는지'는 알 수 없다. ① No, they don't. sleep on one's side: 옆으로 누워서 자다, ② No, they aren't. ③ Because they are not fish. ④ They come out of the water for a deep breath and dive back into the sea.

23 이 글은 'tuskfish가 가장 좋아하는 먹이인 조개를 열기 위해 도구를 사용하는 것'에 관한 글이므로, 주제로는 ②번 'tuskfish는 조개를 열기 위해 도구를 사용하는 똑똑한 물고기이다'가 적절하다.

24 '조개'를 가리킨다.

25 have you ever seen: 현재완료 경험 용법, 지각동사 see+목적어+동사원형: (목적어)가 ~하는 것을 보다

26 주어진 문장의 its size에 주목한다. ②번 앞 문장의 내용을 받고 있으므로 ②번이 적절하다.

27 hundred 다음에는 보통 and를 넣어서 읽고, 쓸 때는 cm과 kg이라고 써도, 읽을 때는 centimeters와 kilograms라고 읽는 것이 적절하다.

Lesson **8**

Up to You

01 ①, ④번은 동사 뒤에 행위자를 나타내는 접미사 '-er'을 붙여 명사형으로 만들 수 있다. ① produce: 생산하다 producer: 생산자 ② invent: 발명하다 inventor: 발명가 ③ protect: 보호하다 protector: 보호자 ④ educate: 교육하다 educator: 교육자 ⑤ collect: 모으다 collector: 수집가

02 ① contribute: 기여하다, 공헌하다 / 모든 사람들이 토론에 참여해 주시기 바랍니다. ② should have+과거분사: ~했어야 했다 / 그는 더 조심했어야 했다. ③ including: 포함해서 / 뷔페식 아침식사를 포함해서 1박에 150달러입니다. ④ active: 활동적인, 적극적인 / 그녀는 지역 정치에 적극 관여하고 있다. ⑤ describe: 기술하다, 묘사하다 / 내 심정은 말로는 다 표현할 수 없다.

03 report: 보도하다 / 신문, TV 또는 라디오를 통해서 무언가에 관한 정보를 주다

04 주어진 문장에서 move는 '(남을) 감동시키다'의 의미로 사용하여 '그러한 친절함에 의해 나는 깊이 감동받았다.'로 해석된다. ① 그들은 꽤 자주 집을 이사한다. ② 그녀는 빠르게 문으로 이동했다. ③ 자동차를 이동시켜 줄 수 있나요? ④ 이 이야기들은 나를 놀라게 했으며 감동시켰다. ⑤ 그의 연설은 청중에게 감동을 주어 눈물을 자아냈다.

05 be grateful for: ~에 감사하다 appreciate: 감사하다 / 도와주셔서 감사합니다

06 thanks to 명사: ~ 덕분에 / 오늘은 좋은 날씨 덕분에 일찍 도착했다.

07 rather than: ~보다는 / 그는 새로운 규칙을 받아들이기 보다는 그만두기로 결정했다.

01 winner   02 (p)articipate

03 catch   04 keep

05 (d)ynamite, (h)eadline, (m)erchant

   (1) headline   (2) merchant   (3) dynamite

06 (1) His new book is due to be published next year.

   (2) The film is described as a highly charged thriller.

(3) I won't make the same mistake again.

(4) It was fine until we got caught in the rain at the picnic.

01 '-or'은 '~하는 사람(행위자)'이라는 의미를 만들어 주는 접미사이다. '-or'과 더불어 동사 뒤에 붙어 행위자를 나타내는 명사형 접미사에는 '-er'이 있다. act: 연기하다, actor: 연기자, win: 우승하다, winner: 우승자

02 engage in: ~에 참가하다 participate in: ~에 참가하다 / 전교생이 자원봉사에 참가해야 한다.

03 catch one's breath: 숨을 고르다 / 숨을 고르기 위해서 Clark 는 앉아야 했다. catch one's eye: 눈길을 끌다 / 내 눈길을 끄는 몇몇 그림들이 있다.

04 keep in touch: 연락하고 지내다 / 너 그와 계속 연락하고 지내니? keep -ing: 계속해서 ~하다 / 왜 계속 그런 식으로 말해?

05 (1) headline: (신문 기사 등의) 표제 / 신문 기사에 큰 글씨로 쓰여진 제목 / 오늘 신문 헤드라인 보셨어요? (2) merchant: 상인 / 대량으로 상품을 파는 사람 / 그 상인은 중국에서 산 물품에 관세를 냈다. (3) dynamite: 다이너마이트 / 강력한 폭약, 폭발물 / 그들은 큰 돌들을 깨기 위해 다이너마이트를 이용했다.

06 (1) due: ~하기로 되어 있는, 예정된 (2) describe A as B: A를 B로 기술하다, 묘사하다 (3) make a mistake: 실수하다 (4) get caught in the rain: 비를 만나다

교과서
Conversation

핵심 Check
p.66~67

1 (1) I should have studied hard.

(2) I should not have been late for school.

2 ②

교과서 대화문 익히기

Check(√) True or False
p.68~69

1 F 2 T 3 T 4 T 5 F 6 F 7 T 8 F

교과서 확인학습
p.71~73

Listen and Speak 1 A
were you late for / stomachache / Are / should have eaten

Listen and Speak 1 B
up, tired / stayed up late / again / not, had to / due / shouldn't have put it off until / the same / try to change, habits

Listen and Speak 1 C
1. wrong / got caught in / sorry to / have taken
2. What's / failed / hear that / should have studied hard
3. lost / I should have chained
4. was late for / should have got up early

Listen and Speak 2 A
going to do during / lots of, about / visit / hope you have

Listen and Speak 2 B
ready for / I'm thinking of giving up / wanted to take part in / good singer / the best singer I know / think so / voice / you for saying, do my best / I hope you win

Listen and Speak 2 C
1. going to sing / hope you move, audience / hope so
2. hope you score a goal
3. participate in / I hope you win / I hope so

Real Life Talk Watch a Video
graduation / looks like, a lot to say / wrote that / else / Some of them, hang out enough with / fault, should have spent more time with / after graduation / hope you keep in touch with / I hope so

Real Life Talk Step 2
1. can't believe / there anything, regret / should have been active / have a second chance / guess / hope you are active
2. believe we're graduating / anything you regret about / should have taken / guess, right / hope you take part in

시험대비 기본평가
p.74

01 ②   02 ①   03 ③

01 B는 학교 축제에서 노래를 부를 거라고 말하고 있다. A는 B가 노래를 불러서 청중을 감동시키는 것을 희망하는 표현을 할 수 있다. move: (남을) 감동시키다

02 'should have 과거분사'는 '~했어야 했는데 (하지 못했다.)'의 의미로 후회를 표현할 때 쓰는 표현이다. 'I should have+과거분사 ~.'는 'I'm sorry I didn't[wasn't] ~.' 또는 'I regret that I didn't[wasn't] ~.'로 바꿔 쓸 수 있다.

03 (C) 내일 무엇을 할지 예정에 대해 질문을 하자 (A) 상대방은 연설 대회에 참가할 것이라고 대답한다. (B) 멋지다고 말하며, 대회에서 우승하기를 기원하는 말을 덧붙인다. (D) 이에 대해 고마움을 표현하고 자신도 우승하기를 바란다고 말한다.

시험대비 실력평가 p.75~76

01 ③	02 ②	03 ⑤	04 ③
05 ④	06 ②	07 ④	08 ③
09 my classmates		10 ⑤	

01 어젯밤에 늦게까지 깨어 있었다는 B의 말에 또 컴퓨터 게임을 했는지 물어보자, 이번에는 아니라는 대답과 함께 역사 과제를 끝내야 했다는 말을 하는 것이 어울리며 'Is it due today?'에서 it은 'my history project'를 가리키는 것이므로 ③이 적절하다.

02 'should not have+과거분사'는 '~하지 말았어야 했는데 (해 버렸다)'의 의미이다. 위의 대화에서 지호가 역사 과제를 마지막 순간까지 미루지 말았어야 했다는 말이 어울리므로 ②가 적절하다. put off: 미루다, 연기하다

03 지호와 G 둘 다 과제를 마지막 순간까지 미루는 문제를 가지고 있으므로, 우리의 나쁜 습관을 바꾸도록 노력하자고 말하고 있는 ⑤번이 빈칸에 어울린다.

04 곧 졸업하는 것에 대해 놀라움을 표현하고, (C) 상대방의 의견에 동의하면서 중학교 생활에서 후회하는 것이 있는지 질문한다. (A) 그렇다고 대답하며 학교 행사에 많이 참여 했어야 했다고 말한다. (B) 고등학교에서 다시 한 번 기회가 있다고 말하자 (D) 그 의견에 동의한다.

05 주어진 문장은 노래 경연 대회에 나가는 것을 포기하려고 하는 재민에게 '너는 내가 아는 노래를 가장 잘하는 사람이야.'라고 말하고 있는 문장이다. 또한 'Do you really think so?'에서 so가 받는 것은 주어진 문장의 내용이므로, 주어진 문장은 ④에 들어가는 것이 적절하다.

06 give up: 포기하다

07 A가 시드니에 많이 가 본 적이 있다고 했는데 A가 언젠가 시드니를 방문할 수 있기를 기원하는 말을 하는 것은 어색하다.

08 주어진 문장의 That은 Linda가 친구들과 충분히 어울리지 않았다는 내용으로 ③이 적절하다.

09 them은 앞에 언급된 my classmates(나의 학급 친구들)을 의미한다.

10 'Some of them said I didn't hang out enough with them.(그들 중 몇몇은 내가 그들과 충분히 어울리지 않았다고 말했어.)'이라고 하고 있으므로 Linda의 친구들은 Linda가 친구들과 많은 시간을 보내지 않았다고 생각한다.

서술형 시험대비 p.77

01 I should not[shouldn't] have eaten more last night.
02 (A) for (B) of
03 I hope you win the contest.
04 up
05 ⓓ, I shouldn't put it off until the last moment. → I shouldn't have put it off until the last moment.
06 I should have been active in classes.

01 밑줄 친 문장은 '어젯밤에 덜 먹었어야 했어.'의 의미로 '어젯밤에 더 먹지 말았어야 했어.'와 같으므로 less 대신에 more를 사용해서 문장을 만들 수 있다. 'should have 과거분사'는 '~했어야 했는데 (하지 못했다.)'의 의미로 후회를 표현할 때 사용하는 표현이며 'should not have+과거분사'는 '~하지 말았어야 했는데 (해 버렸다.)'의 의미이다.

02 (A) be ready for ~: ~의 준비가 되다 (B) I'm thinking of ~: '나는 ~할까 생각 중이다'라는 뜻으로 of 뒤에 동명사를 취해 의도나 계획을 나타낼 때 쓰는 표현이다.

03 'I hope you ~.'는 '나는 네가 ~하기를 바란다[희망한다].'라는 뜻으로 상대방에게 기원하는 말을 할 때 쓸 수 있는 표현이다. win: 이기다 contest: 대회

04 stay up: 안 자다, 깨어 있다

05 지금 '~하지 말아야 한다'의 의미가 아니라 과거에 '숙제를 마지막 순간까지 미루지 말았어야 했다'로 사용해야 하므로, 'should not have+과거분사(~하지 말았어야 했는데 (해 버렸다.))'를 사용해야 한다.

06 'I should have+과거분사 ~.'는 '나는 ~했어야 했다.'라는 뜻으로 과거 사실에 대한 후회를 표현할 때 사용한다. active: 적극적인

교과서

Grammar

핵심 Check p.78~79

1 (1) Living (2) Felt
2 (1) had done (2) had not turned (3) had

01 ①

02 (1) Reading   (2) Not knowing   (3) had   (4) visited

03 ⑤

04 (1) Watching TV, she ate dinner.

    (2) The article said Alfred Nobel had died in France from a heart attack.

01 접속사 없이 '주어+동사'가 이어지고 있으므로 빈칸에는 '접속사+주어+동사'의 역할을 할 수 있는 현재분사로(내가 늦은 것은 능동의 의미이므로) 분사구문이 되어야 한다.

02 (1) 접속사가 없으므로 '접속사+주어+동사'의 역할을 할 수 있는 Reading이 적절하다. (2) 분사구문의 부정은 분사 앞에 'not'이나 'never'를 쓴다. (3) 도착한 것이 그가 떠난 다음이므로 떠난 것을 과거완료로 나타내는 것이 적절하다. (4) 과거완료는 'had+과거분사'의 형태로, 과거 이전에 일어난 일이 과거의 어느 시점까지 영향을 미칠 때 쓴다.

03 돈을 가져간 것이 실토한 것보다 앞서므로 과거완료로 나타내는 것이 적절하다.

04 (1) Watching을 '접속사+주어+동사'의 역할을 하는 분사로 하여 알맞게 배열한다. (2) 프랑스에서 죽은 것이 기사가 쓰여진 것보다 앞선 시제이므로 과거완료로 나타내는 것이 적절하다.

01 ③   02 ④   03 ①   04 ②

05 (1) had already left   (2) had done   (3) had never been   (4) Running   (5) talking   (6) knowing

06 ⑤   07 ②   08 Being   09 ③

10 ④   11 Mom had bought for me

12 ②   13 ④   14 (1) he was   (2) she was   15 had   16 ③   17 ①

01 washes라는 동사가 있고 접속사가 없으므로 listens를 listening으로 분사구문으로 만들어야 한다. She washes away the fatigue of the day listening to music.

02 주어진 문장과 ④번은 결과 용법이다. ①, ② 계속 ③ 경험 ⑤ 완료

03 뒤에 left라는 동사가 있고 접속사가 없으므로 thought를 thinking으로 바꿔 분사구문으로 만들어야 한다. 분사구문이 문장의 중간에 삽입된 형태이다.

04 첫 번째 빈칸에는 접속사가 없으므로 '접속사+주어+동사'의 역할을 할 수 있는 feeling이 적절하다. 두 번째 빈칸에는 밤에 비가 온 것이 앞선 시제이므로 'had rained'가 적절하다.

05 (1) '도착했을 때 이미 떠난 것'이므로 '완료'를 나타내는 과거완료가 적절하다. (2) '자신이 한 짓에 대해 용서를 구했다.'라는

뜻으로 용서를 구하는 시점 이전에 한 것이므로 과거완료가 적절하다. (3) 'Until last week'이 있으므로 그때까지의 경험을 나타내는 과거완료가 적절하다. (4) 접속사가 없으므로 '접속사+주어+동사'의 역할을 할 수 있는 분사구문으로 쓰는 것이 적절하다. (5) 분사구문의 뜻을 명확히 하기 위해 접속사 While을 생략하지 않고 남겨둔 경우이다. (6) 분사구문의 부정은 분사 앞에 'not'이나 'never'를 쓴다.

06 '접속사+주어+동사'의 부사절을 분사구문으로 바꾸어 쓸 수 있다. 이때, 분사구문의 뜻을 명확히 하기 위해 접속사를 생략하지 않기도 하지만 주어를 생략하지는 않는다.

07 We talked about what had happened the previous week. 말하는 시점인 과거보다 더 앞선 시점인 지난주에 일어난 일이므로 과거완료로 쓰는 것이 적절하다.

08 한 문장으로 쓰면 'Because[As] I was nervous, I forgot my lines at the school musical.'이고, 분사구문으로 바꾸면 'Because[As] I was'를 현재분사 Being으로 써야 한다.

09 Sam이 도착한 것은 과거로 쓰고, '가고 없었다'는 '결과'의 의미를 나타내기 위해서는 과거완료의 '결과'로 쓰는 것이 적절하다.

10 'Because she was tired, she came back home early.'를 분사구문으로 바르게 바꾼 것은 ④번이다.

11 사준 것이 잃어버린 것보다 먼저이고 현재 갖고 있지 않은 결과까지 나타내려면 과거완료로 쓰는 것이 적절하다.

12 주어진 문장과 ②번은 '이유'를 나타낸다. ① 양보, ③ 시간, ④ 동시동작, ⑤ 조건

13 주어진 문장과 ④번은 '완료'를 나타낸다. ①, ③ 경험, ② 결과, ⑤ 계속

14 부사절에서 주어가 주절의 주어와 같을 때 '주어+be동사'를 생략할 수 있으며 이것은 분사구문으로 고쳤을 때 being을 생략하고 접속사를 남겨둔 것과 같다.

15 before나 after가 있는 경우 시간의 순서가 분명하기 때문에 흔히 대과거를 나타내는 과거완료 대신에 과거로 쓰기도 한다.

16 부사절과 주절의 주어가 다를 때는 부사절의 주어를 생략하지 않으며 이것을 독립분사구문이라고 한다.

17 '집에 열쇠를 둔 것'이 '그것을 알아차린' 시점보다 앞서므로 알아차린 주절은 과거로 쓰고, 열쇠를 둔 것은 과거완료로 쓰는 것이 적절하다.

01 (1) Getting up too late, I missed the school bus.

    (2) Talking on the phone, he watered the plants.

    (3) Having a problem, ask the teacher.

    (4) Knowing it was wrong, she wouldn't change it.

    (5) Not having any money, I couldn't buy a bike.

    (6) The weather being good, we'll eat out.

02 (1) They couldn't find the treasure because[as,

since] Mr. Joe had hidden it under the sea.

(2) When[As] I arrived at home, Lucky had already fallen asleep.

03 (1) Seen from the mountains, the landscape is green and beautiful.

(2) Being sick, I had to stay home all day.

(3) She had just finished her task when the teacher came in.

(4) They ran to the platform, but the train had just gone.

04 (1) disappointing → disappointed

(2) Taking → Having taken

05 had never been   06 Arriving

07 (1) Leaving right now, you won't miss the train. / If you leave right now, you won't miss the train.

(2) Running to me, she waved her hand. / As she ran to me, she waved her hand.

(3) He had studied Chinese for two years before he went to China.

08 (1) My grandmother had been ill for five days when I visited her.

(2) The ground was covered with snow because it had snowed during the night.

(3) Walking in the park, he met an old friend.

(4) It getting so cold outside, the rain changed into snow.

(5) Made of thick trees, the doors looked unbreakable.

(6) Having eaten dinner, he was not hungry.

01 '접속사+주어+동사'로 이루어진 부사절의 주어가 주절의 주어와 일치할 때 접속사와 주어를 생략하고 동사를 분사(동사원형+-ing)로 만든다. (1) '이유', (2) '동시동작' (3) '조건' (4) '양보' (5) 분사구문의 부정은 분사 앞에 'not'이나 'never'를 쓴다. (6) 주절의 주어와 부사절의 주어가 다르므로 주어를 생략하면 안 된다.(독립분사구문)

02 의미상 어울리는 접속사를 사용하여 한 문장으로 쓰되, 먼저 일어난 사건을 과거완료를 이용하여 쓴다.

03 (1) 과거분사로 시작되는 분사구문은 being이 생략된 것으로 수동의 의미를 갖는다. (2) 현재분사가 분사구문을 이끌도록 한다. (3) 일을 끝마친 것이 앞선 시점이므로 과거완료의 '완료'로 나타낸다. (4) 이미 기차가 출발해서 탈 수 없었으므로 '결과'를 나타내는 과거완료를 이용한다.

04 (1) '실망한'이라는 '수동'의 의미가 되어야 하므로 과거분사 disappointed로 고쳐야 한다. (2) 부사절의 시제가 주절보다 앞선 경우에는 완료분사구문으로 쓴다. 'After he had taken his holiday, he came back refreshed.'를 분사구문으로 고친 것이다.

05 '~에 가 본 적이 없었다'라는 경험을 나타내기 위해서는 과거완료로 쓰는 것이 적절하다. have been to: ~에 가 본 적이 있다

06 'When he arrived ~'를 부사구문으로 고쳐 쓴다.

07 (1), (2) '접속사+주어+동사'로 이루어진 부사절의 주어가 주절의 주어와 일치할 때 접속사와 주어를 생략하고 동사를 분사(동사원형+-ing)로 만들어서 분사구문으로 바꿔 쓴다. (3) 2년 동안 계속 공부했으므로 '계속'을 나타내는 과거완료를 쓴다.

08 (1) 뒤에 'for five days'라는 기간이 나오므로 'had been ill'로 '계속'을 나타내는 것이 적절하다. (2) '밤에 눈이 와서 땅이 눈으로 덮인 것'이므로 눈이 온 것을 과거완료로 쓰고, 눈으로 덮인 것을 과거로 쓰는 것이 적절하다. (3) 산책하는 것은 능동이므로 현재분사를 쓰는 것이 적절하다. (4) 주절의 주어와 부사절의 주어가 다르므로 독립분사구문으로 써야 한다. (5) Being이 생략된 분사구문으로, '만드는' 것이 아니라 '만들어진' 것이므로 Making을 Made로 고쳐야 한다. (6) 시제가 앞서므로 완료분사구문으로 써야 한다.

교과서 Reading

확인문제   p.86

1 T   2 F   3 T   4 F

확인문제   p.87

1 T   2 F   3 T   4 F   5 T   6 F

교과서 확인학습 A   p.88~89

01 How, Be Remembered   02 normal morning

03 sat in his chair   04 caught his eye

06 in surprise   07 take his eyes off

08 his own death   09 from a heart attack

10 my goodness   11 Catching his breath

12 even more shocked   13 described, as

14 had become rich   15 couldn't believe

16 one of his many inventions

17 think of, as   18 disappointed

19 How   20 unbelievable

21 merchant of death   22 in a different way

23 be remembered, the world better

24 to change people's opinions

25 mistakenly

26 who had actually died

27 Thanks to, contribute to   28 to create

29 only five awards   30 sixth award

31 rather than

1 How Will You Be Remembered?

2 It was just a normal morning.

3 Alfred Nobel sat in his chair to read the newspaper.

4 While he was drinking his coffee, a headline caught his eye: *The Merchant of Death, Alfred Nobel, Is Dead.*

5 "What? What is this?"

6 Reading the article, he dropped his cup in surprise.

7 His coffee spilled all over his clothes and desk, but he couldn't take his eyes off the newspaper.

8 The article was about his own death!

9 It said Nobel had died in France from a heart attack.

10 "Oh my goodness! Am I dead?"

11 Catching his breath, Nobel kept reading.

12 Soon, he became even more shocked.

13 The article described him as the inventor of dynamite and other dangerous objects for war.

14 It said that he had become rich from the deaths of others.

15 He couldn't believe his eyes.

16 It was true that dynamite was one of his many inventions.

17 But he never imagined that the world would think of him as "the merchant of death."

18 Nobel was deeply disappointed.

19 "How could this be?

20 This is unbelievable!

21 I'm not a merchant of death.

22 I want to be remembered in a different way.

23 I want to be remembered as a person who made the world better."

24 He decided to change people's opinions about him.

25 In 1888, a French newspaper mistakenly reported Alfred Nobel's death.

26 The person who had actually died was his brother, Ludvig.

27 Thanks to the report, however, Nobel decided to do something to contribute to the world.

28 In 1895, he decided to use his money to create the Nobel Prize.

29 Originally, there were only five awards.

30 A sixth award was added in 1968.

31 Today, when we think of Alfred Nobel, we think of the Nobel Prize, rather than dynamite.

01 ④   02 ②   03 ⑤   04 The article   05 ②   06 ③

07 (A) dynamite   (B) the merchant of death   08 as a person who made the world better   09 He decided to change people's opinions about him.

10 ⑤   11 was added   12 ②

13 from   14 ②, ③, ⑤   15 ②, ③   16 who 또는 that   17 disappointing → disappointed

18 ⑤   19 ④   20 ③   21 ①

22 ③   23 (A) mistakenly   (B) actually   (C) A sixth award was added   24 ⑤

01 ⓐ와 ④: ~하고 있는 동안에(접속사), ① 잠깐 동안(명사), ②, ⑤: [주절 뒤에서 반대·비교·대조를 나타내어] 그런데, 한편(으로는)(접속사), ③ (시간을) 빈둥빈둥 보내다(동사)

02 ② 중반부의 "What? What is this?"와 'he dropped his cup in surprise'를 통해 'embarrassed and confused'를 찾을 수 있다. embarrassed; 당황스러운, confused: 혼란스러워 하는, ① nervous: 불안해[초조해]하는, anxious: 불안해하는, ③ disappointed: 실망한, depressed: 우울한, ⑤ ashamed: 부끄러운

03 '그는 신문에서 눈을 뗄 수 없었다.'고 했다. ignore: 무시하다

04 It은 앞 문장의 'The article'을 가리킨다.

05 very는 원급을 강조하고, ⓑ와 나머지는 비교급을 강조한다.

06 ⓒ와 ③: 대과거 용법(과거에 일어난 두 가지 일 중 더 먼저 일어난 일을 나타냄.), ①, ⑤: 경험 용법, ②, ④: 계속 용법

07 Nobel은 전쟁에 쓰이는 '다이너마이트'와 다른 위험한 물건들을 발명함으로써 부자가 되었지만, 그것들은 많은 사람들을 죽일 수 있었기 때문에 기사에서 그를 '죽음의 상인'으로 기술했다.

08 '다르게' 기억되고 싶다는 것은 '세상을 더 좋게 만든 사람으로' 기억되고 싶다는 것을 가리킨다.

09 decide는 to부정사를 목적어로 취하는 동사이다.

10 사람들이 Nobel을 세상을 더 좋게 만든 사람으로 기억한 것이 아니라, Nobel 자신이 세상을 더 좋게 만든 사람으로 기억되고 싶다고 했을 뿐이다.

11 여섯 번째 상이 '추가되었다'고 해야 하므로 수동태로 쓰는 것이 적절하다.

17

12 이 글은 '한 프랑스 신문의 실수로 인한 보도 덕분에, Nobel이 세상에 공헌하기 위해 무언가를 하기로 결심하고 자신의 돈을 노벨상을 만드는 데 사용하기로 결정했다'는 내용의 글이므로, 제목으로는 ②번 '실수가 귀중한 결과로 이어졌다!'가 적절하다.

13 ⓐ die from: ~으로 죽다, ⓑ from: [원인·이유] ~으로 인해

14 (A)와 ②, ③, ⑤: 현재분사, ①, ④: 동명사

15 (B) think of/regard/look upon/see A as B: A를 B로 생각하다[여기다] ② respect: 존경하다 ③ discuss: 상의[의논/논의]하다

16 주격 관계대명사 'who' 또는 'that'을 쓰는 것이 적절하다.

17 감정을 나타내는 동사의 분사가 형용사로 쓰일 때, 감정을 느끼게 되는 경우에 과거분사를 써야 하므로 disappointed로 고치는 것이 적절하다.

18 (B)와 ①, ②, ③, ④: [역할·자격·기능·성질 따위를 나타내어] ~으로, ⑤: 예를 들면 ~와[같은](= such as, like)

19 '이건 믿을 수 없어! 나는 죽음의 상인이 아니야.'라는 Nobel의 말로 미루어, 앞에 올 내용으로는 'Nobel이 죽음의 상인으로 언급되었다'가 적절하다.

20 ⓐ in surprise: 놀라서, ⓑ off: [분리·이탈] ~으로부터, ~에서 떨어져; ~에서 벗어나, can't take one's eyes off ~: ~에서 눈을 뗄 수 없다

21 ①번 다음 문장의 a headline에 주목한다. 주어진 문장의 the newspaper의 headline을 가리키는 것이므로 ①번이 적절하다.

22 앞에 나오는 내용과 상반되는 내용이 뒤에 이어지므로 however가 가장 적절하다. ② 그 결과, ④ 즉[말하자면], ⑤ 게다가, 더욱이

23 (A) '실수로' Alfred Nobel의 죽음을 보도했다고 해야 하므로 mistakenly가 적절하다. mistakenly: 실수로, purposely: 고의로, (B) '실제로' 죽은 사람이라고 해야 하므로 actually가 적절하다. actually: 실제로, accidentally: 우연히, 뜻하지 않게, (C) '여섯 번째 상이 추가되었다'고 해야 하므로 A sixth award was added가 적절하다. A sixth award: 여섯 번째 상

24 '왜 상을 한 개 더 덧었는지'는 알 수 없다. ① In 1888. ② No. ③ He decided to use his money to create the Nobel Prize. ④ Originally, there were only five awards.

서술형 시험대비   p.96~97

01 As → Is

02 "죽음의 상인, Alfred Nobel 사망하다"라는 기사 제목

03 As[When] he read the article

04 headline

05 the world would think of him as "the merchant of death

06 Nobel's brother → Nobel

07 (A) more shocked   (B) the deaths of others

08 be remembered

09 (A) deeply   (B) unbelievable   (C) to change

10 merchant

11 (A) disappointed   (B) the world better

12 ⓐ eighteen eighty-eight   ⓑ eighteen ninety-five
   ⓒ nineteen sixty-eight

13 (A) the Nobel Prize   (B) dynamite

14 Ludvig

01 'The Merchant of Death'와 'Alfred Nobel'은 동격이므로 Are를 Is로 고치는 것이 적절하다.

02 this는 앞 문장의 'The Merchant of Death, Alfred Nobel, Is Dead'라고 적힌 headline을 가리킨다.

03 접속사 As[When]를 사용하여 고치는 것이 적절하다.

04 신문의 '기사 제목'을 읽고 놀랐기 때문이다.

05 think of A as B: A를 B로 생각하다[여기다]

06 기사에는 'Nobel'이 심장 마비로 프랑스에서 죽었다고 쓰여 있었다.

07 기사에서 Nobel이 '다른 사람들의 죽음'으로 인해 부유해졌다고 말하면서, 그를 전쟁에 쓰이는 다이너마이트와 다른 위험한 물건의 발명가로 기술했기 때문에 Nobel은 훨씬 '더 충격을 받게' 되었다.

08 '기억되고 싶다'고 해야 하므로 수동태로 쓰는 것이 적절하다.

09 (A) '몹시' 실망했다고 해야 하므로 deeply가 적절하다. deep: 깊은; (깊이가) 깊게, deeply: (대단히·몹시의 뜻으로) 깊이[크게], (B) '이건 '믿을 수 없어!'라고 해야 하므로 unbelievable이 적절하다. reasonable: 타당한, 합리적인, unbelievable: 믿을 수 없는, 믿기 어려운, (C) decide는 to부정사를 목적어로 취하는 동사이므로 to change가 적절하다.

10 대량으로 상품을 사거나 파는 사람, 특히 상품을 수입하고 수출하는 사람, merchant: (상품을 대규모로 매매하는) 상인, (특히) 무역상

11 Nobel은 죽음의 상인이라고 언급되어서 몹시 '실망했고', 그래서 사람들이 자신을 '세상을 더 좋게' 만든 사람으로 기억해주기를 원했다.

12 연도는 두 자리씩 끊어 읽고, 십 단위와 단 단위 사이에 보통 하이픈을 쓰는 것이 적절하다.

13 오늘날 우리가 Alfred Nobel을 생각할 때, 우리는 '다이너마이트'보다는 '노벨상'을 떠올린다. B rather than A = B more than A: A라기보다는 B

14 실제로 죽은 사람은 Alfred Nobel의 형인 'Ludvig'였다.

01 ①   02 ④   03 ②

04 unbelievable   05 I'm thinking of giving up

06 (A) take   (B) do   07 ③

08 (A) late   (B) to change   09 due

10 I shouldn't have put it off until the last moment.

11 ③

12 I should have spent more time with my classmates.

13 ③   14 ⑤   15 It being   16 ⑤

17 (1) When Mina returned home, her brother had eaten all her cookies.

  (2) When the waiter finally arrived with the food, the guests had already left the restaurant.

18 (1) Though[Although] it's a thrilling movie

  (2) Because[As] I felt hungry

  (3) If you turn left

19 ⓓ, ⓔ, ⓗ   20 deaths   21 ②

22 The person who had actually died was his brother, Ludvig.

23 ②, ⑤   24 (A) contribute to   (B) the Nobel Prize

25 ⑤   26 ④   27 ③   28 ②

29 ②

---

01 disappointed: 실망한, 낙담한 / 나는 내가 부정적이어서 실망스럽다.

02 create: 창조하다, 만들어 내다 / 그 새로운 공장이 400개가 넘는 일자리를 만들어 낼 것이라고 예상된다.

03 (A) give it a try: 시도하다 / 어렵겠지만 한번 해 볼게요. (B) put off: 미루다, 연기하다 / 그 경기는 날씨가 나빠서 내일까지 미뤄졌다.

04 unbelievable: 믿을 수 없는, 믿기 어려운 / 우리는 파리에서 믿기 어려울 정도로 멋진 시간을 보냈다.

05 'I'm thinking of ~'는 '나는 ~할까 생각 중이다'라는 뜻으로 of 뒤에 동명사를 취해 의도나 계획을 나타낼 때 쓰는 표현이다. give up: 포기하다

06 (A) take part in: ~에 참가하다 (B) do one's best: 최선을 다하다

07 노래 경연대회에 나가는 Jaemin에게 Tina는 Jaemin이 대회에서 우승하기를 기원하는 말을 할 수 있다.

08 (A) stay up: 안 자다, 깨어 있다 late: 늦게 lately: 최근에 (B) try to 동사원형: ~하기 위해 노력하다, try 동사ing: 시험 삼아 ~해 보다

09 due: ~하기로 되어 있는[예정된] / 어떤 특정한 때 예정되어 있거나 계획된

10 should not[shouldn't] have+과거분사: ~하지 말았어야 했다, put off: 미루다, 연기하다

11 주어진 문장의 뜻은 '그 외에는?'의 의미로 졸업 메시지에 많은 친구가 Linda의 미소를 좋아한다 말을 썼다는 말에, 상대방이 '그 외에는?'이라고 말하고 'Some of them said I didn't hang out enough with them.(그들 중 몇몇은 내가 그들과 충분히 어울리지 않았다고 말했어.)'을 이어서 얘기하는 것이 적절하다.

12 should have+과거분사: ~했어야 했다 spend+시간+with ~: ~와 시간을 보내다

13 When I got up, she had already gone to work. 일어나기 전에 이미 가버린 것이므로 일어난 것은 과거로, 가버린 것은 과거완료로 써야 한다.

14 주어진 문장은 '이유'를 나타내는 분사구문이다.

15 'As it was ~'를 부사구문으로 고쳐 쓴다. 주절의 주어와 부사절의 주어가 다르므로 주어를 생략하면 안 된다.(독립분사구문)

16 'As he had not told the truth the previous day, he fell in danger.'를 분사구문으로 쓴 것이므로 telling을 'having told'로 고쳐야 한다.

17 과거완료는 과거보다 한 시제 앞서는 대과거를 나타낼 수 있으므로 앞서는 사건을 과거완료로 쓴다.

18 (1) 내용상 '양보'의 부사절이 적절하다. (2) 내용상 '이유'의 부사절이 적절하다. (3) 내용상 '조건'의 부사절이 적절하다.

19 ⓐ Read → Reading ⓑ Being not → Not being ⓒ Seeing → Seen ⓕ has → had ⓖ stayed → had stayed, had returned → returned

20 수천 명의 사람들의 '죽음'에 대해 책임이 있다고 하는 것이 적절하다. be responsible for: ~에 대해 책임이 있다, ~의 원인이 되다

21 위 글은 '(신문,잡지의) 기사'이다. ③ 수필, ⑤ (책,연극,영화 등에 대한) 논평[비평], 감상문

22 주격 관계대명사 who가 주어 The person을 수식하도록 쓰는 것이 적절하다.

23 ⓑ와 ②, ⑤: 명사적 용법, ①, ④: 형용사적 용법, ③: 부사적 용법

24 한 프랑스 신문의 부정확한 보도 덕분에, Nobel이 세상에 '공헌하기' 위해 무언가를 하기로 결심하고 자신의 돈을 '노벨상'을 만드는 데 사용하기로 결정했다.

25 ⓐ와 ⑤: 때, ① 조건, ②와 ④: 양보, ③ 이유

26 '글쓴이가 UNICEF에 얼마나 많은 돈을 기부했는지'는 대답할 수 없다. ① The writer donated money to children in Africa. ② Because the writer wanted to make a difference for children in need. ③ The writer didn't buy snacks for a month. ⑤ Now the writer really appreciate his or her meals.

27 주어진 문장의 It에 주목한다. ③번 앞 문장의 The article을 받고 있으므로 ③번이 적절하다.

19

28 이 글은 '자신을 '죽음의 상인'이라고 묘사한 기사를 읽고 Nobel이 충격을 받게 되는 내용'의 글이므로, 제목으로는 ②번 '오, 이럴 수가! 내가 '죽음의 상인'이라고?'가 적절하다.

29 ② 숨을 고른 후, Nobel은 '계속 기사를 읽었다.'

p.104~107

단원별 예상문제

01 ③　　　　02 ③　　　　03 (t)ook
04 (1) graduation　(2) director
05 shouldn't have got up　06 ⑤　　07 out
08 ④　　　　09 (A) that　(B) after　10 ⑤
11 (A) to finish　(B) have put it off　12 ①
13 ②, ④　　14 had just left　　15 ②
16 had become
17 (A) dead　(B) shocked　(C) objects　18 ④
19 in order that, might[could] create
20 Because he wanted to honor people who made the world better.
21 ②　　　22 ③, ⑤　　23 ②　　24 ①

01 <보기>의 단어의 관계는 동의어 관계이다. move: 감동시키다, touch: 감동을 주다 ⓒ, ⓓ는 동의어 관계이며 이외의 보기는 반의어 관계이다. ⓐ active: 활동적인, inactive: 활동이 없는 ⓑ including: ~을 포함해서, excluding: ~을 제외하고 ⓒ normal: 보통의, ordinary: 보통의 ⓓ decide: 결정하다, determine: 결정하다 ⓔ satisfied: 만족한, dissatisfied: 불만족한

02 (A) be over: 끝나다 / 우리가 도착했을 때쯤에는 그 모임이 끝났다. (B) get caught in: ~에 사로잡히다 / 교통체증에 걸리면 우리는 3시간이 걸릴 것이다.

03 take eyes off: 눈을 떼다 / 그녀는 나를 흘끗 보기 위해 길에서 눈을 떼었다. take part in: ~에 참가하다 / 약 2만 4천 명이 이 마라톤 대회에 참가하였다.

04 (1) graduate: 졸업하다 graduation: 졸업(식) / 그것은 내가 Oxford 대학을 2019년에 졸업한 후 잡은 첫 직장이었다. (2) direct: 감독하다 director: 감독 / 그는 이 영화의 미술 감독이다.

05 should have 과거분사: ~했어야 했다 should not have 과거분사: ~하지 말았어야 했다 early: 일찍, late: 늦게

06 (C) 방학 동안에 무엇을 할 건지 진수한테 물어보자 (D) 책을 많이 읽을 것이라고 대답하며, 상대방의 방학 동안의 계획을 물어본다. (B) 부산에 계신 조부모님을 방문할 계획이라고 대답한다. (A) 멋진 방학을 보내길 바란다고 기원하는 말을 한다.

07 hang out: 많은 시간을 보내다

08 'should have 과거분사'는 '~했어야 했는데 (하지 못했다.)'의 의미로 후회를 표현할 때 쓰는 표현이다. spend: (시간을) 보내다[들이다]

09 (A) write의 목적어로 that절이 적절하다. 명사절을 연결하는 접속사 that 다음에는 완전한 문장이 나온다. (B) 민호가 'I hope you keep in touch with your classmates after graduation.(네가 졸업한 후에도 학급 친구들과 계속 연락하기를 바라.)'이라고 말하는 것을 볼 때 졸업 후에도 여전히 시간이 있다고 말하는 것이 어울린다.

10 지호가 마지막 순간까지 과제를 미루지 말아야 했는데 미룬 것에 대해 후회를 나타내는 말을 하고 있다. 주어진 문장에서 'the same problem'이 마지막 순간까지 미루는 것을 의미하므로 ⑤가 적절하다.

11 (A) have to 동사원형: ~해야 한다 (B) should not have 과거분사: ~하지 말았어야 했다 put off: 미루다, 연기하다

12 ① 그들의 나쁜 습관을 어떻게 바꿀 것인가?(언급되지 않았다.) ② 역사 과제의 마감은 언제인가?(오늘) ③ Jiho는 어떻게 보이는가?(피곤해 보인다.) ④ 그들이 바꿔야 하는 나쁜 습관은 무엇인가? (마지막 순간까지 일을 미루는 것) ⑤ 지난밤에 Jiho는 무엇을 했는가?(역사 과제를 끝냈다.)

13 ② Walked → Walking ④ 분사구문에서 의미를 분명히 하기 위해 분사 앞에 접속사를 쓰는 경우도 있지만 주절의 주어와 같은 부사절의 주어를 쓰지는 않는다.

14 '버스가 막 떠난 것'으로 '완료'를 나타내는 과거완료로 쓰는 것이 적절하다.

15 ② When Tom opened the door, Alex had already watered the plants.

16 기사가 쓰인 것보다 부유해진 것이 더 먼저 일어난 일이므로 과거완료 시제 (had+과거분사)로 쓰는 것이 적절하다.

17 (A) die는 수동태로 쓸 수 없는 동사이므로 dead가 적절하다. (B) 감정을 나타내는 동사의 분사가 형용사로 쓰일 때, 감정을 느끼게 되는 경우에 과거분사를 써야 하므로 shocked가 적절하다. (C) 다른 위험한 '물건'들이라고 해야 하므로 objects가 적절하다. object: 물건, 물체, subject: (논의 등의) 주제, 과목

18 ⓑ와 ④: 가주어, ① 가목적어, ② 비인칭주어(거리), ③ 그것(앞에 이미 언급되었거나 현재 이야기되고 있는 사물·동물을 가리킴), ⑤ 비인칭주어(막연한 상황)

19 목적을 나타내는 to부정사는 in order that 주어 may[can]을 사용하여 복문으로 고치는 것이 적절하다.

20 '세상을 더 좋게 만든 사람들을 존경해주기 위해서'였다.

21 ② 노벨상은 해마다 물리학, 화학, 생리학 및 의학, 문학, 평화, 경제학의 여섯 부문의 수상자에게 메달과 상장, 상금을 수여하며, 경제학상의 경우, 1968년에 신설되어 1969년부터 상을 수

여했다.

22 그 보도 '덕분에'라고 해야 하므로, ③번 Thanks to와 ⑤번 Because of가 적절하다. ① ~ 대신에, ② ~에도 불구하고, ④ ~에 더하여, ~뿐 아니라

23 이 글은 '한 프랑스 신문의 실수로 인한 보도 덕분에, Nobel이 세상에 공헌하기 위해 무언가를 하기로 결심하고 자신의 돈을 노벨상을 만드는 데 사용하기로 결정했다'는 내용의 글이므로, 주제로는 ②번 '부정확한 보도가 Nobel로 하여금 세상에 공헌하기 위해 무언가를 하기로 결심하게 만들었다'가 적절하다.

24 1888년에, 한 프랑스 신문에서 '실수로' Alfred Nobel의 죽음을 보도했다. on purpose: 고의로[일부러], ⑤ come to one's mind: 생각이 나다, 생각이 떠오르다

서술형 실전문제
p.108~109

01 I hope you take part in many school events

02 (1) I ought to have eaten less last night.

(2) I regret (that) I didn't eat less last night.

(3) I'm sorry (that) I didn't eat less last night.

03 ④ must have spent → should have spent

04 (1) Because[As] he was sick, he went to see a doctor.

(2) You will get a perfect result if you follow these instructions.

(3) There being no bus left, I had to walk home.

(4) He goes to work by train every morning, coming home the same way.

05 (1) had become (2) had changed

06 had died   07 After he caught his breath

08 Nobel   09 made a decision

10 we think of the Nobel Prize, rather than dynamite

11 Alfred Nobel

01 B가 '너는 고등학교에서 다시 한 번 기회가 있어.'라고 말하는 것을 볼 때 빈칸에는 학교 행사에 많이 참여하는 것을 기원하는 말을 하는 것이 적절하다. take part in: ~에 참가하다

02 'should have 과거분사'는 '~했어야 했는데 (하지 못했다)'의 의미로 후회를 표현할 때 사용하는 표현이다. 비슷한 표현으로 'I regret that 주어+과거동사 ~.', 'I feel sorry that 주어+과거 동사 ~.', 'I ought to have 과거분사 ~.'가 있다.

03 'must have p.p.'는 과거에 대한 강한 추측을 나타내어 '~이었음에 틀림없다'의 의미로 사용한다. 흐름상 학급 친구들과 더 많은 시간을 보냈어야 했다며 후회하는 표현이 어울리므로 must가 아니라 should를 사용해야 한다.

04 (1) 의미상 '이유'를 나타내는 분사구문이다. (2) 의미상 '조건'

을 나타내는 분사구문이다. (3) 주절의 주어와 다르므로 독립분사구문으로 바꾼다. (4) 의미상 '연속상황'을 나타내는 분사구문으로 바꾼다.

05 (1) 기사에 쓰여진 내용은 이미 일어난 사건이므로 said의 목적어인 that절은 과거완료로 쓴다. (2) 발견한 것은 이미 변한 것이므로 that절을 과거완료로 쓴다.

06 기사가 쓰인 것보다 죽은 것이 더 먼저 일어난 일이므로 과거완료 시제인 had died로 쓰는 것이 적절하다.

07 '숨을 고른 후'라고 해야 하므로, 접속사 After를 사용하여 고치는 것이 적절하다.

08 'Nobel'을 가리킨다.

09 decide = make a decision

10 B rather than A: A라기보다는 B

11 1888년에, 한 프랑스 신문에서 실수로 'Alfred Nobel'이 죽었다고 보도했지만, 실제로 죽은 사람은 Alfred Nobel의 형인 Ludvig였다.

창의사고력 서술형 문제
p.110

|모범답안|

01 (1) Having nothing to do, I went for a walk to the park.

(2) Being tired, I came back home early.

(3) Not being fish, they need to come up to breathe.

(4) Walking on the street, I saw a famous movie star.

02 (A) donated money to children in Africa

(B) make a difference for children in need

(C) buy snacks for a month (D) my meals

(E) myself

단원별 모의고사
p.111~114

01 ②   02 unbelievable

03 (1) spent, gave (2) hang (3) stay

04 (1) in (2) (h)ope, keep, touch

(3) made, mistake (4) (t)hink of, as

05 (A) tired (B) due (C) change

06 I shouldn't have put it off until the last moment.

07 ④   08 ④   09 ①, ③

10 (C)–(A)–(B)–(D)   11 graduation

12 I hope you keep in touch with your classmates after graduation.

13 (1) When I woke up this morning, the rain had

already stopped.

    (2) The article said Alfred Nobel had died in France from a heart attack.

    (3) Being late for school, Ann ran to catch the school bus.

14 (1) When I got home, I found someone had broken into our house.

    (2) They had finished the pizza before their friends arrived.

    (3) Eating popcorn, he watched TV.

    (4) Turning to the right, you will find the flower shop.

15 ①, ④

16 Catching his breath, Nobel kept reading.

17 ③   18 (A) death (B) imagined 19 ①

20 ③   21 It was added in 1968.

22 participated in the tree planting program 23 ⑤

---

01 be late for ~: ~에 늦다 / 그녀는 매일 직장에 지각한다. be ready for ~: ~의 준비가 되다 / 그렇게 오래 걷고 난 우리는 모두 한잔하고 싶은 생각이 간절했다.

02 unbelievable: 믿을 수 없는, 믿기 어려운 / 그들은 똑같이 그녀에게 놀랐다. 그녀가 그들 중 많은 이들과 같은 나이라는 것이 믿을 수 없었다.

03 (1) spend: (시간을) 보내다[들이다] give up: 포기하다 / 우리는 열쇠를 찾으려고 30분을 보냈고, 결국 포기하고 집에 갔다. (2) hang out: 많은 시간을 보내다 / 나는 종종 커피숍에서 시간을 보낸다. (3) stay up: 안 자다, 깨어 있다 / Josh는 밤새도록 피곤하지 않고 깨어 있을 수 있다.

04 (1) in surprise: 놀라서 (2) hope: 희망하다 keep in touch: 연락하고 지내다 (3) make a mistake: 실수하다 (4) think of A as B: A를 B라고 생각하다

05 (A) 지호는 어젯밤에 늦게까지 깨어 있었으므로 피곤해 보일 것이다. tired: 피곤한 (B) due: ~하기로 되어 있는, 예정된 (C) 지호가 마지막 순간까지 할 일을 미루고, G도 종종 같은 문제를 가지고 있다고 말하는 것으로 보아 나쁜 습관을 바꾸도록 노력하자고 말하는 것이 어울린다.

06 should not have 과거분사: ~하지 말았어야 했다 put off: 미루다, 연기하다 until: ~까지

07 ⓐ for, be ready for ~: ~할 준비가 되다 ⓑ of, think of: ~을 생각하다 ⓒ up, give up: 포기하다 ⓓ in, take part in: ~에 참가하다 ⓔ for, thank you for ~: ~에 대해 감사하다

08 ④ Of course not. → Of course. Tina가 아는 노래를 가장 잘하는 사람이 재민이고, 멋진 목소리를 가졌다고 말하는 것으

로 보아 물론이라고 대답하는 것이 어울린다.

09 재민이는 Tina가 아는 노래를 가장 잘하는 사람이라고 언급되어 있지만 구체적으로 어떤 종류의 노래를 잘 하는지에 대해서는 나와 있지 않았다. 또한 노래 대회가 언제인지도 언급되지 않고 있다.

10 무엇을 읽고 있는지 물어보는 질문에 (C) 학급 친구들에게 받은 졸업 메시지를 읽고 있다고 대답한다. (A) 메시지를 본 민호가 친구들이 Linda에게 할 말이 많은 것 같다고 말하자 (B) 졸업 메시지에 쓰여진 친구들이 Linda의 미소를 좋아한다는 내용을 얘기해 준다. (D) 멋지다고 칭찬하며 그 외에 다른 어떤 내용이 있는지 질문한다.

11 graduation 졸업(식) / 학위나 졸업장이 주어지는 의식

12 'I hope you ~.'는 '나는 네가 ~하기를 바란다[희망한다].'라는 뜻으로 상대방에게 기원하는 말을 할 때 쓸 수 있는 표현이다. keep in touch: 연락하고 지내다 after: ~ 후에

13 (1) 일어났을 때 이미 비가 멈췄다는 것은 어색하며 비가 이미 멈춘 '완료'의 의미를 나타내도록 과거완료로 쓰는 것이 적절하다. (2) 이미 죽었다는 것을 기사로 쓰는 것이므로 죽었다는 내용이 과거완료가 되어야 한다. (3) 접속사가 없으므로 'Ann was'를 being으로 바꾸어 분사구문으로 만든다.

14 (1) '결과'를 나타내는 과거완료를 이용한다. (2) '완료'를 나타내는 과거완료를 이용한다. (3) '동시동작'의 분사구문을 이용한다. (4) '조건'의 분사구문을 이용한다.

15 ① Being nervous on the stage, the actor forgot his lines. ④ Jimmy borrowed some money because he had lost his bag.

16 After he caught his breath를 분사구문으로 고쳐 Catching his breath라고 쓰는 것이 적절하다. catch one's breath: 숨을 고르다, keep+동사-ing: 계속 ~하다

17 ⓑ와 ③: 진주어에 해당하는 명사절을 이끄는 접속사, ① 보어절을 이끄는 접속사, ②와 ④: 목적절을 이끄는 접속사, ⑤ 동격절을 이끄는 접속사

18 그가 죽은 뒤에 세상이 그를 '죽음'의 상인으로 생각할 것임을 깨달았고, 그는 그럴 것이라고는 결코 '상상하지' 못했기 때문이다.

19 주어진 문장의 who had actually died에 주목한다. ①번 앞 문장의 내용과 상반되는 내용을 말하는 것이므로 ①번이 적절하다.

20 ⓐ와 ②, ⑤: 부사적 용법, ①, ④: 명사적 용법, ③: 형용사적 용법

21 여섯 번째 상은 1968년에 추가되었다.

22 '나무 심기 프로그램에 참가한 것'을 가리킨다.

23 글쓴이가 나무에 관심을 가지지 않았던 것은 나무 심기 프로그램에 참가하기 전이고, 현재는 '나무들이 우리에게 정말 중요하다는 것을 알고 있다.'

Picture the Future

Reading

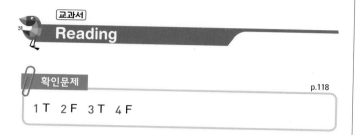

확인문제   p.118

1 T   2 F   3 T   4 F

확인문제   p.119

1 T   2 F   3 F   4 T   5 F

교과서 확인학습 A   p.120~121

01 Picture   02 It's

03 shakes, Five more minutes

04 stops shaking   05 appears, be late for

06 Clear   07 become clear

08 scans Minji's body   09 health condition

10 comes out from   11 comes, dries

12 with today's clothes   13 for breakfast

14 The usual   15 presses, on

16 prints out   17 rushes out

18 A few minutes later   19 send a drone to

20 a million   21 driverless flying car

22 in comfortable chairs   23 to select

24 by putting, on a sensor   25 will be delivered

26 150-story

27 give a presentation with   28 doesn't have to

29 Thanks to, feel like   30 is ready

31 talk about   32 washes the dishes

33 called chess   34 agrees

35 3-D chess board   36 lots of fun

37 whispers to   38 Remind, to take

교과서 확인학습 B   p.122~123

1 Picture the Future

2 It's 7 a.m.

3 The bed shakes and Minji Kim yells, "Five more minutes!"

4 The bed stops shaking.

5 Suddenly, Minji's mom appears on a screen on the wall and says, "You're going to be late for school!"

6 Minji rubs her eyes and says, "Clear the windows."

7 The dark windows become clear and the sun shines brightly through them.

8 In the bathroom, a red light scans Minji's body.

9 A voice says, "54 kilograms. Your health condition is excellent."

10 When she steps in the shower, water comes out from the top and sides.

11 After her shower, warm air comes out and dries her.

12 When she gets out, a drawer opens with today's clothes.

13 In the kitchen, her father says, "Good morning, Honey. What do you want for breakfast?"

14 Minji says, "The usual, please."

15 Mr. Kim presses a few buttons on the cooking machine.

16 The machine prints out some bacon, eggs and bread.

17 Mr. Kim says goodbye and rushes out the door.

18 A few minutes later, Minji's father appears on a screen and shouts, "I forgot my glasses!"

19 Ms. Kim smiles and answers, "No problem. I'll send a drone to your office."

20 Mr. Kim says, "Thanks a million!"

21 Ms. Kim and Minji get into a driverless flying car.

22 They sit in comfortable chairs around a table.

23 Ms. Kim touches the car window to select the groceries for this week.

24 She pays for them by putting her finger on a sensor.

25 They will be delivered to her house.

26 The car lands at Minji's school on top of a 150-story building.

27 Today Minji will give a presentation with Dona, a student in America.

28 But Minji doesn't have to go to America.

29 Thanks to a VR classroom, they will feel like they are in the same classroom.

30 When Minji's family comes back home, dinner is ready.

31 They eat and talk about their day.

32 After a delicious dinner, the cleaning robot clears the table and washes the dishes.

33 Minji says, "I learned a game called chess today. Do you want to play?"

34 Everyone agrees.

35 A 3-D chess board appears on the table.

36 They have lots of fun.

37 Right before Minji goes to bed, she whispers to her watch.

38 "Remind Daddy to take his glasses tomorrow."

 서술형 실전문제 p.124~126

01 (u)sual   02 of

03 (1) story   (2) comfortable   (3) clear

04 (1) He couldn't finish college because of his bad health condition.

(2) A man suddenly appeared from behind a tree.

(3) The moon shone brightly in the sky.

05 (R)emind

06 ⓐ to read → reading, ⓒ By use → By using

07 driverless 08 ⑤

09 (1) It is right before Minji goes to bed that she whispers to her watch.

(2) It is water that[which] comes out from the top and sides.

(3) It is a few buttons that[which] Mr. Kim presses on the cooking machine.

(4) It is on top of a 150-story building that[where] the car lands.

10 Do you have a client named Peters?

11 be delivered

12 (A) a drone   (B) his office

13 She pays for them by putting her finger on a sensor.

14 150-stories → 150-story

15 need not   16 a VR classroom

17 to shake → shaking   18 the windows

19 (A) scans   (B) clothes   (C) a few

20 Warm air comes out and dries her.

21 drawer

01 usual: 일상의, 늘 하는; 늘 먹던 것 / 그녀는 늘 하는 온갖 변명들을 늘어놓았다. 늘 먹던 걸로 주세요.

02 be tired of ~: ~에 싫증이 나다 / 우리는 그가 전화하는 것을 기다리는 것에 싫증이 났다. on top of: ~의 꼭대기에 / 그 집은 언덕 꼭대기에 위치해 있다.

03 (1) story: (건물의) 층 / 그의 사무실은 30층 건물의 꼭대기 층에 있다. (2) comfortable: 편안한, 안락한 / 침대가 너무 편하고 따뜻해서 일어나고 싶지 않았다. (3) clear: 치우다 / 식탁 치우는 거 거들어 줄래?

04 (1) health condition: 건강 상태 (2) appear: 나타나다 (3) shine: 빛나다, 비추다

05 remind A to 동사원형: A에게 ~할 것을 상기시키다 / 누군가가 그들이 해야만 하는 것을 기억하게 만들다 / 나에게 오늘 밤 우유를 살 것을 상기시켜 줘.

06 ⓐ stop 동명사: ~하기를 멈추다 / 나는 읽기를 멈추고 불을 껐다. ⓑ thanks to 명사: ~ 덕분에 / 최근의 호우 덕택에 가뭄이 가셨다. ⓒ by 동사ing: ~함으로써 / 인터넷을 사용함으로써 너는 쇼핑을 집에서 할 수 있다.

07 driverless: 운전자가 필요 없는

08 조동사가 있는 문장의 수동태는 '조동사+be+과거분사'의 형태로 나타낸다.

09 'It ~ that ...' 강조 구문으로 강조하며, 'It is/was ~ that ...'의 형태로, 강조하고자 하는 부분을 'It is/was'와 that 사이에 넣고, 나머지 부분을 that 뒤에 쓴다. 또한 'It ~ that ...' 강조 구문에서 강조하는 대상이 사람일 때는 that 대신에 who[whom], 사물이나 동물일 때는 which로 바꿔 쓸 수 있으며, 시간 또는 장소의 부사(구/절)일 경우, when(시간) 또는 where(장소)로 바꿔 쓸 수 있다.

10 named가 뒤에서 a client를 수식하도록 쓴다. 앞에 'who is'가 생략된 형태로 볼 수 있다.

11 식료품이 집으로 '배달될' 것이라고 해야 하므로 수동태로 써야 하고, 조동사 수동태는 '조동사+be+과거분사'의 형태로 쓰는 것이 적절하다.

12 민지의 엄마가 '그의 사무실'로 안경과 함께 '드론'을 보낼 것이다.

13 by+동사-ing: ~함으로써

14 150-story는 '150층의, 150층짜리'라는 뜻으로 두 개의 단어가 하이픈(-)으로 연결된 복합 형용사이며, '층'을 나타내는 명사 story를 '단수'로 쓰는 것이 적절하다.

15 don't/doesn't have to+동사원형 = don't/doesn't need to+동사원형 = need not+동사원형: ~할 필요가 없다, need not에서 need가 조동사이므로 'needs not'으로 쓰지 않도록 주의해야 한다.

16 'VR(가상 현실) 교실' 덕분에, 그들이 같은 교실에 있는 것처럼

침대가 '흔들기를' 멈춘다고 해야 하므로 to shake를 shaking으로 고치는 것이 적절하다. stop ~ing: ~하기를 그만두다, stop+to부정사: ~하기 위해 멈추다(to부정사의 부사적 용법 목적)

18 '창문'을 가리킨다.

19 (A) 민지의 몸을 '정밀 검사한다'라고 해야 하므로 scans가 적절하다. scan: 정밀 검사[촬영]하다, skip: 깡충깡충 뛰다, 건너뛰다, (B) 오늘의 '옷'이 나타난다고 해야 하므로 clothes가 적절하다. cloths: cloth(옷감, 직물)의 복수, clothes: 옷, 의복, (C) 버튼 '몇 개'라고 해야 하므로 a few가 적절하다. a few+복수명사, a little+셀 수 없는 명사

20 샤워 후에는, '따뜻한 공기가 나와 그녀를 말린다.'

21 박스 같은 형태로 물건들을 안에 넣도록 디자인된 책상, 상자 또는 다른 가구의 부분, drawer: 서랍

단원별 예상문제   p.127~130

01 (1) on   (2) for   (3) out   (4) to
02 ②   03 ⑤   04 ③
05 (1) (t)ired of   (2) Remind, to   (3) stopped (t)alking
06 ③   07 ②   08 Pressing the button
09 will be decorated
10 (Being) Tired after a long walk, Minji went to bed early.
11 (1) Appearing on a screen on the wall, Minji's mom says, "You're going to be late for school!"
    (2) As[Because/Since] she was late, she hurried to work.
    (3) If you are an architect, what will you choose from nature?
12 (1) This movie will be loved by many teens.
    (2) The environment should not be destroyed (by us).
    (3) The fruit can be made into delicious jam (by them).
    (4) What you promised has to be delivered (by you).
13 ⓐ, ⓓ, ⓔ   14 ③
15 the groceries (for this week)
16 I learned a game which[that] is called chess today.
17 ②   18 ①   19 The usual, please.
20 ③   21 ③, ⑤
22 is appeared → appears   23 ④

---

01 (1) on top of: ~의 꼭대기에 / 그 탑은 언덕 꼭대기에 위치해 있다. (2) pay for: ~의 값을 지불하다 / 현실은 이 사업에 지불

할 충분한 돈이 없다는 것이다. (3) print out: (프린트로) 출력하다 / 이 문서를 출력해 주시겠어요? (4) send A to B: A를 B에 보내다 / 그는 수십 개의 장미를 그의 여자친구에게 생일날 보냈다.

02 ②의 영영풀이는 yell의 영영풀이이다. ① select: 선택하다 / 어떤 것이나 누군가를 무엇이 최선인지, 가장 적절한지 등에 관해 조심스러운 생각으로 고르다 ② whisper: 속삭이다 / to speak or say something very quietly, using your breath rather than your voice 목소리보다는 숨을 사용해서 매우 조용하게 말하다 yell: 소리치다, 외치다 / to shout or say something very loudly, especially because you are frightened, angry, or excited 특히 겁이 나거나, 화나거나, 흥분해서 매우 크게 소리치거나 말하다 ③ press: 누르다 / 기계가 시작하거나, 종이 울리도록 하기 위해서 버튼이나 스위치 등을 누르다 ④ shine: 빛나다, 비추다 / 밝은 빛이 생기게 하다 ⑤ appear: 나타나다 / 특히 갑자기 보이거나, 도착하거나, 어느 장소에 존재하기 시작하다

03 select: 선택하다 choose: 고르다, 선택하다 / 부모들이 배우는 데 어려움을 가진 아이들을 위한 올바른 학교를 고르는 것은 중요하다.

04 ③은 'ful', 나머지는 모두 'less'가 들어간다. ① careless: 부주의한 / 사고가 나는 데는 부주의한 운전자 한 명만 있으면 된다. ② driverless: 운전자가 필요 없는 / 회사는 현재 운전자가 필요 없는 차를 실험 중이다. ③ harmful: 해로운 / 흡연은 건강에 해로운 효과를 준다. ④ useless: 쓸모없는 / 그것에 대해 걱정해 봐야 소용없다. ⑤ endless: 끝없는 / 음악은 많은 사람에게 한없는 즐거움의 원천이 된다.

05 (1) be tired of ~: ~에 싫증이 나다 (2) remind A to 동사원형: A에게 ~할 것을 상기시키다 (3) stop 동명사: ~ 하기를 멈추다

06 (A) give a presentation: 발표를 하다 / 나는 발표하기 위해 얼마나 시간이 있는지 항상 묻는다. (B) step: 서다, (발을) 디디다 / 문 앞에 서면 문이 저절로 열립니다.

07 ② word → words / a few+복수명사(긍정), few+복수명사(부정), a little+셀 수 없는 명사(긍정), little+셀 수 없는 명사(부정)

08 'If you press the button, ~'을 분사구문으로 만든다.

09 장식되어야 하는 것이므로 수동태를 이용하고 '조동사+be+과거분사'의 형태로 쓴다.

10 민지가 피곤하게 된 것으로 수동의 의미이므로 과거분사 Tired가 되어야 한다.

11 (1) '연속동작'의 분사구문으로 쓴다. (2) 내용상 '이유'의 부사절이 적절하다. (3) 내용상 '조건'의 부사절이 적절하다.

12 (1) 조동사가 있는 문장의 수동태는 '조동사+be+과거분사'의 형태로 나타낸다. (2) 부정문의 경우 '조동사+not+be+과거분사'의 형태로 나타낸다. (3) 일반인이 주어일 경우 'by+목적격'을 생략할 수 있다. (4) 수동태로 바꿀 때 주어가 단수로 바뀌므로 'have to'를 'has to'로 써야 하는 것에 주의한다.

13 ⓑ today → today's ⓒ is appeared → appears ⓕ catching → to catch

14 ③번 다음 문장의 them에 주목한다. 주어진 문장에서 Ms. Kim이 선택한 식료품을 가리키므로 ③번이 적절하다.

15 민지의 엄마가 선택한 '이번 주 식료품'을 가리킨다.

16 주격 관계대명사와 be동사(which[that] is)가 생략되어 있다. 요즘에도 체스라고 불리는 것이므로 생략된 부분의 시제를 '현재시제'로 쓰는 것이 적절하다.

17 이 글은 '미래 사회에서 민지의 가족이 저녁 시간을 보내는 모습'을 보여주는 글이므로, 주제로는 ②번 '미래의 삶의 한 장면'이 적절하다.

18 ⓐ for breakfast: 아침식사로, ⓑ 요리 기계에 버튼이 부착되어 있는 것이므로 on이 적절하다.

19 usual 일상의, 늘 하는; 늘 먹던 것

20 민지가 옷을 고르기 위해 서랍을 여는 것이 아니라, 서랍이 열리며 오늘의 옷이 나타난다.

21 ⓐ와 ③, ⑤: 동명사, ①, ②, ④: 현재분사

22 appear는 수동태로 쓸 수 없는 자동사이므로, is appeared를 appears로 고치는 것이 적절하다.

23 '민지가 엄마에게 뭐라고 말하는지'는 대답할 수 없다. ① It shakes. ② No, she yells, "Five more minutes!", instantly: 즉시, 즉각, ③ She appears on a screen on the wall and says, "You're going to be late for school!" ⑤ She says, "Clear the windows."

교과서 파헤치기

Lesson
7

단어 TEST Step 3 p.04

1 million, 100만, 수많은 2 Arctic, 북극 (지방)
3 blow, (입으로) 불다 4 complete, 완성하다
5 breathe, 숨을 쉬다 6 smash, 때려 부수다, 깨뜨리다
7 whale, 고래 8 distance, 거리 9 surface, 수면, 표면
10 fool, 속이다, 기만하다 11 calculate, 계산하다
12 tool, 도구 13 forecast, 예측, 예보
14 octopus, 문어 15 species, (분류상의) 종
16 dive, 뛰어들다, 다이빙하다

단어 TEST Step 1 p.02

01 태양의 02 평균의, 보통의 03 피
04 발견하다, 찾아내다 05 아마
06 때려 부수다, 깨뜨리다 07 완성하다
08 경치, 풍경 09 기사 10 완전히
11 해외에, 해외로 12 (음식을) 제공하다, 차려 주다
13 거리 14 적 15 (분류상의) 종
16 수면, 표면 17 속이다, 기만하다; 바보
18 예측, 예보 19 문어
20 경이, 경탄, 놀라움; 궁금하다
21 100만; 100만의, 수많은 22 둘러싸다
23 소통하다 24 온도, 기온 25 괴물
26 조개 27 대걸레로 닦다
28 인근의, 가까운 곳의 인근에, 가까운 곳에 29 숨을 쉬다
30 계산하다 31 발견하다 32 단단히, 꽉
33 도구 34 진공청소기로 청소하다
35 포기하다 36 ~ 없이 지내다 37 한 줄로
38 ~로 가득 차다 39 차츰 사라지다 40 마침내, 결국
41 ~로 덮여 있다 42 이맘때는, 이맘때쯤이면
43 ~와 다르다

대화문 TEST Step 1 p.05~07

Listen and Speak 1 A
almost at the top of / wonder how high / It's about, high / high mountain, keep going

Listen and Speak 1 B
at, on / look, cold / is the coldest place on / how cold it is / average, is, in, in / then, colder than / Although it's, doesn't / interesting, too

Listen and Speak 1 C
1. finally / excited, look around / wonder where / in front of, police station / Let's
2. finally here / look around / wonder where the information center / behind / right
3. Let's / I wonder where, is / next to / Let's go

Listen and Speak 2 A
so, outside / about going on a picnic / check, weather / forecast says it'll be rainy / another time

Listen and Speak 2 B
to do / go hiking, join me / Where do you want to / thinking of going / scenery, this time of / I heard that it's covered with, autumn leaves / How long, take / The Internet says it takes / on

Listen and Speak 2 C
1. What, doing / reading / anything interesting / This article says scientists have discovered
2. the newspaper / anything interesting / This article says, was seen in the East Sea

Real Life Talk Watch a Video
Check out / camels, in a line in / hot, dry / wonder how long camels can go without / out / The Internet says, without water / Camels are, interesting / travel with them

Real Life Talk Step 2
1. Where, coldest place / South Pole / I wonder how cold / says, average temperature, about / amazing
2. biggest, solar system / Jupiter / I wonder how big

단어 TEST Step 2 p.03

01 enemy 02 fat 03 abroad
04 blood 05 surround 06 average
07 completely 08 scenery 09 discover
10 distance 11 complete 12 article
13 finally 14 forecast 15 surface
16 clam 17 guess 18 smash
19 million 20 mop 21 wonder
22 nearby 23 blow 24 fool
25 vacuum 26 tool 27 calculate
28 monster 29 octopus 30 probably
31 solar 32 temperature 33 tightly
34 breathe 35 be covered with
36 give up 37 in the end 38 melt away
39 in a line 40 fall asleep 41 go without
42 be full of 43 be different from

/ The Internet says, times bigger than

3. hottest desert on / how hot it is / says, reach up to / amazing

---

Listen and Speak 1 A

B: We're almost at the top of the mountain.

G: I wonder how high this mountain is.

B: It's about 2,000m high.

G: Wow! This is a really high mountain.

B: Yes, it is. Let's keep going.

Listen and Speak 1 B

B: Look at the baby penguins on TV. They're so cute.

G: Yes, but they look very cold out there.

B: Yeah, the South Pole is the coldest place on Earth.

G: I wonder how cold it is there.

B: The average temperature is about -58℃ in July and -26℃ in December.

G: Oh, then, July is colder than December there. Interesting!

B: Yes. Although it's very cold there, it doesn't snow much.

G: That's interesting, too!

Listen and Speak 1 C

1. A: We're finally here.

 B: Yes, I'm so excited. Let's look around.

 A: I wonder where the bus stop is.

 B: It's in front of the police station.

 A: You're right. Let's go.

2. A: We're finally here.

 B: Yes, I'm so excited. Let's look around.

 A: I wonder where the information center is.

 B: It's behind the library.

 A: You're right. Let's go.

3. A: We're finally here.

 B: Yes, I'm so excited. Let's look around.

 A: I wonder where Green Park is.

 B: It's next to the school.

 A: You're right. Let's go.

Listen and Speak 2 A

B: The weather is so nice outside.

G: Yeah. How about going on a picnic this afternoon?

B: Good idea. Can you check the weather?

G: Oh, no! The weather forecast says it'll be rainy in the afternoon.

B: Let's go another time, then.

Listen and Speak 2 B

B: Sumin, what are you going to do on Sunday?

G: I'm going to go hiking. Do you want to join me?

B: I'd love to. Where do you want to go?

G: I'm thinking of going to Namsan.

B: Oh, the scenery there is so beautiful this time of year.

G: Right. I heard that it's covered with red autumn leaves now.

B: Great. How long does the shortest hiking course take?

G: The Internet says it takes about two hours.

B: Okay, see you on Sunday!

Listen and Speak 2 C

1. A: What are you doing?

 B: I'm reading the newspaper.

 A: Is there anything interesting?

 B: This article says scientists have discovered a new planet.

2. A: What are you doing?

 B: I'm reading the newspaper.

 A: Is there anything interesting?

 B: This article says a whale family was seen in the East Sea.

Real Life Talk Watch a Video

Suji: Check out this picture!

Tony: Wow! The camels are walking in a line in the desert.

Suji: Yeah. The desert looks very hot and dry.

Tony: I wonder how long camels can go without water in the desert.

Suji: Let's find out on the Internet.

Tony: Okay. The Internet says they can go about two weeks without water.

Suji: Wow, that's amazing! Camels are really interesting animals.

Tony: I want to travel with them in the desert someday.

Real Life Talk Step 2

1. A: Where is the coldest place on Earth?

 B: I thinks it's the South Pole.

 A: I wonder how cold it is.

 B: The book says the average temperature of the South Pole is about -49°C.

 A: That's amazing!

2. A: Which planet is the biggest in the solar system?

B: I thinks it's Jupiter.

A: I wonder how big it is.

B: The Internet says Jupiter is over 11 times bigger than Earth.

A: That's amazing!

3. A: Where is the hottest desert on Earth?

B: I thinks it's the Sahara Desert.

A: I wonder how hot it is.

B: The newspaper says the temperature of the Sahara Desert can reach up to 50°C.

A: That's amazing!

본문 TEST Step 1
p.11~12

01 Under, Sea

02 Two-thirds, planet, covered, oceans

03 full, wonder, millions, species

04 Every, learning new things

05 Let's find out, sea   06 Sweet Dreams

07 guess what, whales, doing

08 looks like, up, group   09 actually sleeping

10 stand on, tails while   11 sleep near, surface

12 Since, need, up, breathe   13 Also, fall asleep

14 wake, deep breath, into   15 Enjoy, Meal

16 smart, take, look at

17 whose, clams, tool, open

18 hide, cannot, easily discovered

19 blows, until, clam appears

20 clam, closed tightly, so   21 doesn't give up

22 smashes, against, rock

23 In, end, opens, served   24 Three, Jump

25 probably, fly down, catch   26 seen, jump out of

27 have, careful, giant, around

28 grow up to   29 let its size fool

30 fish, quick, smart

31 spot, flying, calculate, distance

32 flies nearby, jumps, catches

본문 TEST Step 2
p.13~14

01 Under, Sea

02 Two-thirds, is covered by

03 are full of, millions of species

04 new things

05 Let's find out, sea animals

06 Sweet

---

07 what these whales are doing

08 looks like, in a group   09 actually sleeping

10 stand on their tails while they sleep

11 near the surface

12 Since, need to come up to breathe

13 fall asleep completely

14 for a deep breath, dive back into

15 Enjoy, Meal   16 take a look at

17 whose favorite food, open

18 hide, cannot be easily discovered

19 blows, until, appears   20 is closed tightly

21 give up   22 smashes, against

23 In the end, is served   24 Jump

25 have, seen, fly down

26 have, ever seen, jump out of the water

27 have to, is around   28 up to

29 let, fool   30 quick and smart

31 spot, calculate, speed, distance

32 nearby, jumps, catches

본문 TEST Step 3
p.15~16

1 바다 아래에

2 우리 행성의 3분의 2는 대양들로 덮여 있다.

3 대양들은 신기한 것으로 가득 차 있고 수많은 종의 서식지이다.

4 매일 우리는 그들에 관한 새로운 것들을 배우고 있다.

5 몇몇 흥미로운 바다 동물들을 알아보자.

6 좋은 꿈 꿔라

7 여러분은 그림 속 이 고래들이 무엇을 하고 있는지 추측할 수 있는가?

8 그들이 무리를 지어 서 있는 것처럼 보인다.

9 그러나 그들은 실제로는 잠을 자고 있다!

10 혹등고래들은 잠을 자는 동안 꼬리로 서 있다.

11 그들은 수면 근처에서 잠을 잔다.

12 그들은 물고기가 아니기 때문에 숨을 쉬기 위해 위로 나올 필요가 있다.

13 또한 그들은 완전히 잠들지 않는다.

14 그들은 잠에서 깨면 심호흡을 하러 물 밖으로 나왔다가 바다로 다시 뛰어든다.

15 맛있게 먹어라

16 만약 물고기가 똑똑하지 않다고 생각한다면 'tuskfish'를 보아라.

17 가장 좋아하는 먹이가 조개인 이 작은 물고기는 조개를 열기 위해 도구를 사용한다.

18 조개는 대개 모래 아래에 숨어 있어서 쉽게 발견할 수 없다.

19 'tuskfish'는 조개가 나타날 때까지 모래에 입김을 분다.

20 조개가 단단히 닫혀 있어서 물고기는 이것을 먹을 수 없다.

21 그러나 'tuskfish'는 포기하지 않는다.

22 'tuskfish'는 돌에 조개를 내리친다.

23 마침내 조개가 열리고 밥상이 차려진다.

24 하나, 둘, 셋, 뛰어라!

25 여러분은 아마 새가 물고기를 잡기 위해 바다로 날아 내려가는 것을 본 적이 있을 것이다.

26 그러나 물고기가 새를 잡기 위해 물 밖으로 뛰어오르는 것을 본 적이 있는가?

27 자, 새들은 'giant trevally'가 주변에 있을 때 조심해야 한다.

28 이 물고기는 170센티미터에 80킬로그램까지 자랄 수 있다.

29 그러나 그 크기에 속지 마라.

30 이 물고기는 빠르고 똑똑하다.

31 이것은 날고 있는 새를 발견하고 그 새의 속도와 거리를 계산할 수 있다.

32 새가 근처에 날고 있을 때, 'giant trevally'는 물 밖으로 뛰어올라 새를 잡는다.

본문 TEST Step 4-Step 5 p.17~20

1 1 Under the Sea

2 Two-thirds of our planet is covered by oceans.

3 They are full of wonder and are home to millions of species.

4 Every day, we are learning new things about them.

5 Let's find out about some interesting sea animals.

6 Sweet Dreams

7 Can you guess what these whales are doing in the picture?

8 It looks like they are standing up in a group.

9 But they are actually sleeping!

10 Humpback whales stand on their tails while they sleep.

11 They sleep near the surface.

12 Since they are not fish, they need to come up to breathe.

13 Also, they don't fall asleep completely.

14 When they wake up, they come out of the water for a deep breath and dive back into the sea.

15 Enjoy Your Meal

16 If you think fish are not smart, take a look at the tuskfish.

17 This small fish whose favorite food is clams uses a tool to open them.

18 Clams usually hide under the sand, so they cannot be easily discovered.

19 The tuskfish blows on the sand until a clam appears.

---

20 The clam is closed tightly, so the fish cannot eat it.

21 But the tuskfish doesn't give up.

22 It smashes the clam against a rock.

23 In the end, the clam opens and dinner is served.

24 One, Two, Three, Jump!

25 You have probably seen a bird fly down to the sea to catch a fish.

26 But have you ever seen a fish jump out of the water to catch a bird?

27 Well, birds have to be careful when a giant trevally is around.

28 This fish can grow up to 170cm and 80kg.

29 But don't let its size fool you.

30 This fish is quick and smart.

31 It can spot a flying bird and calculate its speed and distance.

32 When the bird flies nearby, the giant trevally jumps out of the water and catches it.

구석구석지문 TEST Step 1 p.21

After You Read A. Read and Correct

1. learned about oceans

2. Two-thirds, is covered by

3. millions of species

4. There are many interesting facts

5. For example, stand on their tails while, near the surface

Word Power

1. good spot to park

2. spot, in the audience

3. Don't be fooled by

4. makes, fool wise

Think and Write

1. Fun Animal

2. will introduce, whale

3. the Arctic Ocean, a round head

4. usually eats, clams

5. An interesting fact, that, white all over

6. That's why, call it, white whale

7. When, is born, gray

8. grows up, becomes white

9. with my own eyes

After You Read A. Read and Correct

1. I learned about oceans today.

2. Two-thirds of our planet is covered by oceans.

3. They are home to millions of species.

4. There are many interesting facts about sea animals.

5. For example, humpback whales stand on their tails while they sleep, and they sleep near the surface.

Word Power

1. He found a good spot to park the car.

2. I can spot you in the audience.

3. Don't be fooled by his cute looks.

4. Experience makes even fool wise.

Think and Write

1. My Fun Animal: Beluga whale

2. I will introduce the beluga whale.

3. It lives in the Arctic Ocean. It has a round head.

4. It usually eats fish and clams.

5. An interesting fact about the beluga whale is that it is white all over.

6. That's why people call it the white whale.

7. When it is born, it is gray.

8. But when it grows up, its body becomes white!

9. I want to see this animal with my own eyes!

Lesson
8

01 보호하다, 지키다　02 활동적인, 적극적인

03 기여하다, 공헌하다　　　　　　　04 상인

05 ~하기로 되어 있는, 예정된

06 믿을 수 없는, 믿기 어려운　　　07 실수, 잘못

08 다이너마이트　09 잘못　　　10 졸업하다

11 (신문 기사 등의) 표제　　　　　12 고맙게 생각하다

13 기술하다, 묘사하다　　　　　　14 기사

15 심장 마비　　16 ~을 포함해서　17 후회; 후회하다

18 졸업(식)　　19 습관　　　　　20 발명품

21 사실　　　　22 발명가　　　　23 충격을 받은

23 의견　　　　24 실망한, 낙담한　25 원래는, 처음에는

26 참가하다　　27 관객　　　　　28 보통의, 정상적인

29 상, 시상　　30 완벽한

31 쏟아지다, 흐르다, 쏟다　　　　32 실수로

33 복통　　　　34 포기하다　　　35 미루다, 연기하다

36 A를 B라고 생각하다　　　　　37 눈을 떼다

38 숨을 고르다　39 ~보다는　　　40 연락하고 지내다

41 ~에 참가하다　42 A를 B로 기술하다, 묘사하다

---

01 normal　　　02 opinion　　　03 actually

04 describe　　05 fault　　　　06 graduate

07 appreciate　08 including　　09 perfect

10 shocked　　11 protect　　　12 move

13 audience　　14 merchant　　15 regret

16 disappointed 17 mistake　　　18 habit

19 award　　　20 mistakenly　21 spill

22 due　　　　23 originally　　24 contribute

25 deeply　　　26 invention　　27 article

28 headline　　29 stomachache 30 heart attack

31 unbelievable 32 dynamite　　33 graduation

34 trust　　　　35 be late for　36 in surprise

37 put off　　　38 take part in　39 rather than

40 give up　　　41 stay up　　　42 keep in touch

43 think of A as B

---

1 dynamite, 다이너마이트　2 spill, 쏟아지다, 흐르다, 쏟다

3 appreciate, 고맙게 생각하다

4 describe, 기술하다, 묘사하다　5 regret, 후회하다

6 score, 득점하다   7 invention, 발명품
8 contribute, 기여하다, 공헌하다   9 merchant, 상인
10 due, ~하기로 되어 있는, 예정된   11 graduation, 졸업(식)
12 unbelievable, 믿을 수 없는, 믿기 어려운
13 audience, 관객   14 headline, (신문 기사 등의) 표제
15 move, 감동시키다   16 report, 보도하다

대화문 TEST Step 1
p.26~28

Listen and Speak 1 A
were you late for / stomachache / Are, okay / should have eaten less

Listen and Speak 1 B
up, tired / stayed up late / play, again / not, had to finish / due / shouldn't have put it off until, last moment / the same / try to change, habits

Listen and Speak 1 C
1. wrong / got caught in / sorry to hear / have taken
2. What's / failed / hear that / should have studied hard
3. wrong / lost / to hear / I should have chained
4. was late for / sorry to hear that / should have got up early

Listen and Speak 2 A
going to do during / lots of, What about / planning to visit / hope you have

Listen and Speak 2 B
ready for / I'm thinking of giving up / thought, wanted to take part in / good singer / the best singer I know / think so / course, voice / you for saying, do my best / I hope you win

Listen and Speak 2 C
1. are, going to / going to sing / hope you move, audience / hope so
2. going to play / hope you score a goal / too
3. participate in, speech contest / I hope you win / I hope so

Real Life Talk Watch a Video
reading / graduation messages / looks like, a lot to say / wrote that, smile / else / Some of them, hang out enough with / fault, busy / should have spent more time with / after graduation / right / hope you keep in touch with, after graduation / I hope so

Real Life Talk Step 2
1. can't believe, graduating / there anything, regret / should have been active in classes / have a second chance / guess / hope you are active

2. believe we're graduating / anything you regret about / should have taken part in / second chance / guess, right / hope you take part in

대화문 TEST Step 2
p.29~31

Listen and Speak 1 A
G: Mike, why were you late for class?
B: I had a bad stomachache.
G: Oh, no! Are you okay now?
B: Yeah. I should have eaten less last night.

Listen and Speak 1 B
G: Jiho, what's up? You look tired.
B: Yeah. I stayed up late last night.
G: Did you play computer games again?
B: No, not this time. I had to finish my history project.
G: Is it due today?
B: Yeah. I shouldn't have put it off until the last moment.
G: Hmm, I understand. I often have the same problem.
B: Really? Well, let's try to change our bad habits.

Listen and Speak 1 C
1. A: What's wrong?
   B: I got caught in the rain.
   A: Oh, I'm sorry to hear that.
   B: I should have taken an umbrella.
2. A: What's wrong?
   B: I failed the test.
   A: Oh, I'm sorry to hear that.
   B: I should have studied hard.
3. A: What's wrong?
   B: I lost my bike.
   A: Oh, I'm sorry to hear that.
   B: I should have chained it.
4. A: What's wrong?
   B: I was late for school.
   A: Oh, I'm sorry to hear that.
   B: I should have got up early.

Listen and Speak 2 A
G: Jinsu, what are you going to do during the vacation?
B: I'm going to read lots of books. What about you?
G: I'm planning to visit my grandparents in Busan.
B: Sounds great. I hope you have a wonderful vacation.

G: Jaemin, are you ready for the singing contest?

B: Well, I'm thinking of giving up, Tina.

G: Why? I thought you really wanted to take part in the contest.

B: I don't think I'm a good singer.

G: Come on. You're the best singer I know.

B: Do you really think so?

G: Of course. You have a really nice voice.

B: Thank you for saying so, I'll do my best.

B: I hope you win the contest.

Listen and Speak 2 C

1. A: What are you going to do tomorrow?

B: I'm going to sing in the school festival.

A: Great! I hope you move the audience.

B: Thanks. I hope so, too.

2. A: What are you going to do tomorrow?

B: I'm going to play soccer.

A: Great! I hope you score a goal.

B: Thanks. I hope so, too.

3. A: What are you going to do tomorrow?

B: I'm going to participate in the speech contest.

A: Great! I hope you win the contest.

B: Thanks. I hope so, too.

Real Life Talk Watch a Video

Minho: Linda, what are you reading?

Linda: I'm reading graduation messages from my classmates.

Minho: Oh, it looks like they had a lot to say to you.

Linda: Many of them wrote that they like my smile.

Minho: That's nice. What else?

Linda: Some of them said I didn't hang out enough with them.

Minho: That's not your fault. You were always busy.

Linda: Yeah, but I should have spent more time with my classmates.

Minho: You still have time after graduation.

Linda: You're right.

Minho: I hope you keep in touch with your classmates after graduation.

Linda: Thanks. I hope so, too.

Real Life Talk Step 2

1. A: I can't believe we're graduating soon.

B: Yeah. Is there anything you regret about your middle school life?

A: Yes. I should have been active in classes.

B: Well, you have a second chance in high school.

A: I guess you're right.

B: I hope you are active in classes in high school.

2. A: I can't believe we're graduating soon.

B: Yeah. Is there anything you regret about your middle school life?

A: Yes. I should have taken part in many school events.

B: Well, you have a second chance in high school.

A: I guess you're right.

B: I hope you take part in many school events in high school.

본문 TEST Step 1   p.32~33

01 How, Be Remembered   02 just, normal morning

03 sat in, chair to

04 While, headline caught, eye

05 What, this

06 article, dropped, in surprise

07 spilled, over, take, off

08 article, his own death

09 died, from, heart attack   10 my goodness, dead

11 Catching, breath, kept reading

12 even more shocked

13 described, as, inventor, other

14 become rich, deaths, others

15 couldn't believe, eyes

16 true, one of, inventions

17 imagined, think of, as

18 was deeply disappointed 19 How could, be

20 This, unbelievable   21 merchant of death

22 remembered in, different way

23 be remembered, world better

24 to change people's opinions

25 newspaper mistakenly reported, death

26 who had actually died

27 Thanks to, however, contribute

28 decided, use, to create

29 Originally, only five awards

30 sixth award, added

31 think, rather than dynamite

본문 TEST Step 2   p.34~35

01 How, Be Remembered   02 just, normal morning

03 sat in his chair to read

04 While, headline caught his eye

33

05 What   06 Reading, in surprise

07 spilled, take his eyes off

08 about his own death

09 had died, from a heart attack

10 my goodness

11 Catching his breath, kept reading

12 even more shocked

13 described, as, other dangerous objects

14 had become rich, deaths of others

15 couldn't believe

16 It, that, one of his many inventions

17 think of, as, merchant of death

18 deeply disappointed   19 How, be

20 unbelievable   21 merchant of death

22 in a different way

23 be remembered as, the world better

24 to change people's opinions

25 mistakenly reported

26 who had actually died

27 Thanks to, decided to, contribute to

28 to create

29 Originally, only five awards

30 sixth award, added

31 think of, rather than

16 다이너마이트가 그의 많은 발명품 중 하나인 것은 사실이었다.

17 하지만 그는 세상이 그를 '죽음의 상인'으로 생각할 거라고는 결코 상상하지 못했다.

18 Nobel은 몹시 실망했다.

19 "어떻게 이럴 수가 있지?

20 이건 믿을 수 없어!

21 나는 죽음의 상인이 아니야.

22 나는 다르게 기억되고 싶어.

23 나는 세상을 더 좋게 만든 사람으로 기억되고 싶어."

24 그는 자신에 대한 사람들의 견해를 바꾸기로 결심했다.

25 1888년에, 한 프랑스 신문에서 실수로 Alfred Nobel의 죽음을 보도했다.

26 실제로 죽은 사람은 Alfred Nobel의 형인 Ludvig였다.

27 하지만 그 보도 덕분에, Nobel은 세상에 공헌하기 위해 무언가를 하기로 결심했다.

28 1895년에, 그는 자신의 돈을 노벨상을 만드는 데 사용하기로 결정했다.

29 원래 다섯 종류의 상만 있었다.

30 여섯 번째 상은 1968년에 추가되었다.

31 오늘날 우리가 Alfred Nobel을 생각할 때, 우리는 다이너마이트보다는 노벨상을 떠올린다.

1 How Will You Be Remembered?

2 It was just a normal morning.

3 Alfred Nobel sat in his chair to read the newspaper.

4 While he was drinking his coffee, a headline caught his eye: *The Merchant of Death, Alfred Nobel, Is Dead.*

5 "What? What is this?"

6 Reading the article, he dropped his cup in surprise.

7 His coffee spilled all over his clothes and desk, but he couldn't take his eyes off the newspaper.

8 The article was about his own death!

9 It said Nobel had died in France from a heart attack.

10 "Oh my goodness! Am I dead?"

11 Catching his breath, Nobel kept reading.

12 Soon, he became even more shocked.

13 The article described him as the inventor of dynamite and other dangerous objects for war.

14 It said that he had become rich from the deaths of others.

15 He couldn't believe his eyes.

1 당신은 어떻게 기억될까요?

2 그저 평범한 아침이었다.

3 Alfred Nobel은 신문을 읽기 위해 의자에 앉았다.

4 커피를 마시는 동안 한 기사 제목이 그의 눈길을 끌었다. "죽음의 상인, Alfred Nobel 사망하다"

5 "뭐라고? 이게 뭐지?"

6 기사를 읽으며 그는 놀라서 컵을 떨어뜨렸다.

7 커피가 그의 옷과 책상 온 곳에 쏟아졌지만 그는 신문에서 눈을 뗄 수 없었다.

8 기사는 그 자신의 죽음에 관한 것이었다!

9 기사에는 Nobel이 심장 마비로 프랑스에서 죽었다고 쓰여 있었다.

10 "오, 이럴 수가! 내가 죽었다고?"

11 숨을 고른 후, Nobel은 계속 읽었다.

12 곧, 그는 훨씬 더 충격을 받게 되었다.

13 기사는 그를 전쟁에 쓰이는 다이너마이트와 다른 위험한 물건의 발명가로 기술했다.

14 기사에는 그가 다른 사람들의 죽음으로 인해 부유해졌다고 쓰여 있었다.

15 그는 자신의 눈을 믿을 수 없었다.

16 It was true that dynamite was one of his many inventions.

17 But he never imagined that the world would think of him as "the merchant of death."

18 Nobel was deeply disappointed.

19 "How could this be?

20 This is unbelievable!

21 I'm not a merchant of death.

22 I want to be remembered in a different way.

23 I want to be remembered as a person who made the world better."

24 He decided to change people's opinions about him.

25 In 1888, a French newspaper mistakenly reported Alfred Nobel's death.

26 The person who had actually died was his brother, Ludvig.

27 Thanks to the report, however, Nobel decided to do something to contribute to the world.

28 In 1895, he decided to use his money to create the Nobel Prize.

29 Originally, there were only five awards.

30 A sixth award was added in 1968.

31 Today, when we think of Alfred Nobel, we think of the Nobel Prize, rather than dynamite.

구석구석지문 TEST Step 1 p.42

After You Read A. Read and Correct

1. APRIL
2. The Merchant of Death, Dead
3. died, in, from a heart attack
4. invented dynamite, other dangerous objects
5. became rich, the deaths of others
6. is responsible for, thousands of people
7. remember, as, the merchant of death

Word Power

1. invented special shoes for
2. over, inventions, his life
3. the inventor, the plane

Think and Write Step 2

1. Looking back, that, donated, to children
2. because, to make a difference, in need
3. To save, for a month
4. donated the money to
5. left food on my plate
6. really appreciate my meals
7. proud of myself

구석구석지문 TEST Step 2 p.43

After You Read A. Read and Correct

1. WORLD NEWS / APRIL 13, 1888
2. The Merchant of Death, Alfred Nobel, Is Dead
3. Alfred Nobel died yesterday in France from a heart attack.
4. He invented dynamite and other dangerous objects for war.
5. He became rich from the deaths of others.
6. He is responsible for the deaths of thousands of people.
7. The world will remember him as "the merchant of death."

Word Power

1. Tim invented special shoes for the beach.
2. Thomas Edison made over 1,000 inventions in his life.
3. Who is the inventor of the plane?

Think and Write Step 2

1. Looking back this year, I'm glad that I donated money to children in Africa.
2. I did this because I wanted to make a difference for children in need.
3. To save money, I didn't buy snacks for a month.
4. I donated the money to UNICEF.
5. Before I donated, I sometimes left food on my plate.
6. Now I really appreciate my meals.
7. I'm proud of myself.

Lesson S

01 해결책	02 ~ 후에
03 맑게[투명하게] 하다; 투명한, 맑은	04 건강 상태
05 내려앉다, 착륙하다; 육지, 땅	06 나타나다
07 선택하다 08 욕실	09 누르다
10 특별한 11 밝게	12 문지르다, 비비다
13 정밀 검사[촬영]하다	
14 일상의, 늘 하는; 늘 먹던 것	15 샤워실, 샤워
16 속삭이다 17 센서, 감지기	18 빛나다, 비추다
19 미래 20 식료품 및 잡화	21 편안한, 안락한
22 흔들리다, 흔들다 23 서랍	24 (건물의) 층
25 소리치다, 외치다 26 운전자가 필요 없는	
27 ~함으로써 28 ~에 발을 디디다	
29 ~인 것처럼 느끼다	30 ~에 싫증이 나다
31 돌아오다 32 ~하기를 멈추다	
33 A에게 ~할 것을 상기시키다	34 발표를 하다
35 ~의 꼭대기에 36 ~의 값을 지불하다	
37 (프린트로) 출력하다	38 A를 B에게 보내다
39 ~ 덕분에 40 ~할 필요가 없다	

01 shine	02 appear	03 story
04 usual	05 bathroom	06 clear
07 special	08 future	09 grocery
10 health condition		11 sensor
12 land	13 press	14 after
15 rub	16 shake	17 driverless
18 scan	19 brightly	20 select
21 drawer	22 shower	23 whisper
24 yell	25 comfortable	26 solution
27 step in	28 feel like	29 come back
30 be tired of ~	31 pay for	32 by -ing
33 on top of	34 don't have to 동사원형	
35 stop -ing	36 give a presentation	
37 print out	38 thanks to ~	
39 remind A to 동사원형	40 send A to B	

1 story, (건물의) 층   2 shine, 빛나다, 비추다
3 land, 착륙하다   4 select, 선택하다   5 bathroom, 욕실
6 comfortable, 편안한   7 grocery, 식료품 및 잡화
8 appear, 나타나다   9 press, 누르다
10 whisper, 속삭이다   11 select, 선택하다
12 sensor, 센서, 감지기   13 yell, 소리치다, 외치다
14 drawer, 서랍   15 rub, 문지르다, 비비다
16 shake, 흔들다

01 Picture, Future	02 It's, a.m.
03 shakes, yells, minutes	04 stops shaking
05 Suddenly, appears, going, late	
06 rubs, eyes, says, Clear	
07 become, shines brightly, through	
08 light scans, body	
09 voice, health condition, excellent	
10 steps, out, top, sides	
11 warm, comes out, dries	
12 gets out, with, clothes	
13 kitchen, says, for breakfast	
14 says, usual	
15 presses, few, cooking machine	
16 machine prints out	17 says, rushes out
18 later, appears, shouts, forgot	
19 smiles, answers, problem, send	
20 says, Thanks, million	
21 get into, driverless flying	
22 sit in comfortable, around	
23 touches, select, groceries for	
24 pays, by putting, sensor	25 will be delivered to
26 lands, on top, story	
27 give, presentation with, in	28 doesn't have to go
29 Thanks to, like, same	
30 When, comes back, ready	31 talk about, day
32 delicious, clears, washes, dishes	
33 learned, called chess, play	34 Everyone agrees
35 3-D, board appears on	36 lots of fun
37 Right before, whispers, watch	
38 Remind, to take, glasses	

01 Picture, Future	02 It's
03 shakes, yells, Five more minutes	
04 stops shaking	05 appears, be late for

06 rubs her eyes, Clear

07 become clear, shines brightly

08 scans Minji's body

09 voice, health condition

10 steps in, comes out from, top, sides

11 comes out, dries

12 gets out, with today's clothes

13 for breakfast 14 The usual

15 presses a few, on 16 prints out

17 rushes out

18 A few minutes later, forgot

19 send a drone to 20 a million

21 driverless flying car

22 in comfortable chairs around

23 to select, groceries

24 pays for, by putting, on a sensor

25 will be delivered 26 lands, 150-story

27 give a presentation with 28 doesn't have to

29 Thanks to, feel like, same classroom

30 comes back, is ready 31 talk about

32 delicious dinner, washes the dishes

33 called chess, to play 34 agrees

35 3-D chess board appears 36 lots of fun

37 whispers to 38 Remind, to take

본문 TEST Step 3   p.51~52

1 미래를 상상하다

2 오전 7시이다.

3 침대가 흔들리고 김민지가 "5분만 더!"라고 소리를 지른다.

4 침대가 흔들기를 멈춘다.

5 갑자기, 민지의 엄마가 벽 스크린에 나타나 말한다. "학교에 늦겠구나!"

6 민지는 눈을 비비며 "창문을 투명하게 해 줘."라고 말한다.

7 어두운 창문이 투명해지며 창문으로 햇살이 밝게 비춘다.

8 욕실에서 빨간 빛이 민지의 몸을 정밀 검사한다.

9 목소리가 "54킬로그램. 건강 상태가 매우 좋습니다."라고 말한다.

10 그녀가 샤워실 안에 발을 디디자, 물이 위와 양측에서 나온다.

11 샤워 후에, 따뜻한 공기가 나와 그녀를 말린다.

12 그녀가 나가자, 서랍이 열리며 오늘의 옷이 나타난다.

13 부엌에서 민지의 아빠가 "좋은 아침이구나, 얘야. 아침으로 무엇을 먹고 싶니?"라고 말한다.

14 민지는 "늘 먹던 걸로 주세요."라고 말한다.

15 아빠가 요리 기계의 버튼 몇 개를 누른다.

16 기계는 베이컨, 달걀, 빵을 만들어 낸다.

---

17 아빠는 작별 인사를 하고 문 밖으로 급히 나간다.

18 몇 분 후에, 민지의 아빠가 스크린에 나타나 소리친다. "안경을 깜빡했어요!"

19 민지의 엄마가 미소 지으며 답한다. "괜찮아요. 드론을 당신의 사무실로 보낼게요."

20 민지의 아빠가 "정말 고마워요!"라고 말한다.

21 민지의 엄마와 민지는 운전자가 필요 없는 비행 자동차에 탄다.

22 두 사람은 탁자 주변의 편안한 의자에 앉는다.

23 민지의 엄마가 이번 주 식료품을 선택하기 위해 자동차 창문을 터치한다.

24 그녀는 센서에 손가락을 대서 식료품 값을 지불한다.

25 식료품은 집으로 배달될 것이다.

26 자동차는 150층 빌딩의 꼭대기에 있는 민지의 학교에 내린다.

27 오늘 민지는 미국에 있는 학생 Dona와 함께 발표를 할 것이다.

28 하지만 민지가 미국에 갈 필요는 없다.

29 VR(가상 현실) 교실 덕분에, 그들은 같은 교실에 있는 것처럼 느낄 것이다.

30 민지의 가족이 집에 돌아오자 저녁이 준비된다.

31 그들은 식사를 하며 그 날에 관해 이야기한다.

32 맛있는 저녁 식사 후에, 청소 로봇이 식탁을 치우고 설거지를 한다.

33 민지가 "오늘 체스라고 불리는 놀이를 배웠어요. 해 보실래요?"라고 말한다.

34 모두가 동의한다.

35 탁자 위에 삼차원 체스판이 나타난다.

36 그들은 아주 즐거운 시간을 보낸다.

37 민지는 자러 가기 직전에, 자신의 손목시계에 속삭인다.

38 "아빠께 내일 안경을 가져가시라고 상기시켜 드려."

본문 TEST Step 4-Step 5   p.53~56

1 Picture the Future

2 It's 7 a.m.

3 The bed shakes and Minji Kim yells, "Five more minutes!"

4 The bed stops shaking.

5 Suddenly, Minji's mom appears on a screen on the wall and says, "You're going to be late for school!"

6 Minji rubs her eyes and says, "Clear the windows."

7 The dark windows become clear and the sun shines brightly through them.

8 In the bathroom, a red light scans Minji's body.

9 A voice says, "54 kilograms. Your health condition is excellent."

10 When she steps in the shower, water comes out from the top and sides.

11 After her shower, warm air comes out and dries her.

12 When she gets out, a drawer opens with today's clothes.

13 In the kitchen, her father says, "Good morning, Honey. What do you want for breakfast?"

14 Minji says, "The usual, please."

15 Mr. Kim presses a few buttons on the cooking machine.

16 The machine prints out some bacon, eggs and bread.

17 Mr. Kim says goodbye and rushes out the door.

18 A few minutes later, Minji's father appears on a screen and shouts, "I forgot my glasses!"

19 Ms. Kim smiles and answers, "No problem. I'll send a drone to your office."

20 Mr. Kim says, "Thanks a million!"

21 Ms. Kim and Minji get into a driverless flying car.

22 They sit in comfortable chairs around a table.

23 Ms. Kim touches the car window to select the groceries for this week.

24 She pays for them by putting her finger on a sensor.

25 They will be delivered to her house.

26 The car lands at Minji's school on top of a 150-story building.

27 Today Minji will give a presentation with Dona, a student in America.

28 But Minji doesn't have to go to America.

29 Thanks to a VR classroom, they will feel like they are in the same classroom.

30 When Minji's family comes back home, dinner is ready.

31 They eat and talk about their day.

32 After a delicious dinner, the cleaning robot clears the table and washes the dishes.

33 Minji says, "I learned a game called chess today. Do you want to play?"

34 Everyone agrees.

35 A 3-D chess board appears on the table.

36 They have lots of fun.

37 Right before Minji goes to bed, she whispers to her watch.

38 "Remind Daddy to take his glasses tomorrow."

MEMO

적중100

영어 기출 문제집

정답 및 해설

동아 | 이병민